IMAGES
of America

HARNEY COUNTY

I0806082

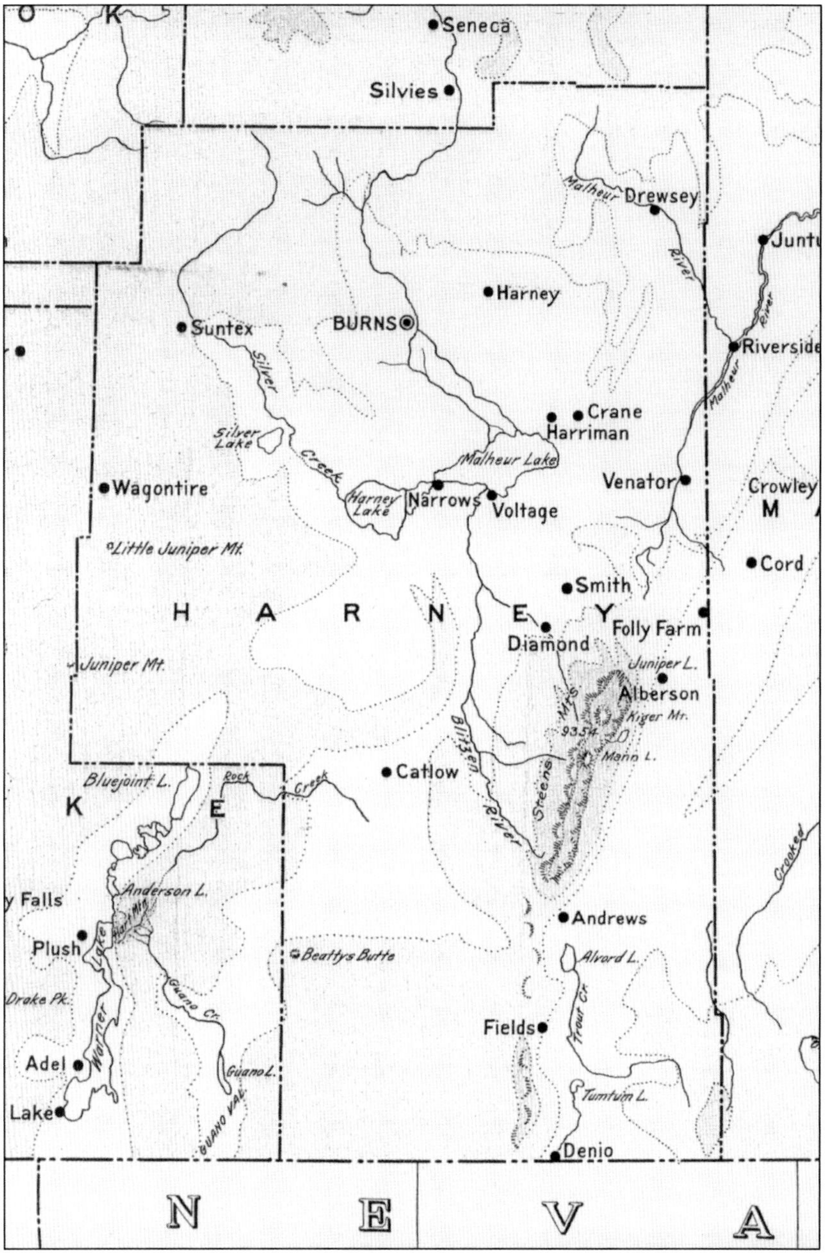

This 1935 map from the Life Zones of Oregon shows the location of many of the early-day settlements within Harney County. (Courtesy Claire McGill Luce Western History Room.)

On the Cover: The cowboys pictured here were participants of the Harney County Rodeo between 1920 and 1929. Those identified, from left to right, include: (first row) John Culp and Blackie Reed; (second row) Linn Baker and Charles Frazier; (third row) Rankin Crow, Billy Pete, Lee Shepard, and Alvin Woodruff (wearing cap); (on horses) Troy Osborn, Gus Bardwell, and Buck Miller. (Photograph by R. W. Heck; courtesy Claire McGill Luce Western History Room.)

IMAGES
of America

HARNEY COUNTY

Karen Nitz for the Harney County Library
Claire McGill Luce Western History Room

ARCADIA
PUBLISHING

Copyright © 2008 by Karen Nitz for the Harney County Library Claire McGill Luce Western History Room
ISBN 978-0-7385-5922-3

Published by Arcadia Publishing
Charleston, South Carolina

Printed in the United States of America

Library of Congress Catalog Card Number: 2008926395

For all general information contact Arcadia Publishing at:
Telephone 843-853-2070
Fax 843-853-0044
E-mail sales@arcadiapublishing.com
For customer service and orders:
Toll-Free 1-888-313-2665

Visit us on the Internet at www.arcadiapublishing.com

This book is dedicated to the memory of Claire McGill Luce, without whose generous bequest to Harney County, the Western History Room would not have been constructed. Also to all the residents of Harney County, past and present, who have shaped the character of the county.

Contents

ACKNOWLEDGMENTS

The idea for a small booklet to showcase some of the resources available at the newly created Claire McGill Luce Western History Room, housed within the Harney County Library, quickly snowballed into a full-fledged book.

This book would not have been possible without the contributions of many individuals. Jolyn Wynn, Harney County library director, along with the Harney County Library Foundation, organized the funding for the Claire McGill Luce Western History Room, which is a repository for historical records, oral histories, rare and out-of-print publications, newspaper microfilm, genealogy resources, photographs, and more dealing with the settlement of the West, particularly Oregon and Harney County. Sandra Crittenden tirelessly supervised the archiving of the various collections in order to allow researchers access. Sandra and volunteer Mary Manning assisted with the initial research. Martha Corrigan helped with additional research and Claire Larson with proofreading. Members of the Harney County Historical Society and Museum have generously shared their knowledge along with their photograph collections, some of which will be cataloged and housed in the Western History Room.

It was my intention at the outset to involve the community in providing photographs that have not previously been published. A big thank you to all the following families who took the time to share their photographs and memories: Beverly Adams, LaDonna Baker, Pauline Brayman, Frank and Sharon Catterson, Paul Cronin, Dale Eggleston, Louanne Fugal, Grant Gunderson, Harney County Educational Service District, Dick Jenkins, Conly Marshall, Letha Melton and Argetta Williams, Jack and Bonnie Smith, Suzanne Crowly Thomas from the Holy Family Catholic Church of Burns, Max Tyler, Merle Weil, Linda and Ron Whiting, Lurie Whiting, and Nancy and Terry Williams. This book could not have been possible without you.

Finally, thanks to my family Roy, Andy, Allison, and Amanda for putting up with me during these last few hectic months, and to my parents, Darrel and Darlene, for all those roads trips during my childhood, which inspired a lasting interest in the places and people around me.

INTRODUCTION

The geographic isolation of Harney County fostered a sense of independence among the early settlers, as well as a great sense of community. Harney County was officially established in February 1889, being partitioned off from the southern half of Grant County. The expansive size of the county precluded convenient travel between the farthest reaches of the southern limits of the county to the Grant County seat in Canyon City.

The establishment of Camp Harney on August 10, 1867, was the first permanent occupation of the Harney Valley by white men. Previous to the coming of the camp, the Harney Valley had been visited by fur traders, immigrants looking for a shorter route to the Willamette Valley, gold seekers, and military surveyors planning to establish strategic wagon routes. Several temporary military camps, including Camp Curry, Camp Wright, and Camp Alvord, served the area. Skirmishes between the Paiute, Bannock, and Modoc Indians eventually led to the formation of the Malheur Indian Reservation in 1872. Much of this land was later encroached upon by settlers until only a small portion of the original reserve remained.

As word spread of the riches to be found in this region, cattlemen and sheep men amassed great herds of stock. Notables such as Peter French, Hugh Glenn, John Devine, W. B. Todhunter, John Catlow, Mace McCoy, and the Pacific Livestock Company were important figures in the settlement of the far reaches of the county. Basque and Scottish herders employed to tend the great cattle and sheep herds. The Homestead Act lured land seekers to the valley in hopes of establishing productive claims.

A. H. Robie ushered in the era of the lumberman to supply the building needs of Camp Harney. Thus were the beginnings of the importance of timber from the forested mountains flanking the north and west of Harney County. In 1929, the construction of the Edward Hines Lumber Company would lead to the establishment of the city of Hines. Timber cutting and lumber production were the lifeblood of the northern part of the county into the 1980s when such a way of life came to a screeching halt.

Transportation was a key factor in the settlement of the county. The coming of the railroad that first came to Crane then later to Burns influenced the growth of some settlements and the decline of others. The coming of automobiles and paved roads served to lessen the isolation of much of the county. Aircrafts were employed to more easily cover vast distances and to also serve as workhorses in the air.

In such an isolated environment, community pride was exhibited in grand parades, rodeos, outdoor recreation, and cultural and civic groups such as the Sagebrush Symphony Orchestra.

Photographs included in this book that are not directly credited are from the combined collections of the Claire McGill Luce Western History Room and the Harney County Historical Museum. The collection includes photographs donated by local historian Eugene Luckey and author Edward Gray. Most of the photographs in this book were likely taken by prolific Harney County photographer Rufus W. Heck. His career in Harney County spanned the years between 1907 and 1945. Other notable early-day photographers working in Harney County include W. N. Jorgensen, John McMullen, A. D. Browning, and Bob Lemons.

One

Around the Country

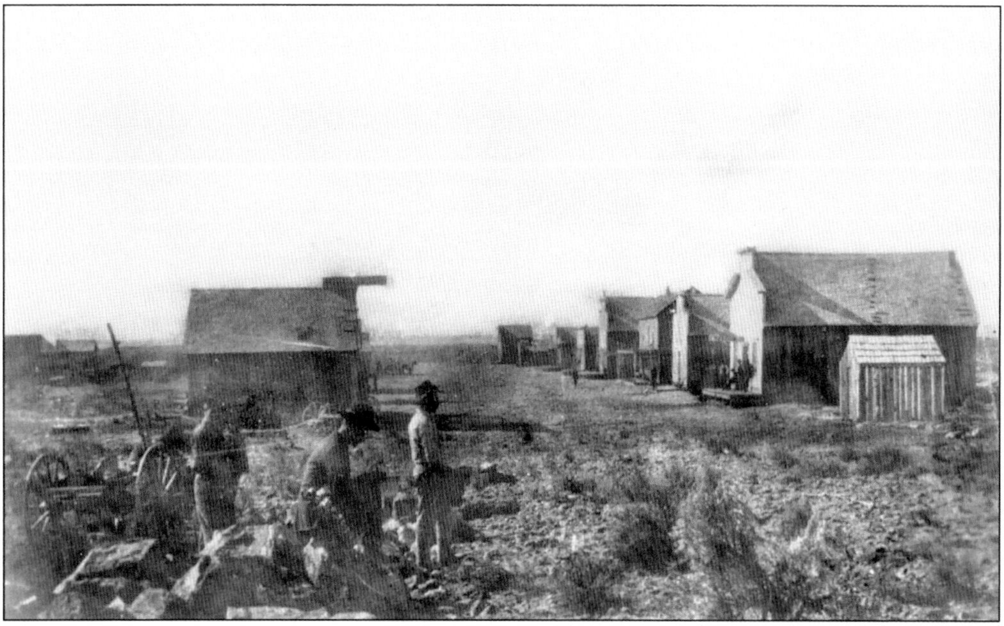

George McGowan, in partnership with Pete Stenger, operated the first mercantile business in the town of Burns. The post office was located here in 1884 after a fire burned the building of the office located two and a half miles southwest at Egan. In honor of a favorite poet from his native land of Scotland, McGowan, with Stenger's approval, settled upon the name of Burns for the new community.

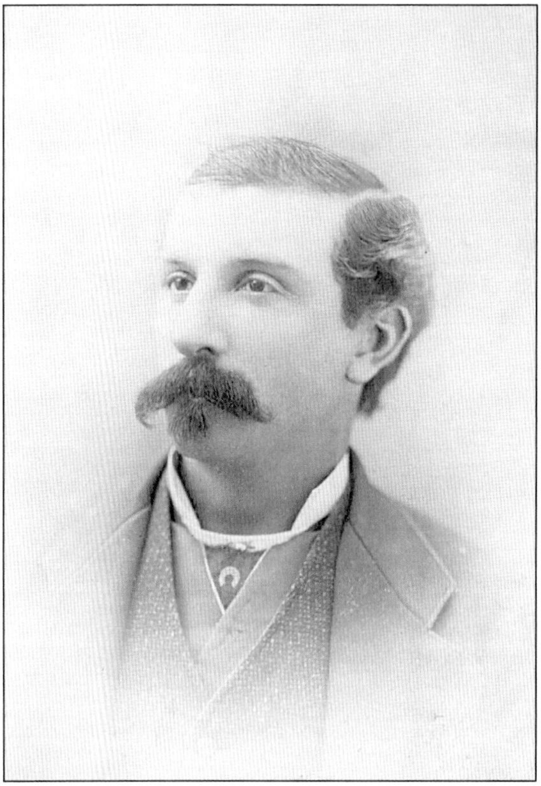

Peter Stenger came to Harney County around 1875 as a stock raiser and quickly established himself in a variety of other ventures. He partnered with George McGowan in the merchandise business, and the pair built a larger store near the Stenger home in Burns in 1883. After the partnership dissolved, Stenger retained the original store while McGowan proceeded to open a hardware business. Stenger served as one of the town's original councilmen. (Photograph by Jeb Brown.)

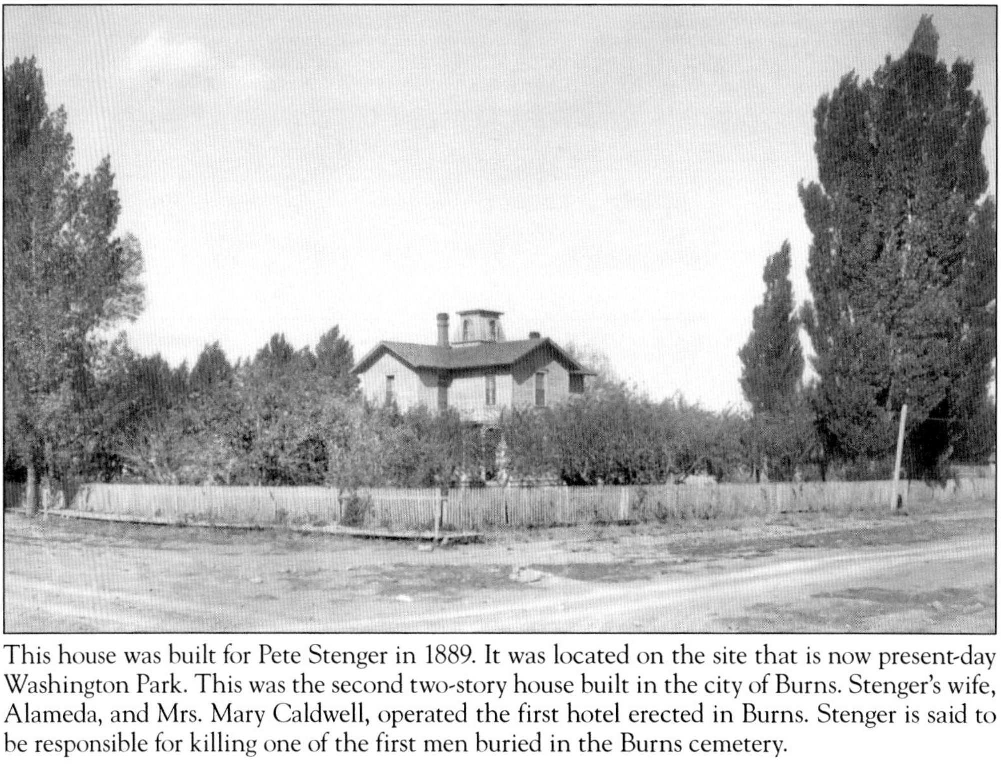

This house was built for Pete Stenger in 1889. It was located on the site that is now present-day Washington Park. This was the second two-story house built in the city of Burns. Stenger's wife, Alameda, and Mrs. Mary Caldwell, operated the first hotel erected in Burns. Stenger is said to be responsible for killing one of the first men buried in the Burns cemetery.

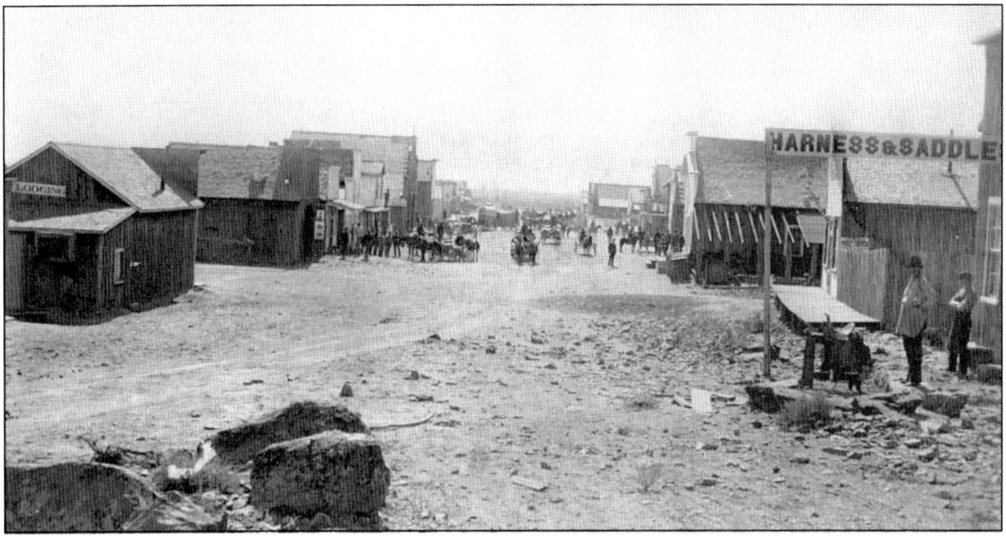

Harney County was officially created from a portion of Grant County in February 1889. The Oregon Supreme Court, following charges of election fraud by Burns and Harney City voters, decided the location of the county seat. In July 1890, Burns was declared the winner by a margin of six votes. This 1889 photograph of Main Street (now Broadway Street) in Burns illustrates the growth that the community was experiencing during this time.

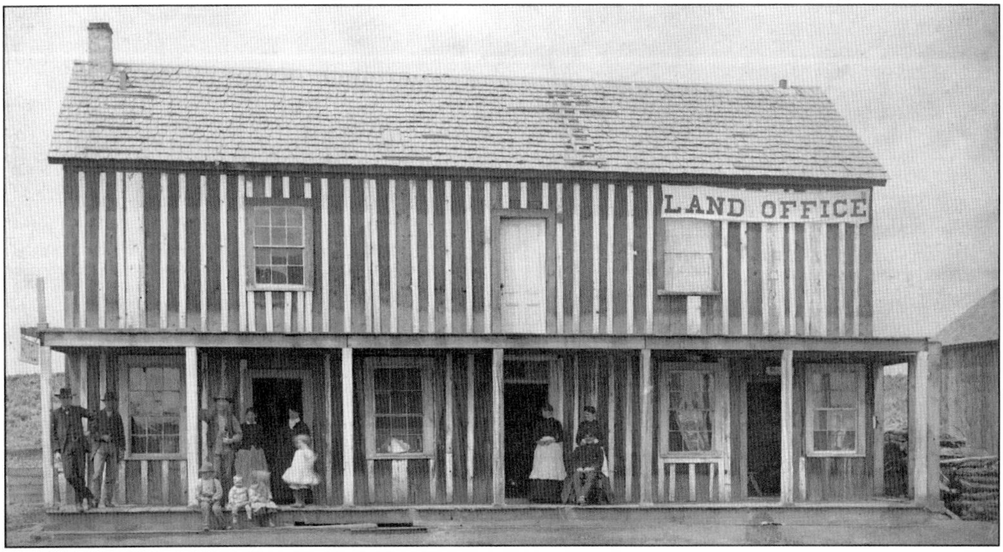

By 1889, the town began to prosper. There was a population of 350, with 115 children in the school district. The town included business such as hotels and a liquor store, in addition to merchants such as a barber, surveyor, blacksmith, physician, lumber supplier, lawyer, and carpenters who all provided business. This hotel, constructed about 1879, served double duty as the U.S. Land Office.

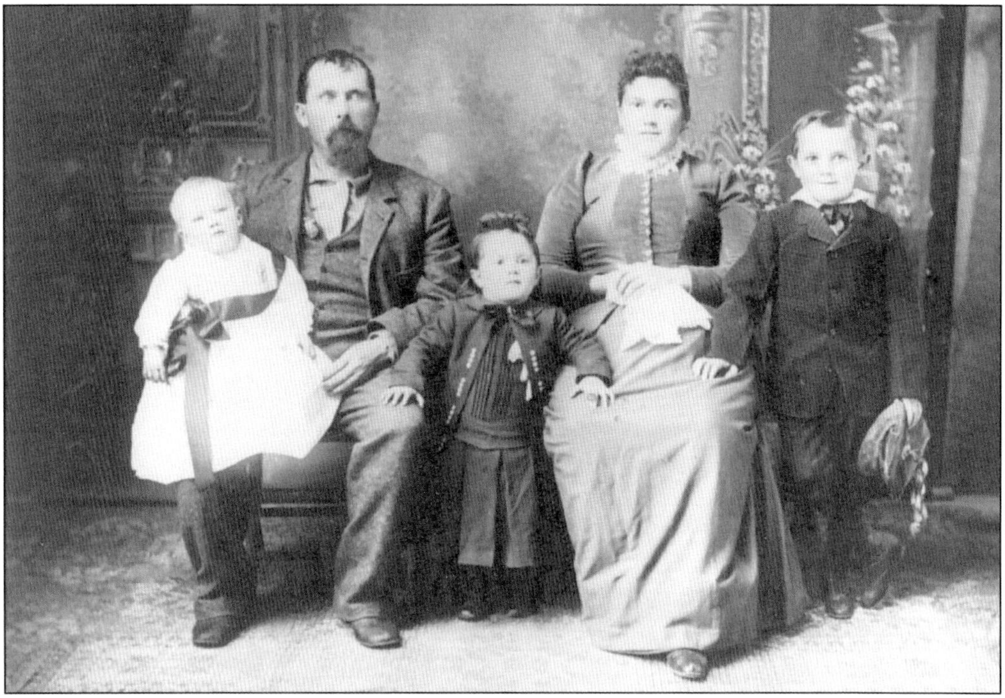

Anthony A. Cowing was the first official sheriff of Harney County. Appointed by Governor Pennoyer, he served from the county's inception in 1889 through 1892. After leaving the sheriff's office, Cowing was appointed by Pres. Grover Cleveland to serve as receiver at the U.S. Land Office in Burns from 1894 to 1898. Cowing is pictured here with wife Mattie Colby Cowing and children Clyde, Audrey, and John Edward around 1892. (Courtesy Sharon Catterson.)

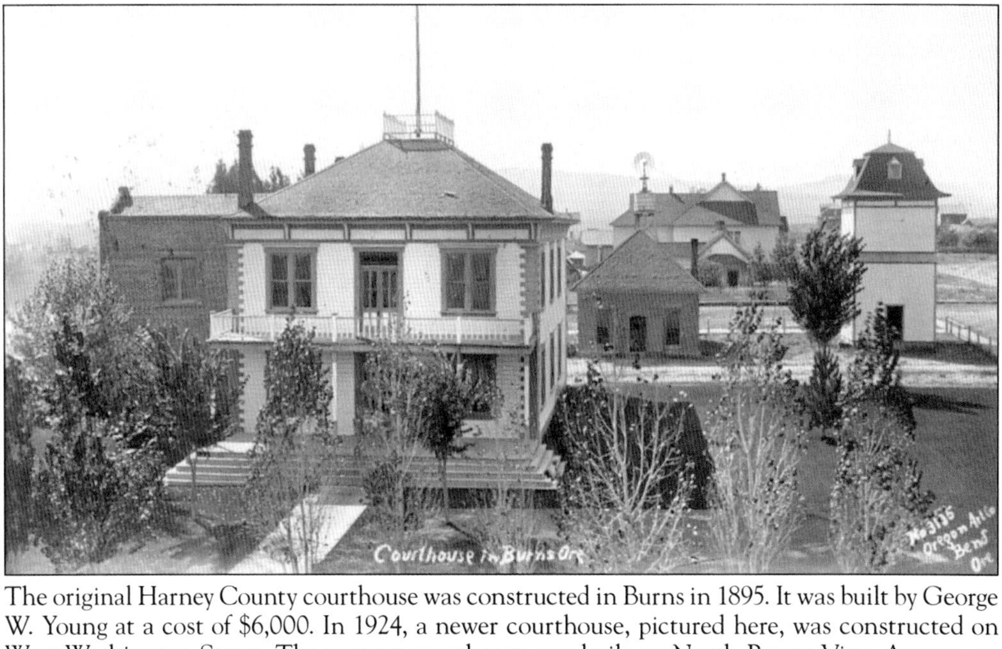

The original Harney County courthouse was constructed in Burns in 1895. It was built by George W. Young at a cost of $6,000. In 1924, a newer courthouse, pictured here, was constructed on West Washington Street. The present courthouse was built on North Buena Vista Avenue on the site of the original building in 1940. (Photograph by Oregon Art Company.)

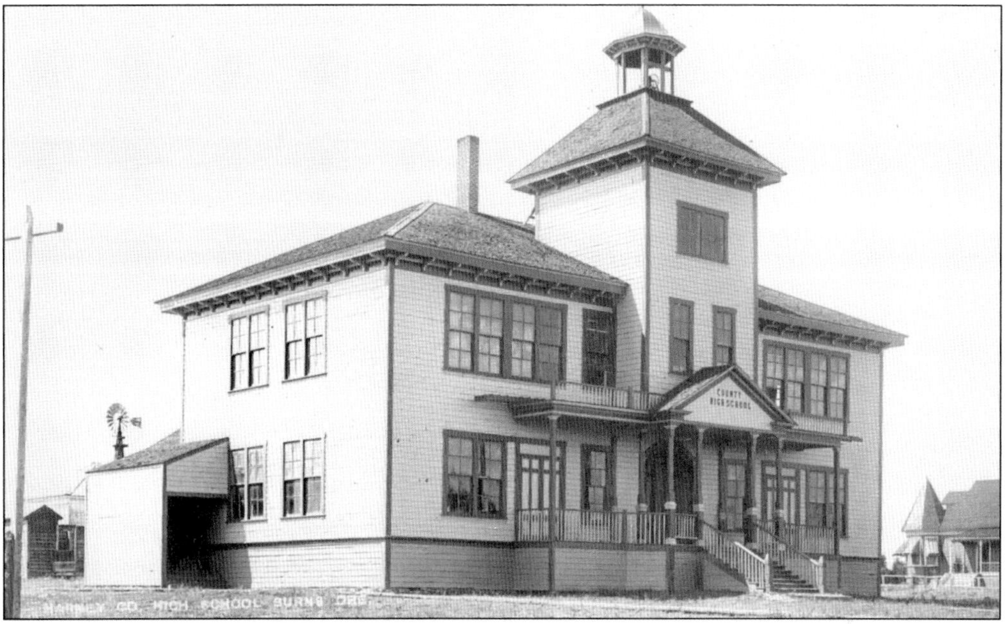

In 1895, this school was built to serve the students of Burns. The building was two stories high with four classrooms located on each floor. In 1896, there were 46 students in the primary grades and 30 registered in higher grades. Grade school was last held in this building during the 1912–1913 school year.

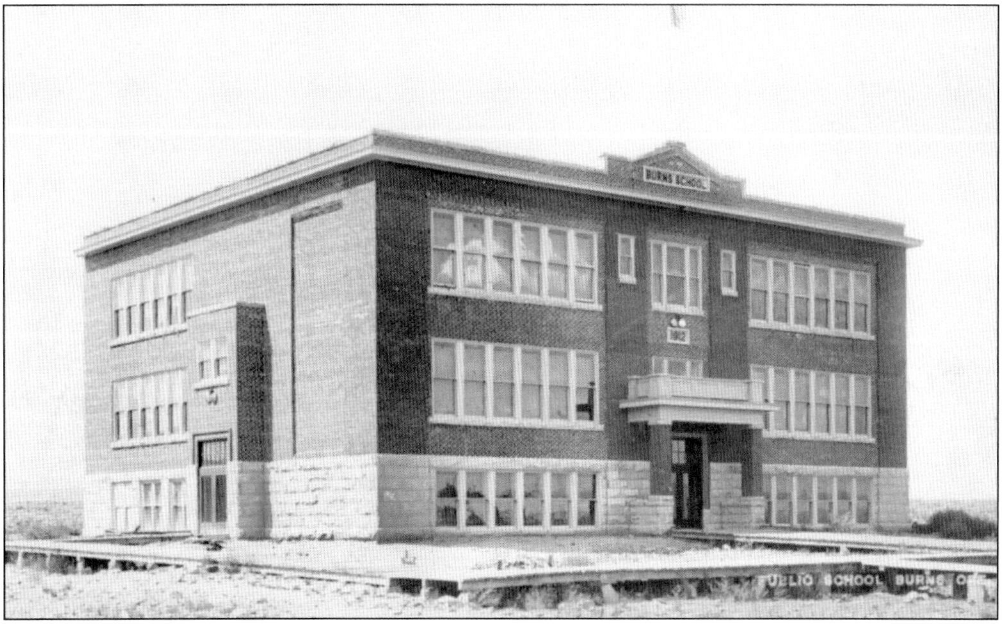

In 1912, the Burns School District constructed this new high school. The building was 83 feet wide by 112 feet long and two stories high with a basement. It contained eight classrooms, a principal's room, and a 40-foot by 70-foot gymnasium as well as a similarly sized auditorium. After a new high school was built, this structure served as the junior high. Today it houses school district offices.

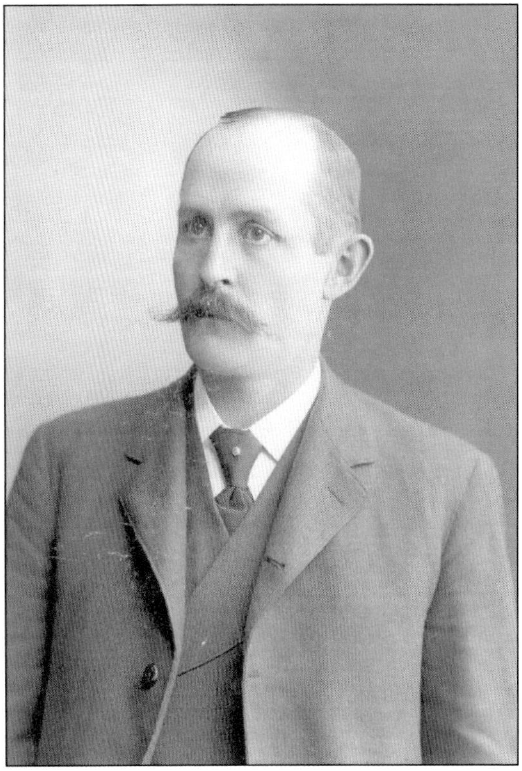

Charles H. Voegtly, an early pioneer merchant, arrived in Burns in 1886. He acquired 160 acres of land in what was later to become the city of Burns. The elaborate house he had constructed in 1907 still stands and is the Sage Country Inn, a bed and breakfast. When the railroad reached town in 1924, the depot was sited in the center of the Voegtly property, through where the tracks cut diagonally. (Photograph by Stevens and Son Company.)

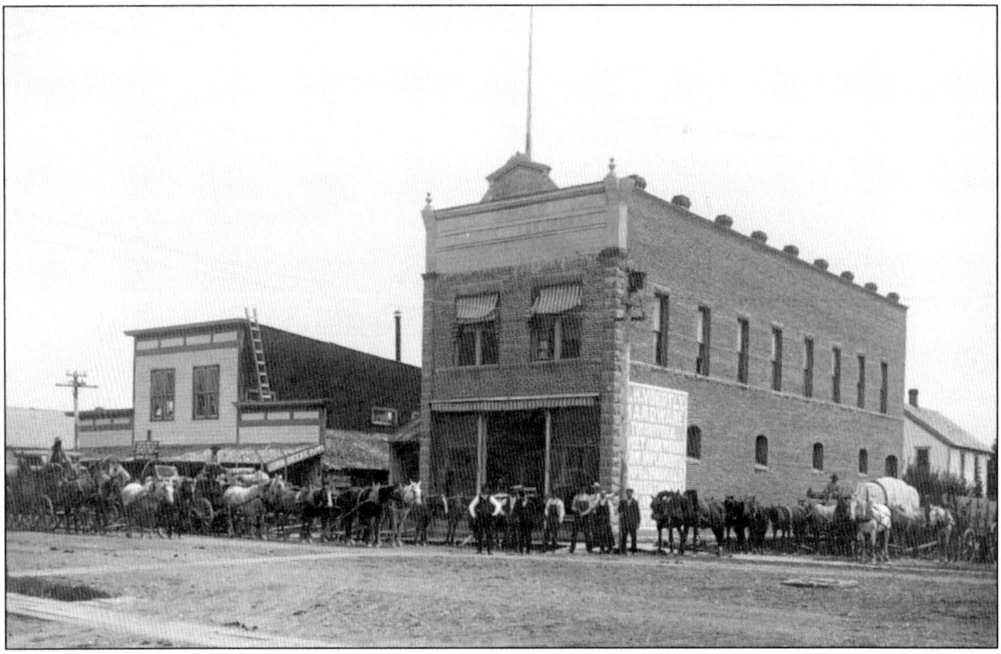

The Voegtly Hardware building, financed by businessman C. H. Voegtly in 1899, is located on the corner of Broadway Street and East Adams in Burns. Built by Harry Smith using locally manufactured red bricks, this building gained the first elevator in Burns in 1912. The hardware business was in operation through 1929. Wenzel's Cash and Grocery later occupied the building.

Frank Welcome poses as a young boy in 1888 with the "Welcome Saddle" made by his father, Jacob Charles (J. C.) Welcome. The Welcomes started a harness and saddle shop in the city hall building upon arriving in Harney County in 1888 and later relocated to the upper end of Main Street. The Welcome spring snap and saddle tree were patented by J. C. (Courtesy Louanne Fugal.)

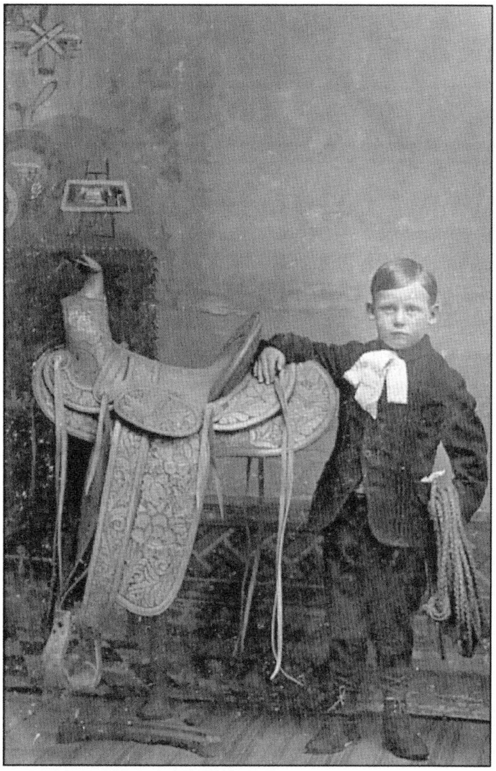

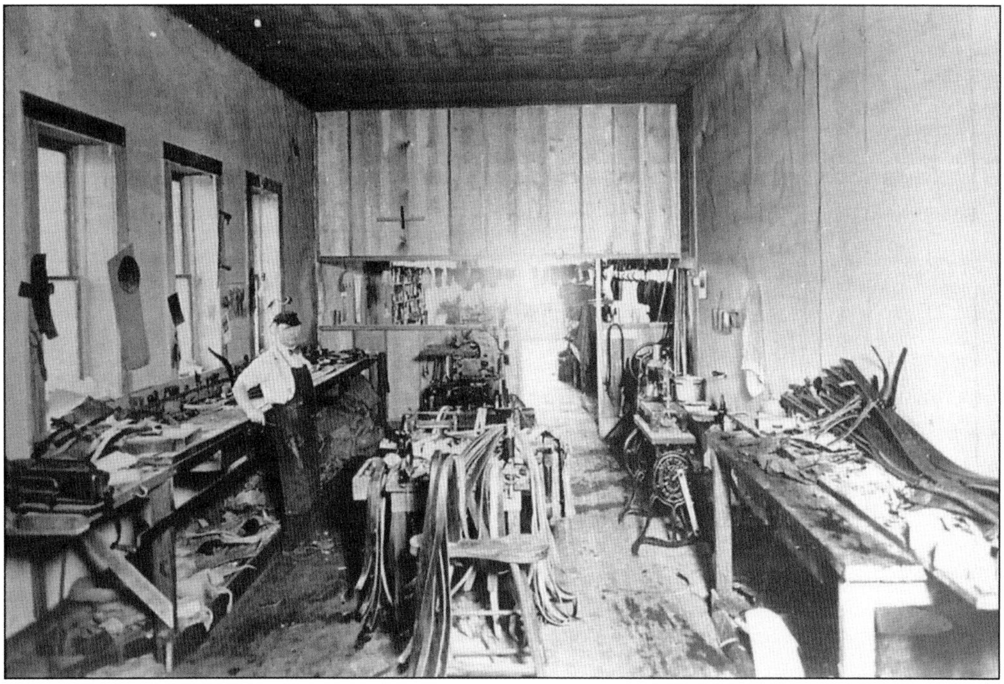

In an era when most transportation was by horseback, there was a great demand for quality leatherwork. Frank Welcome is pictured in the early 1900s in the saddle and harness shop originally started by his father. Frank continued to operate the business until 1924. (Courtesy Lurie Whiting.)

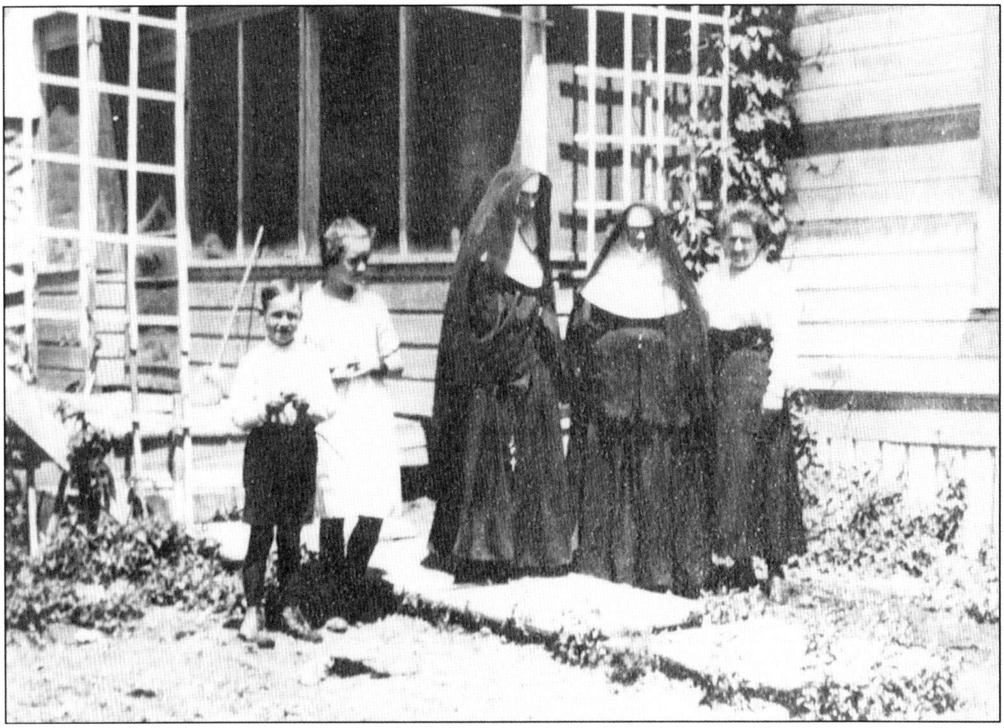

During October 1918, Sisters of St. Joseph from Tipton, Indiana, arrived in Burns to look into the prospects of establishing a Catholic hospital in the community. Pictured during that visit are, from left to right, Wally Welcome, Eleanor Welcome Jenkins, Sisters of St. Joseph, and Mrs. Frank Welcome. (Courtesy Holy Family Catholic Church, Burns.)

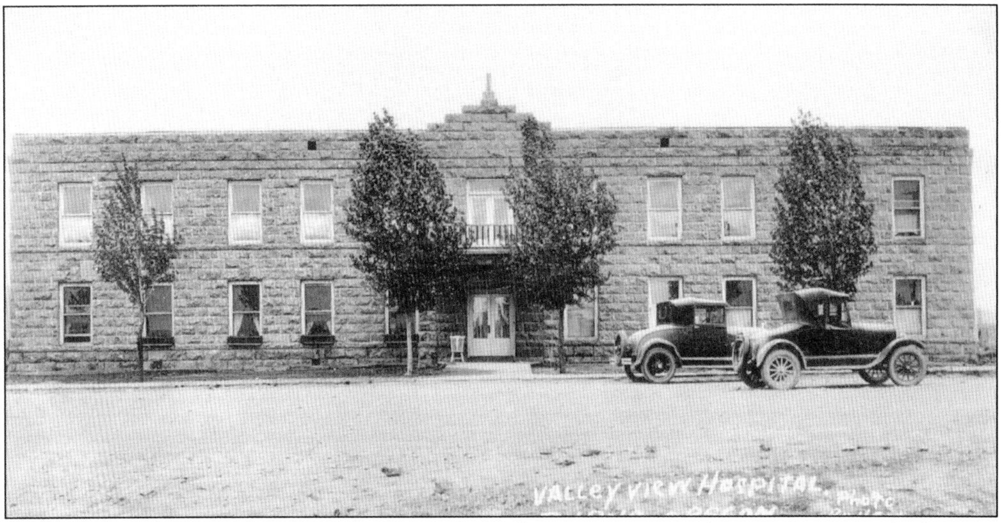

St. Joseph's Hospital, which later operated as Valley View Hospital, was constructed of native stone and equipped in 1922. Financial troubles forced the sale of the building and the sisters left Burns. Dr. B. F. Smith later bought the building and operated a successful practice here. The building served the medical needs of the Edward Hines Lumber Company as well. A new hospital was built in another location in 1950. This structure still stands at the north end of Egan Street. (Photograph by R. W. Heck.)

Fr. Hugh J. McDevitt planned to build a small wood-frame church, but many townspeople persuaded him to build a stone church worthy of what they thought Burns would become. The old Catholic Church, shown here with Father McDevitt, was completed in 1902. The interior decoration of the old church was completed in 1909. In 1911, a brick rectory was added. Franciscans served the parish only until 1923. (Courtesy Holy Family Catholic Church, Burns.)

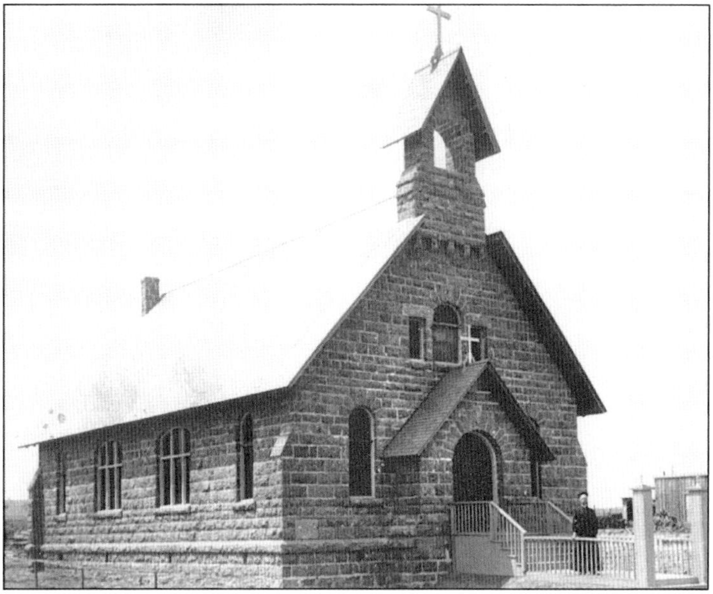

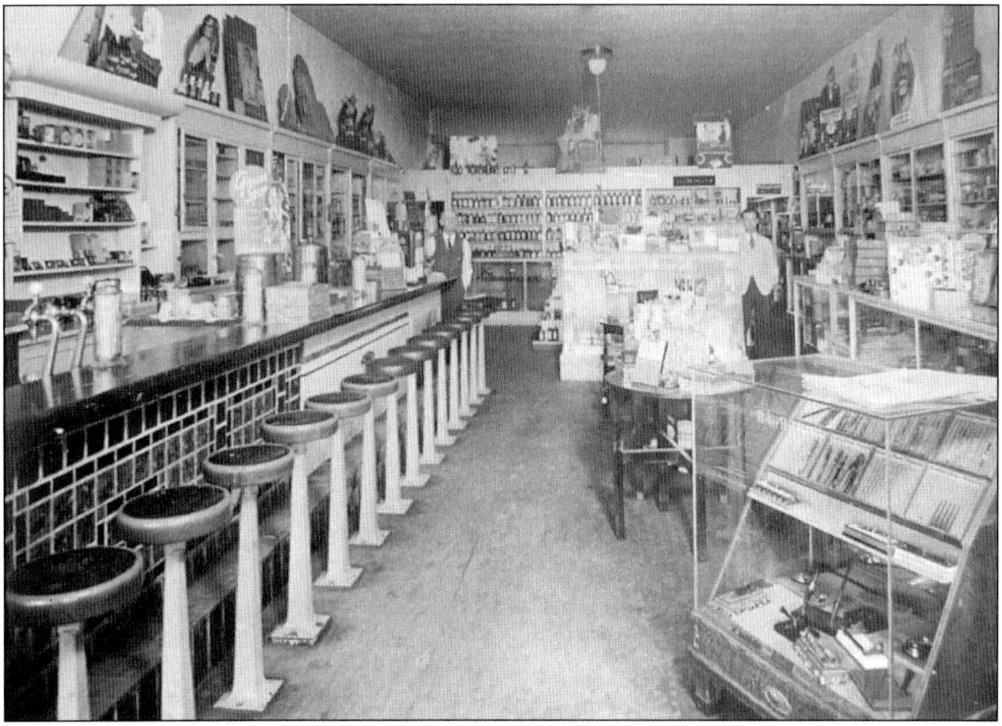

The Home Drug Company was located in a brick building on the east side of North Broadway Street in Burns. Pictured is the pharmacist and owner Jacob C. Welcome Jr., standing at the rear to left, and nephew Wally Welcome shown with the vast array of goods displayed in the store in 1936. (Courtesy Lurie Whiting.)

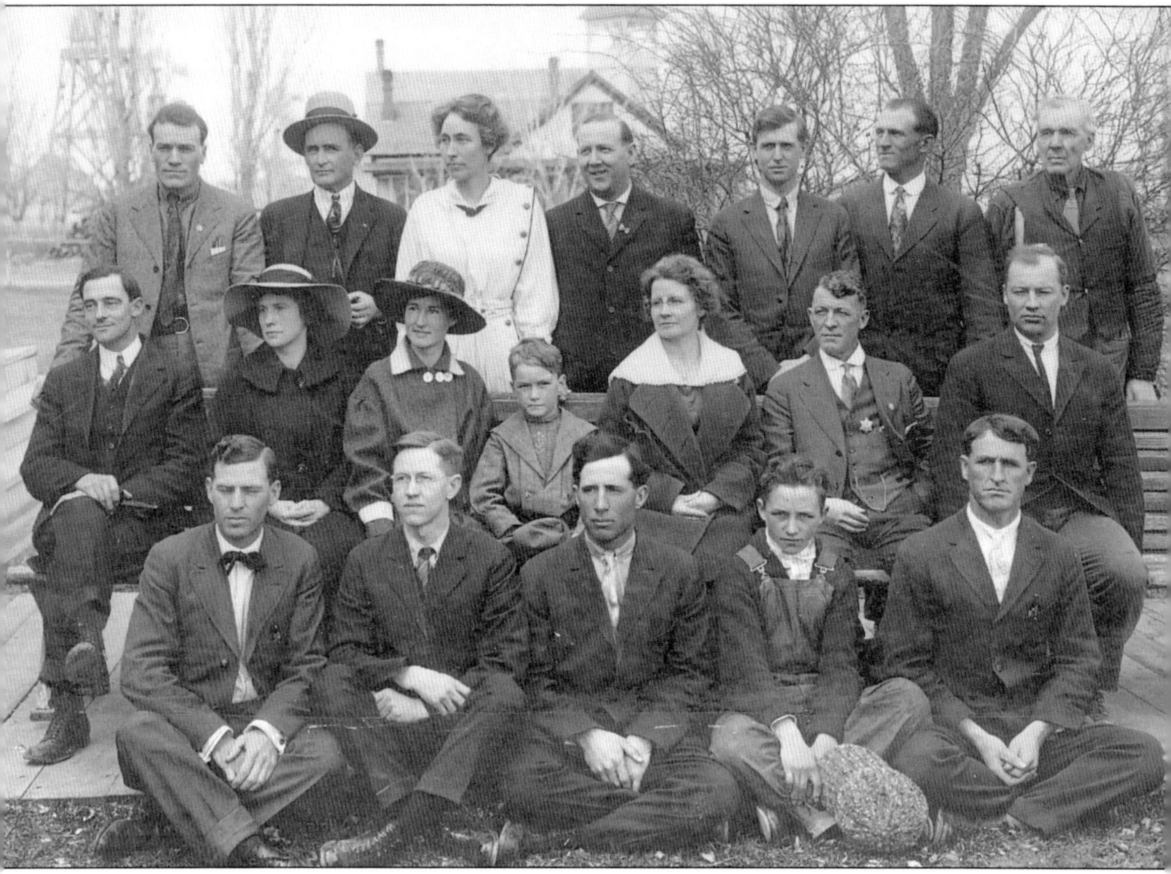

Austin Goodman was elected Harney County sheriff in 1914. Archie Cody murdered Goodman in 1924 at Folly Farm after Cody was suspected of passing a bad check. Cody was captured, tried, and convicted and was sentenced to hang at the state penitentiary. Cody was hanged April 16, 1926, at the age of 30. Goodman is pictured here with the Harney County Court officers in 1916. Pictured are, from left to right, (first row) Irwin Dillman, Ches Dalton, John Caldwell, Ed Goodman, and Pat Davis; (second row) Billy Carroll, Dolly Buchanan, Florence Winans, F. Dalton, unidentified, Austin Goodman, and Harry Buck; (third row) Roe Buchanan, Tom Sprague, Pearl Fiske, unidentified, Allen Biggs, Frank Triska, and M. J. Gould.

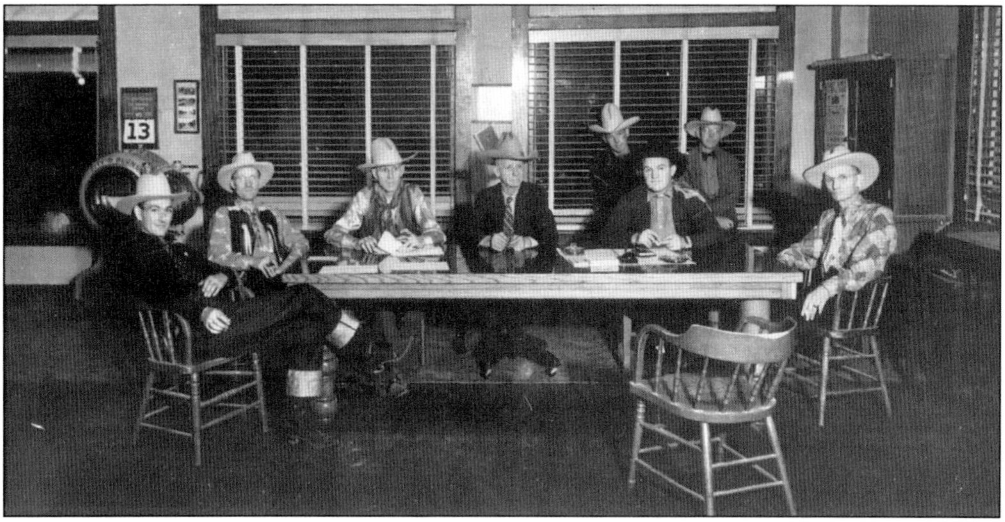

The frontier spirit is evident in every aspect of county life. The city fathers of Burns sport 10-gallon hats and traditional Western garb even while conducting official business. The group is gathered in the upstairs council chambers of the city hall in 1940. Pictured from left to right are (sitting) Ed Brown, George Hughet, Lee Miller, Jake Welcome (mayor), Polly Thornburg, and C. J. Girts; (standing) Mac ? and Dick O'Brian (police chief).

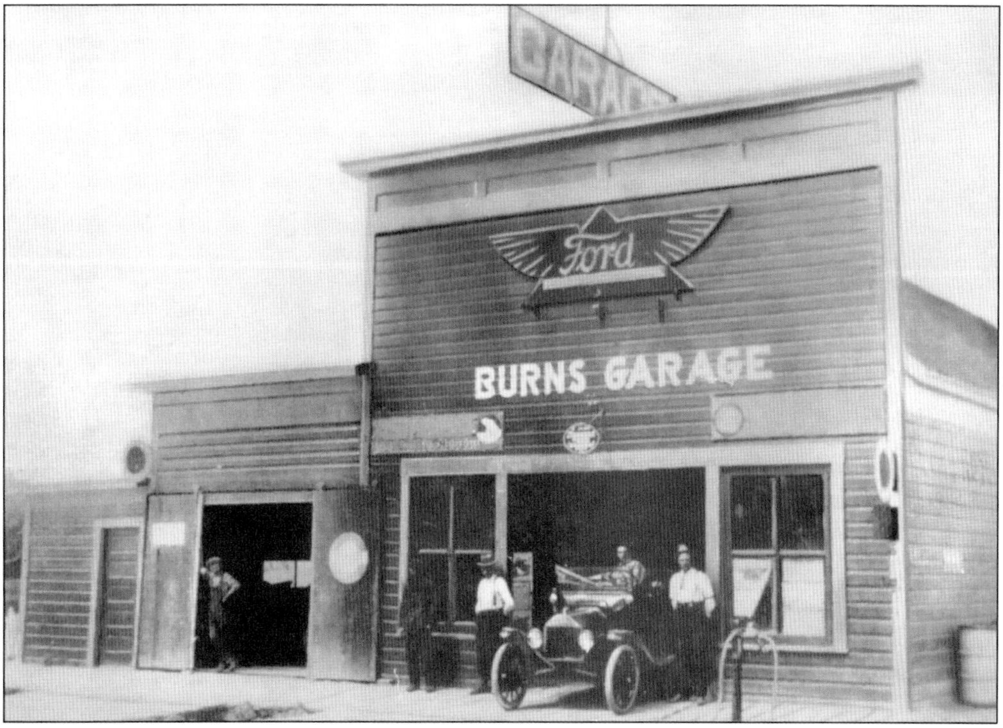

The Burns Ford Garage was established in 1910 by Archie McGowan, son of city founder George McGowan. It has remained at the same location for nearly 100 years. The business is the oldest existing Ford dealership operating in the same location on the entire West Coast. The building has undergone some cosmetic changes over the years and is planning an expansion to celebrate the centennial anniversary.

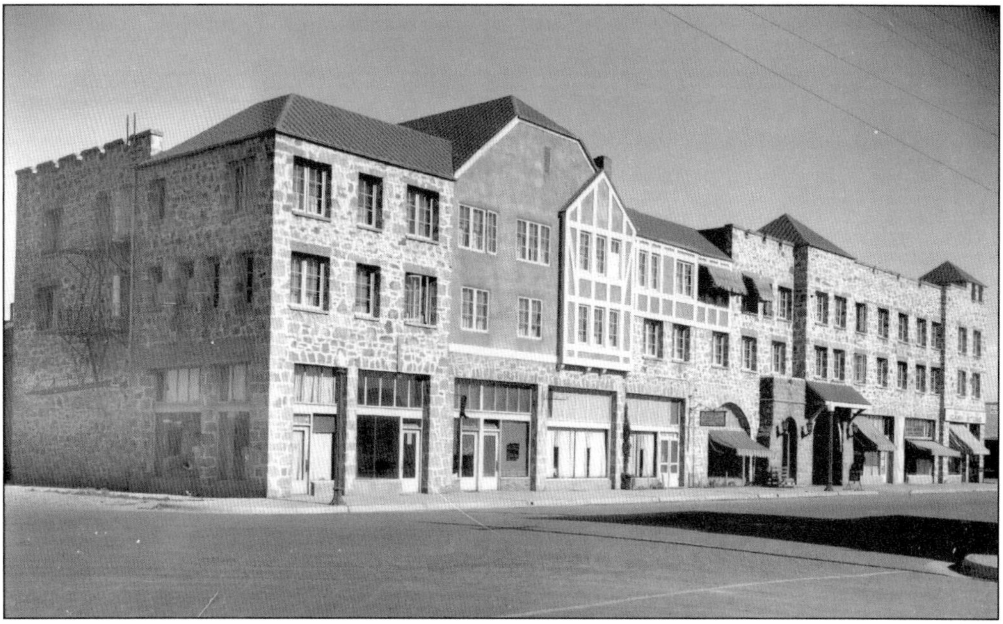

Construction of the three-story native stone Welcome Hotel was completed in 1929. Owned and managed by A. C. Welcome and his wife, Vella, the hotel boasted 53 guest rooms, 32 with a bath and radio, and 11 apartments. The ground floor of the hotel housed a variety of businesses. F. W. Pettibone, general manager of the Edward Hines Western Pine Company, was the first guest to register at the new establishment. (Photograph by R. W. Heck.)

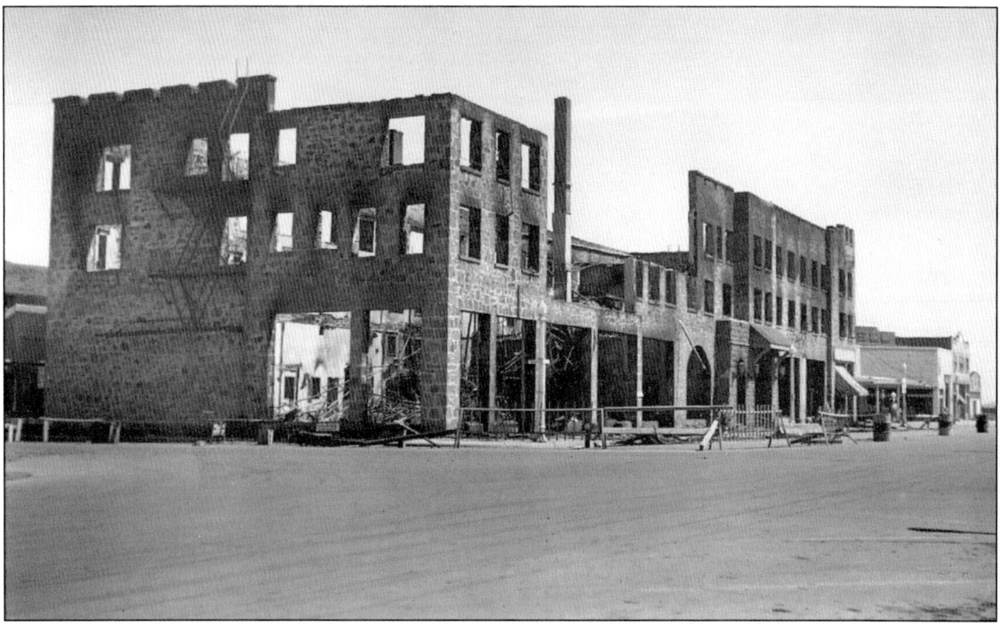

Pictured is the Welcome Hotel following a devastating fire that occurred at 4:30 a.m. on July 15, 1937. The city's local water storage tank was nearly emptied by the time the final flames were extinguished. The Burns Post Office, within the hotel building, fell to the flames and interrupted mail service to and from the city. Losses due to the fire totaled more than a quarter of $1 million. (Photograph by R. W. Heck.)

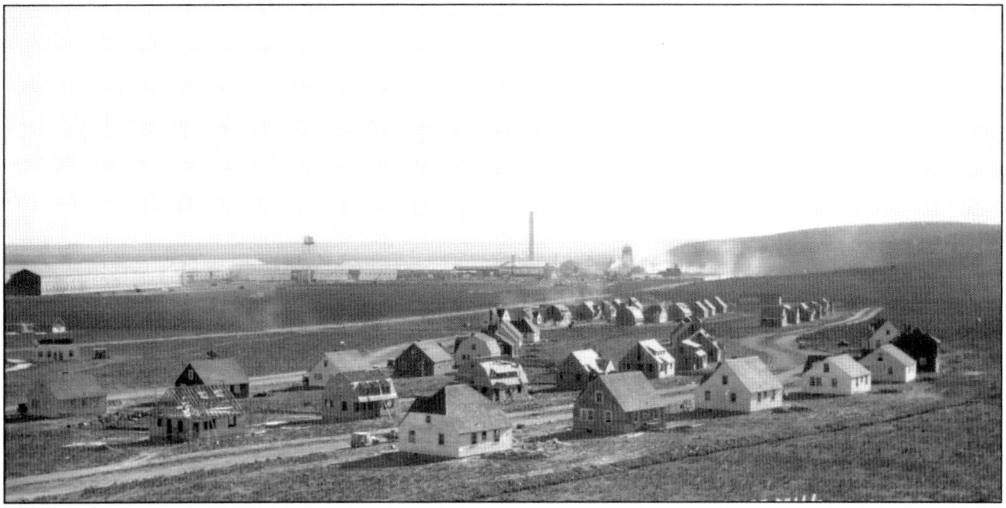

The community of Hines, originally known as the "Greater Burns Subdivision," sprang up to accommodate the workers employed by the Edward Hines Lumber Mill located about two miles south of Burns. Founded in 1929, the town was established on 2,000 acres north and west of the Mill site and was purchased by Mississippi realtors Stafford, Derbes, and Roy. Billed as Oregon's first scientifically planned community, the town was built around a circular park. (Photograph by R. W. Heck.)

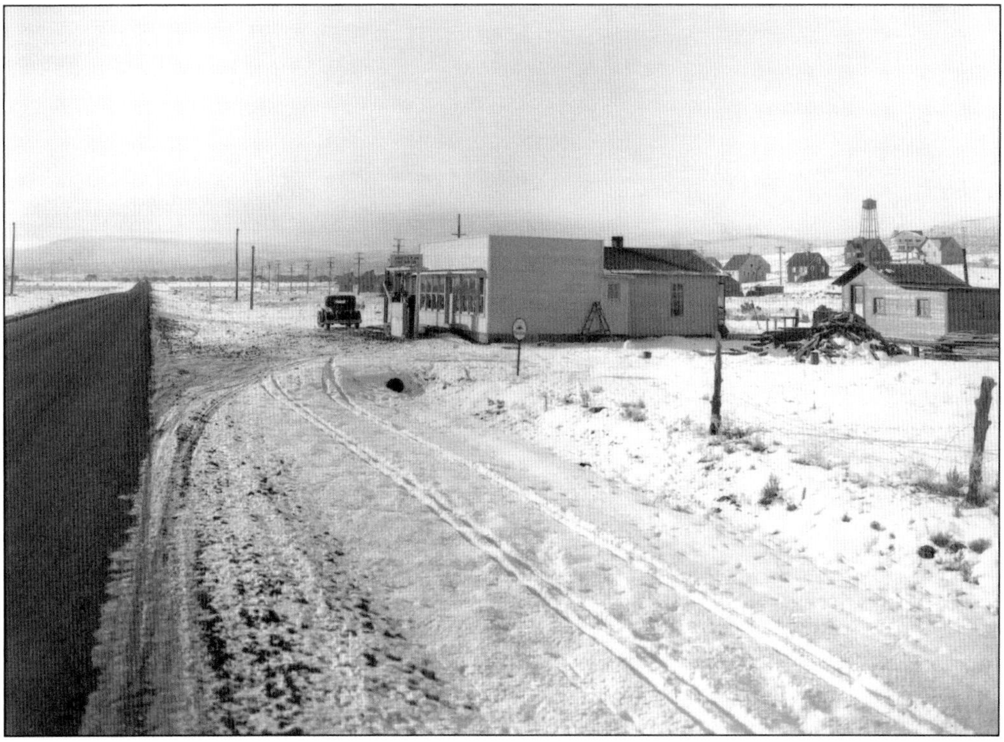

Shorty's Place was located along Highway 20 in the 1930s between the cities of Burns and Hines near the location of the original site of Egan. In 1880, Egan was comprised of a post office, store, and saloon. George McGowan purchased the store and moved it and the post office to Burns in 1883. The saloon burned down, and Egan ceased to exist. (Photograph by R. W. Heck.)

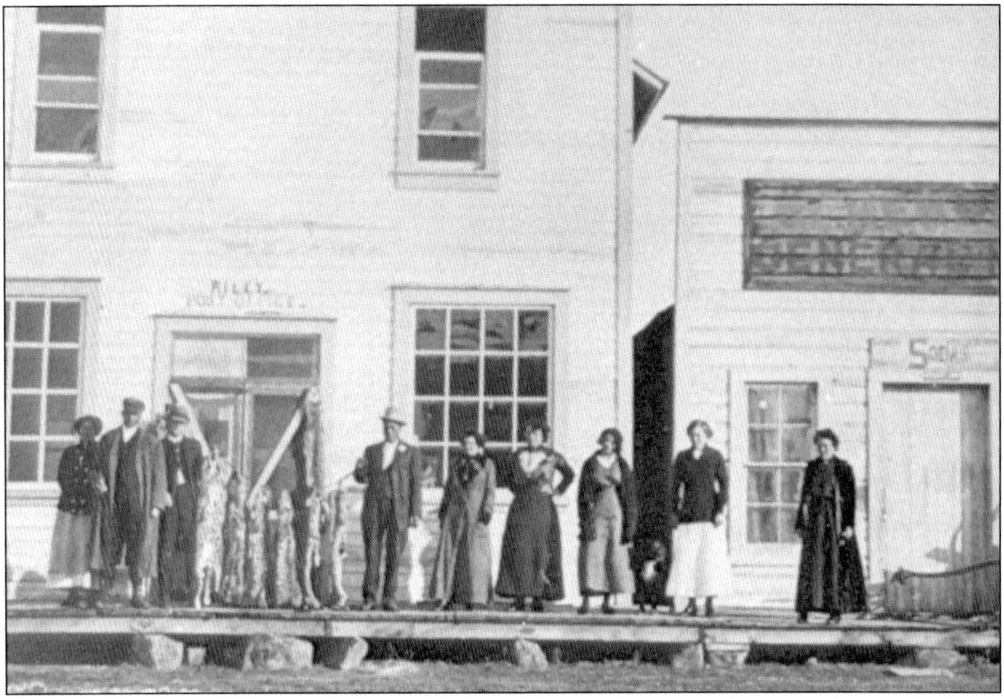

The Hembree Mercantile at Riley, located on Highway 20 about 25 miles west of Burns, is shown here about 1912. The store served as the location of the Riley Post Office from 1902 to 1918. Guy Hembree operated the store and served as postmaster. The post served the settlers of the Silver Creek Valley.

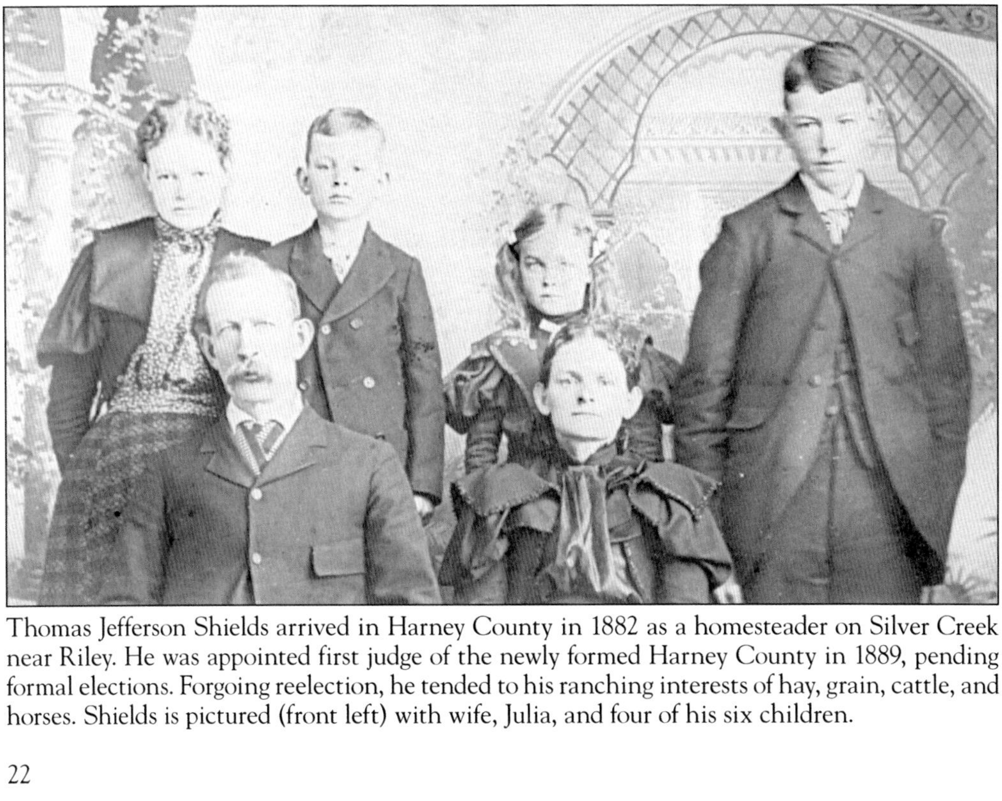

Thomas Jefferson Shields arrived in Harney County in 1882 as a homesteader on Silver Creek near Riley. He was appointed first judge of the newly formed Harney County in 1889, pending formal elections. Forgoing reelection, he tended to his ranching interests of hay, grain, cattle, and horses. Shields is pictured (front left) with wife, Julia, and four of his six children.

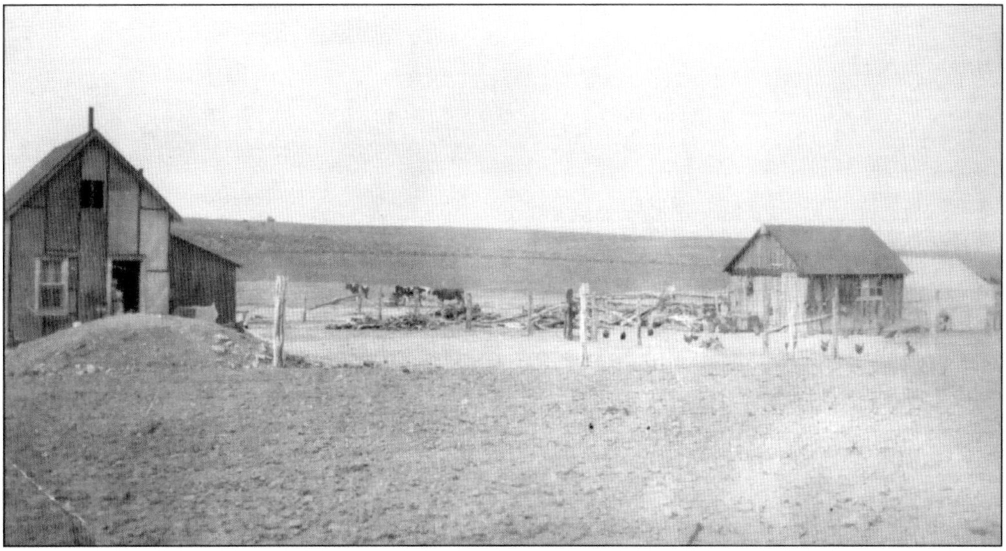

Wagontire, named for local landmark Wagontire Mountain, is situated on the extreme western edge of Harney County along the route from Riley to Lakeview. The Wagontire Post Office, formerly known as Egli, was officially established in 1919. Loretta Addington served as the first postmistress and worked at an addition (pictured) built on the side of their cabin that contained the mailboxes. She received about $30 per month from a percentage of the postmarks that she stamped. (Courtesy May Tyler.)

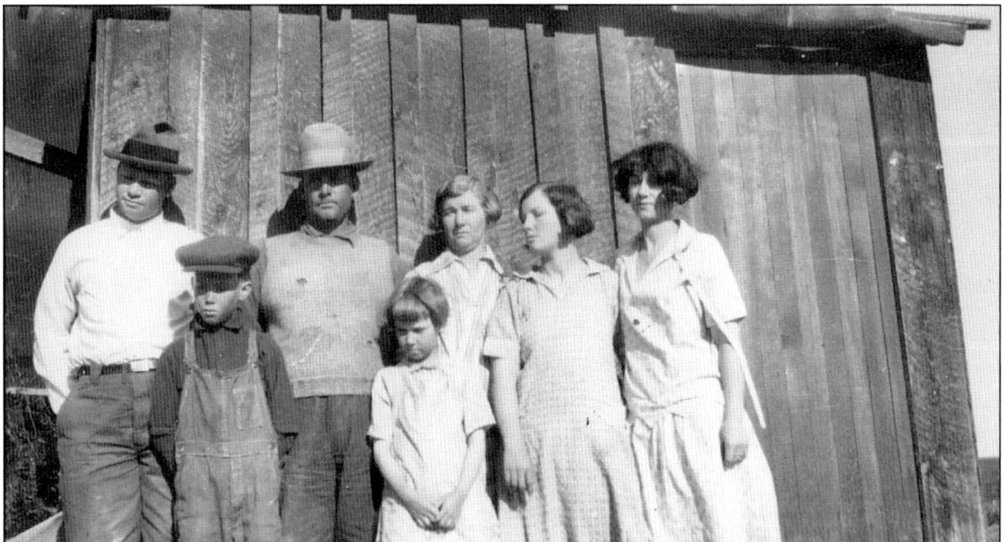

Pictured in 1927 is the Addington family of Wagontire. The following, from left to right, are (first row) Virgil and Vera; (second row) Melvin, Luther, Loretta, Lola, and Lena. Luther Addington hauled freight and lumber from Bend. As nearby homesteaders moved on, he seized the opportunity to enlarge his holdings by moving abandoned outbuildings to his own ranch. (Courtesy May Tyler.)

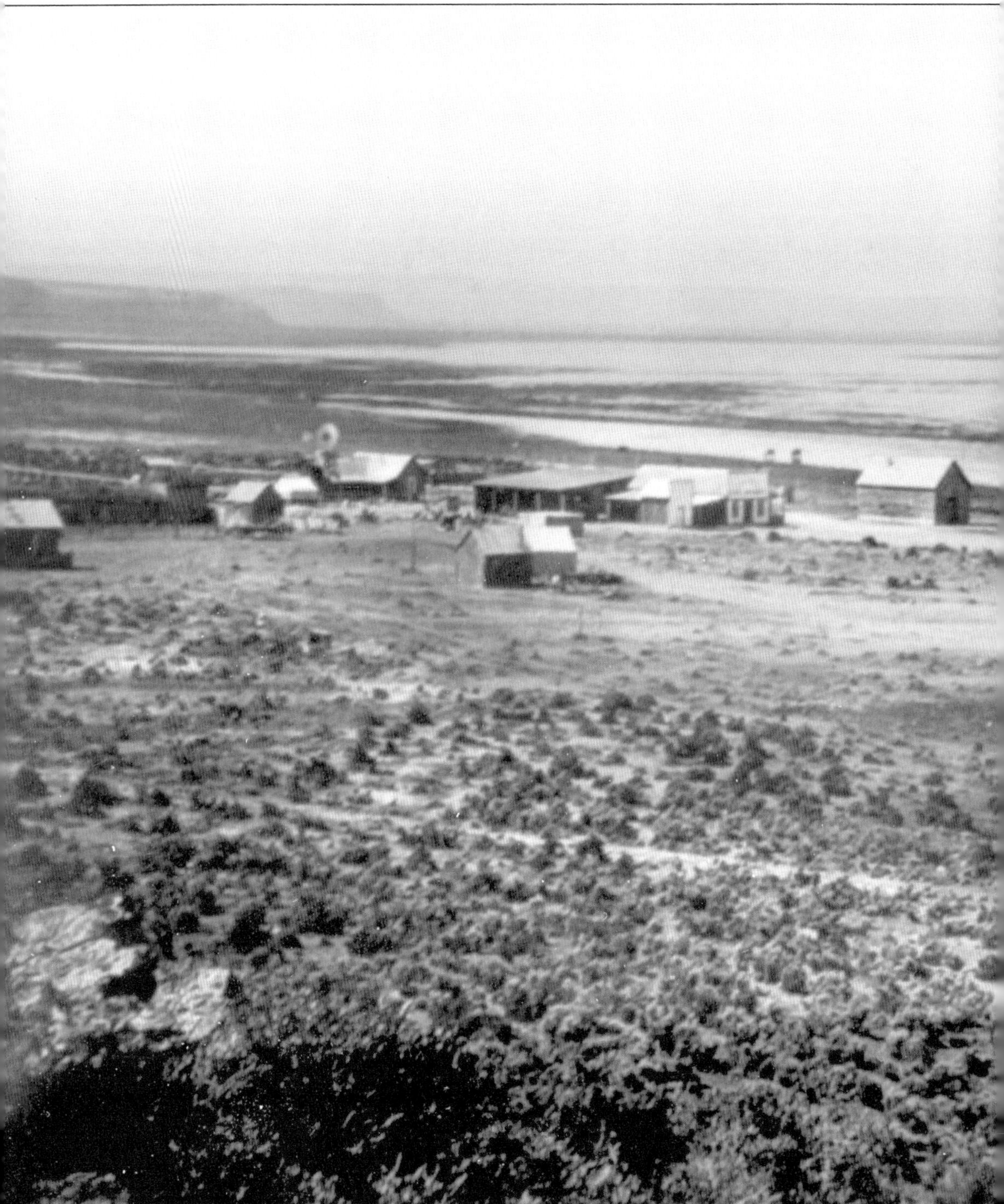

This is a view of the Narrows, which is located about 30 miles south of Burns along Highway 205. Looking south toward Harney Lake, this is the community as it appeared near the height of the settlement's population. By 1910, the town consisted of two hotels, a general store, schoolhouse, dance hall, jail, at least three saloons, a post office, two livery stables, a garage, and various

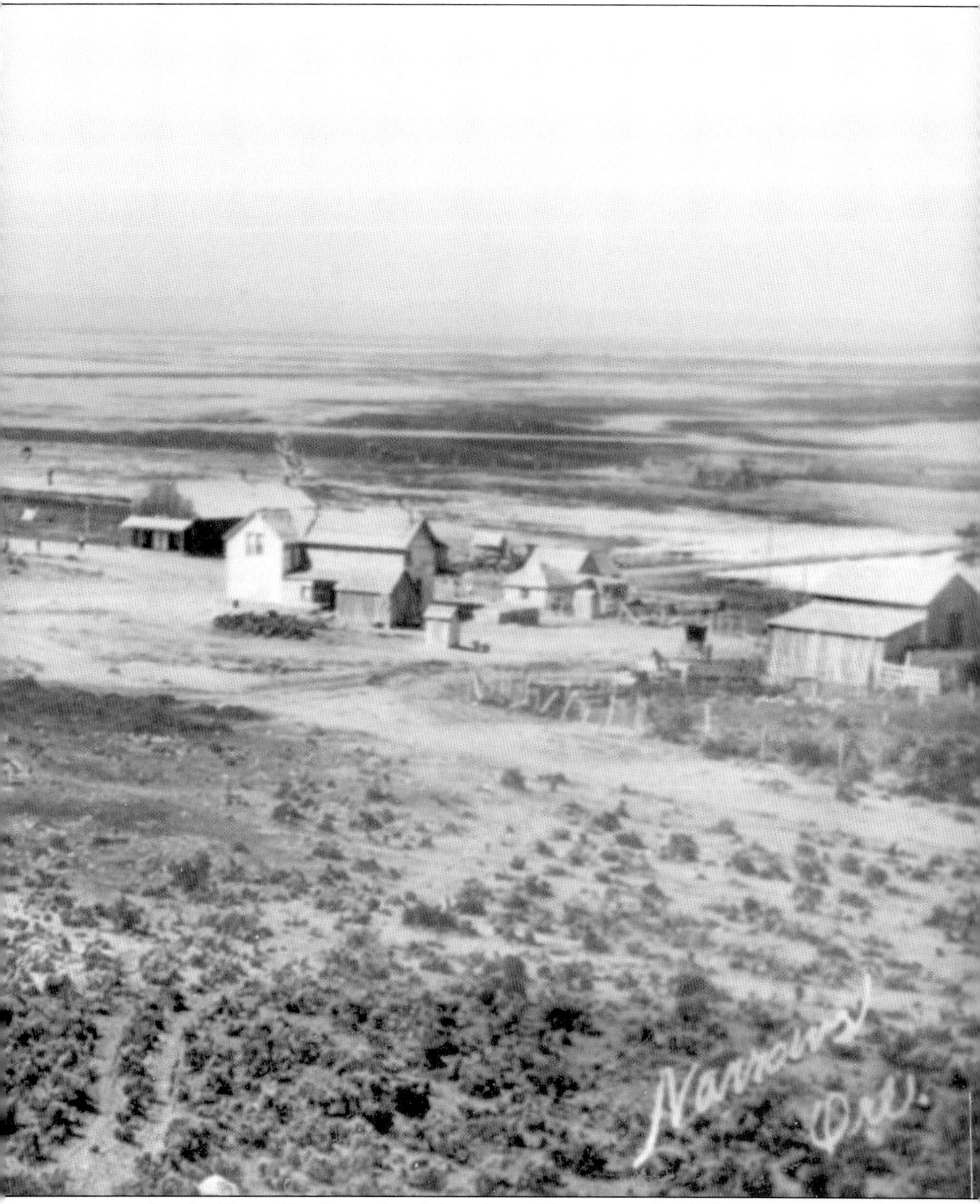

storage and outbuildings. Residences lined the edges of the surrounding hills. Poor success with dryland farming and the growing shift toward automobile transportation were factors in the decline of the community beginning as early as the 1920s. By the 1940s, the settlement was nearly abandoned.

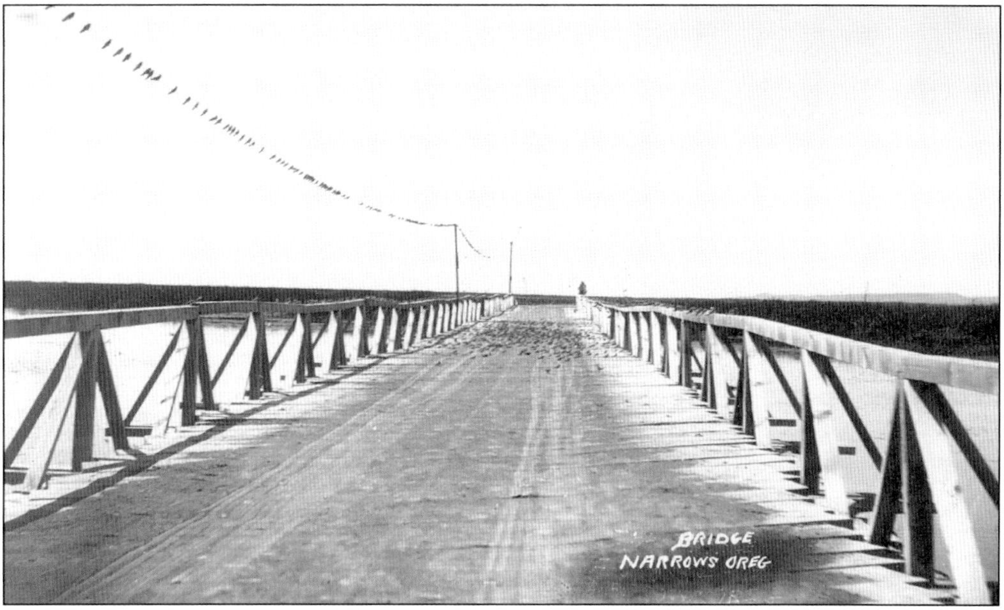

In the winter of 1891–1892, this 300-foot-long bridge was built at the Narrows, crossing the gap between Mud and Malheur Lakes. The bridge on the main road between Burns and Frenchglen was used to cross the narrow channel between the lakes. In dry years, Harney and Mud Lakes have little or no water; however, in wet years such as those that occurred in the 1980s, the three lakes combined to cover a total of 280 square miles. In 1942, a new bridge was constructed.

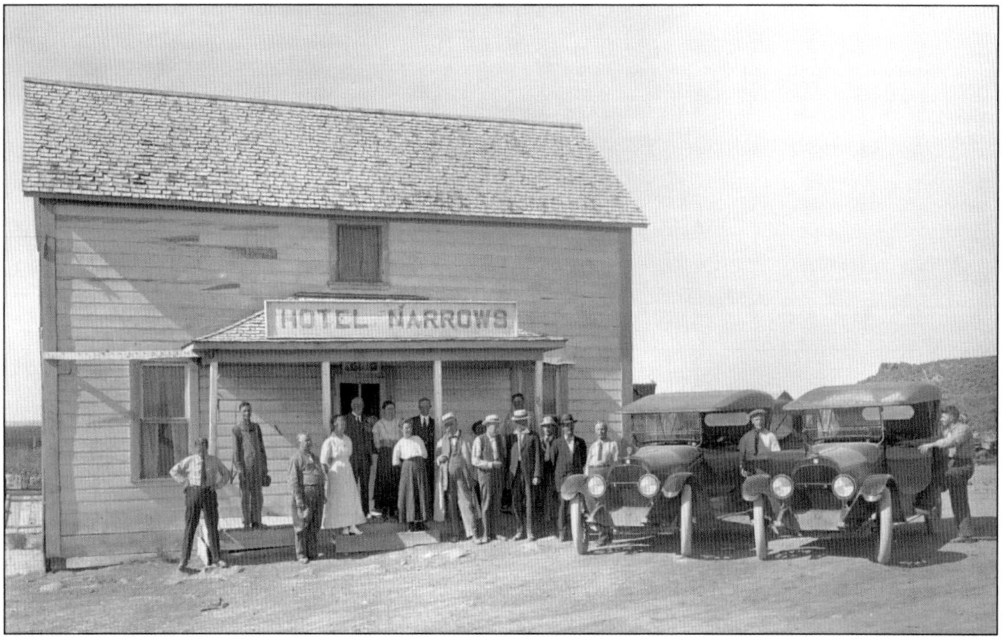

Albert Hembree was the first settler to establish a hotel and general store at the Narrows, located at the narrow channel that connects Harney and Malheur Lakes. In 1892, the post office was transferred to the Narrows from nearby Springer; Hembree served as postmaster until 1897 when he sold out and turned the post office over to Charles Haines. The Narrows Hotel is shown here with an unidentified group around 1920.

Charles Haines, pictured here in the 1890s, operated a very successful mercantile business at the Narrows. He was an astute businessman who supplied the needs of local homesteaders and stockmen. A story is told of Haines taking a sheepherder down to his basement saloon, getting him drunk, then selling the man a load of supplies and a wheelbarrow to take it home in. Charles Haines left an estate valued at $365,000 upon his death in 1916. (Photograph by R. W. Heck.)

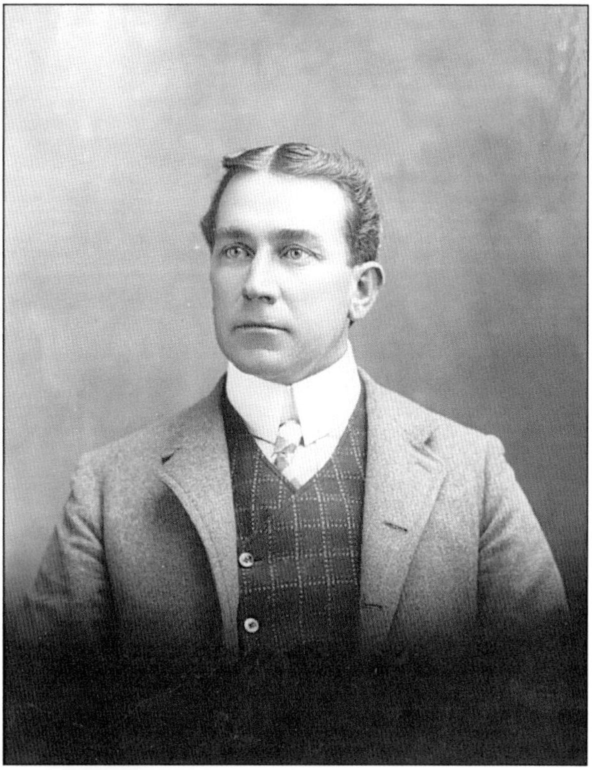

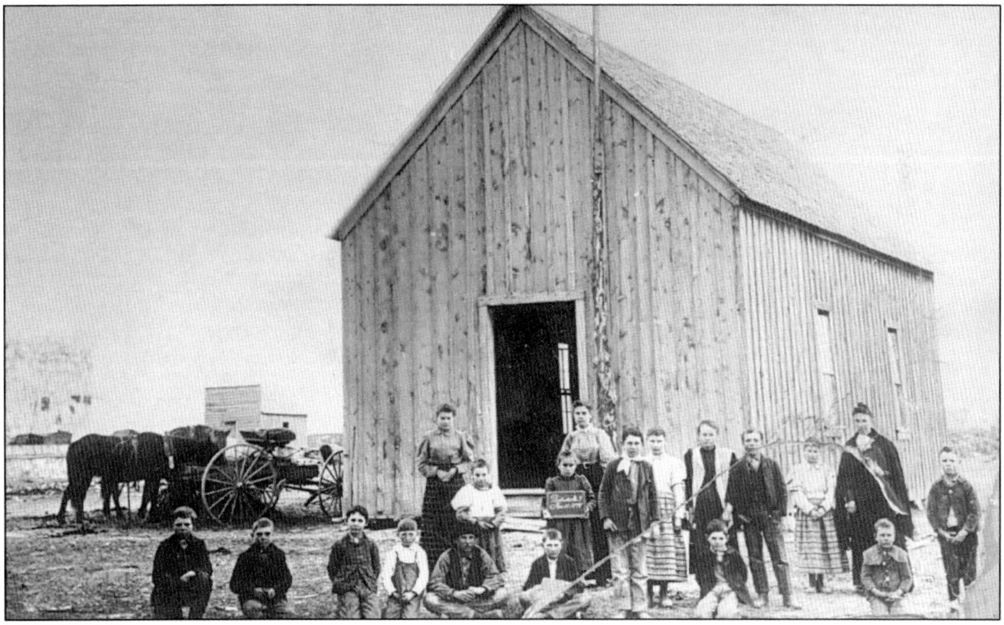

This was the first school that was located at the Narrows. Mrs. McKenzie, the teacher poses with students, including Judy McKenzie, Josephine McKenzie, Homer Bringle, Walter Bringle, Burt Leroy Oliver, and Roy Oliver. The slate held by the small boy in the middle reads "District 9 November 11, 1898." Some records show that the district was not formally established until 1903. In 1940, the Narrows District was consolidated with the Sod House District.

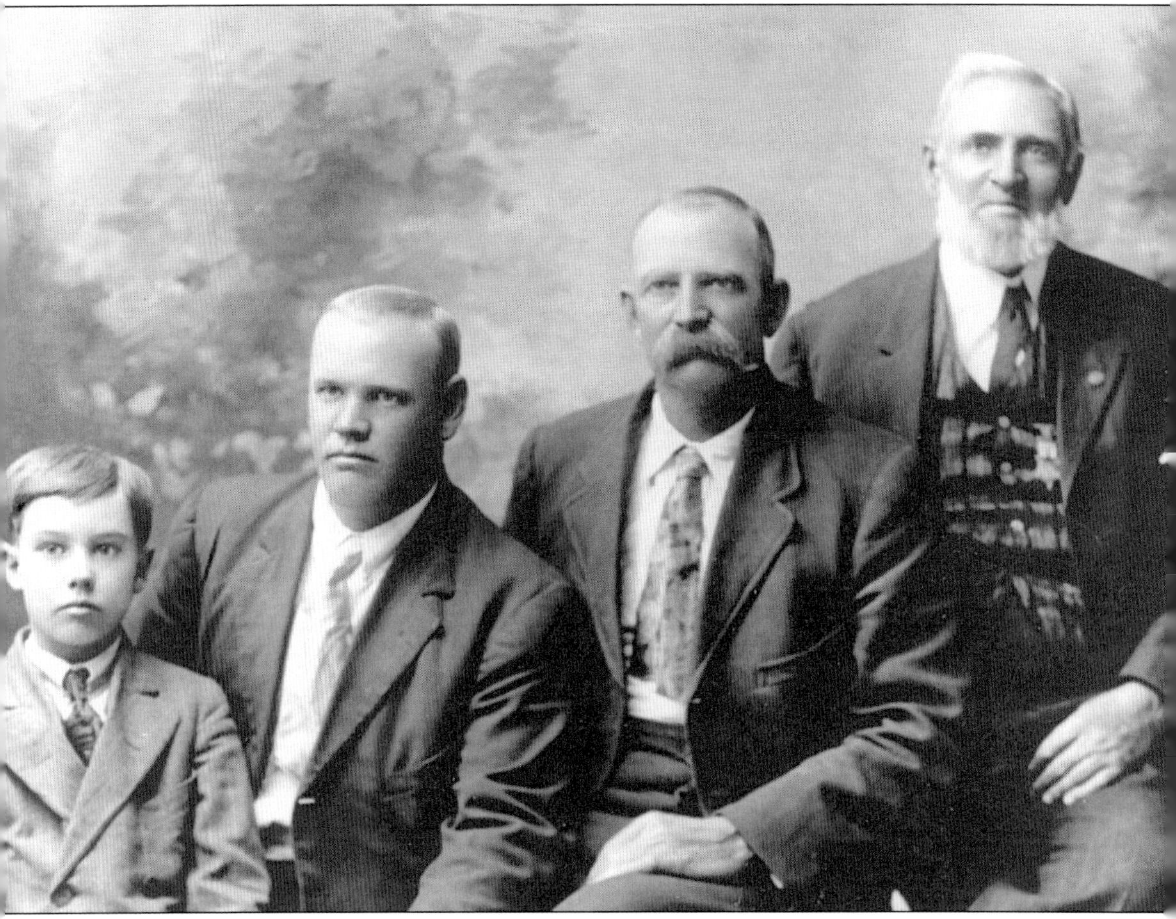

Lewis B. Springer, shown here in a four-generation portrait taken around 1910, first settled in Harney County in 1885. Pictured from left to right are Wilbur, Eddie, Alva, and Lewis Springer. Lewis was a veteran of the Civil War and also served as a wagon master on at least two of five trips across the Great Plains. In 1888, Lewis along with his son Alva and son-in-law George Marshall settled at Sod House Spring. Men named Chapman and Weaver originally inhabited the location and constructed the first shelter made of sod. An 1890 Harney County Tax Assessor Roll notes that Lewis owned six horses, 30 head of cattle, and property value of $615. Alva had seven horses, 30 head of cattle, and property value of $560. The Springer Post Office opened in 1889 with Lewis serving as postmaster. The post office was closed in 1892 with the mail being transferred to the Narrows Post Office.

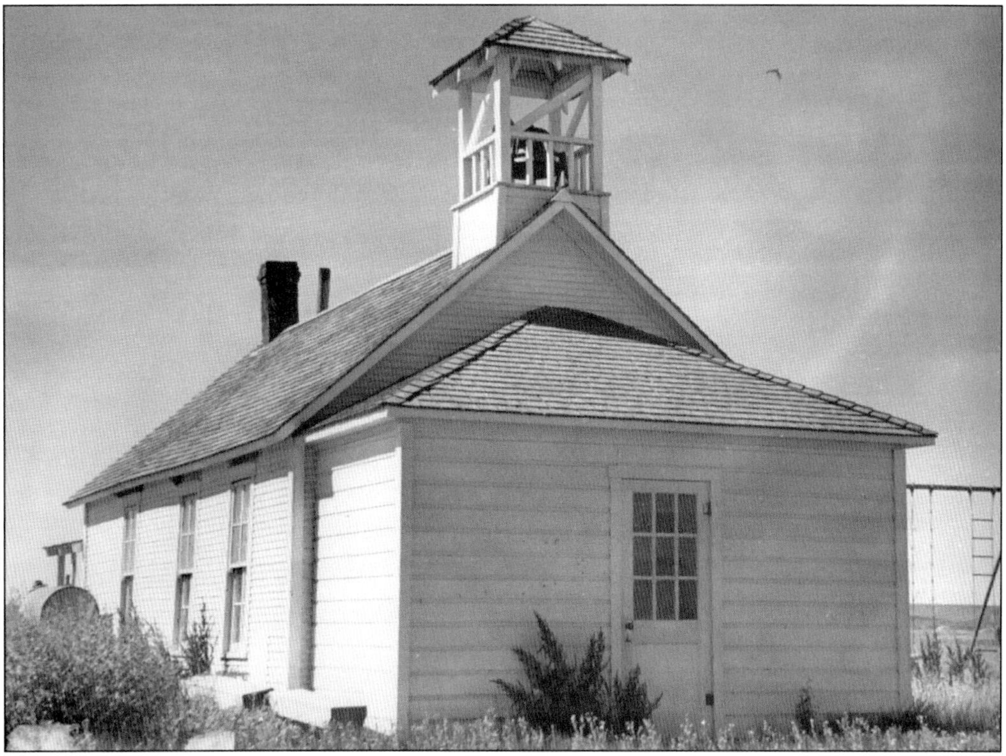

The Sod House School District was established in 1908. During a disagreement about the location of the schoolhouse, the structure was burned. The Pacific Livestock Company donated a quarter section of land for the construction of a new schoolhouse. Enid Cawlfield served as teacher during the years 1910–1911. At this time she had 30 students in eight grades. Some of her students were children of the Dunn, Cawlfield, Marshall, Witzel, Springer, Haines, and Comegys families. (Courtesy Harney County ESD.)

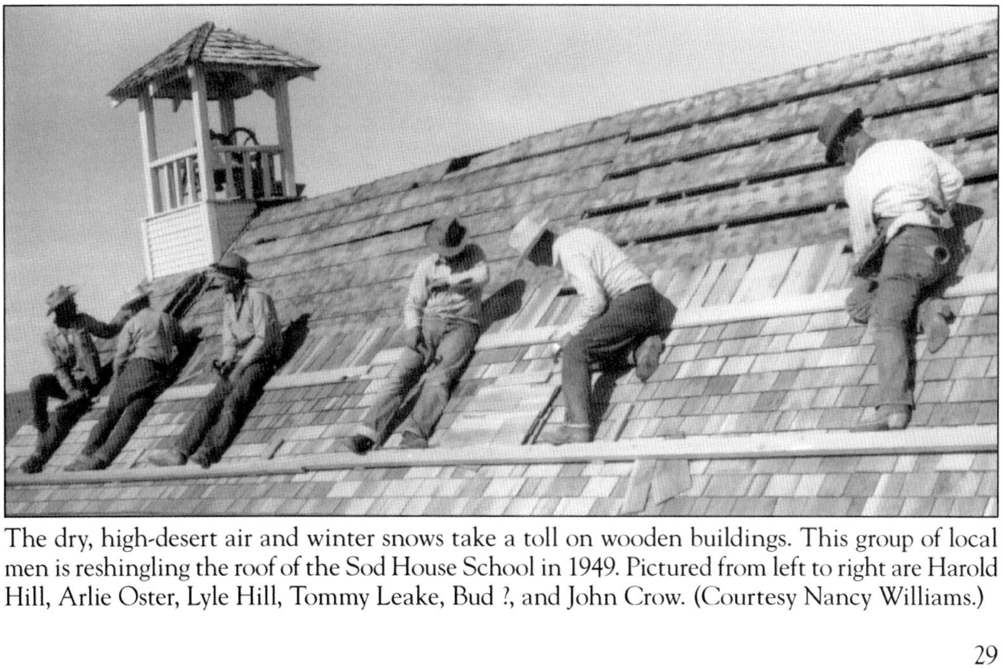

The dry, high-desert air and winter snows take a toll on wooden buildings. This group of local men is reshingling the roof of the Sod House School in 1949. Pictured from left to right are Harold Hill, Arlie Oster, Lyle Hill, Tommy Leake, Bud ?, and John Crow. (Courtesy Nancy Williams.)

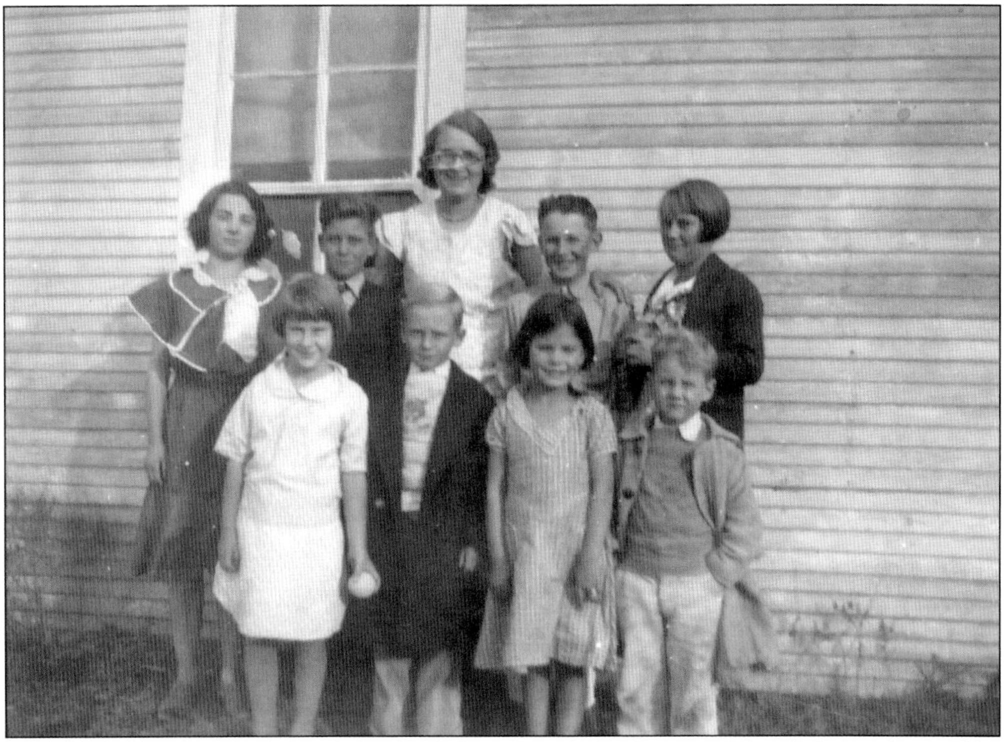

Edna Haines taught the Sod House School class of 1933–1934. Pictured from left to right are (first row) Mary Osborn, Buddy Harris, Mavis Dunn, and Buster Harris; (second row) Olive Cooley, Harold Hill, Edna Haines, Jess Bonyard, and Virginia Osborn. (Courtesy Nancy Williams.)

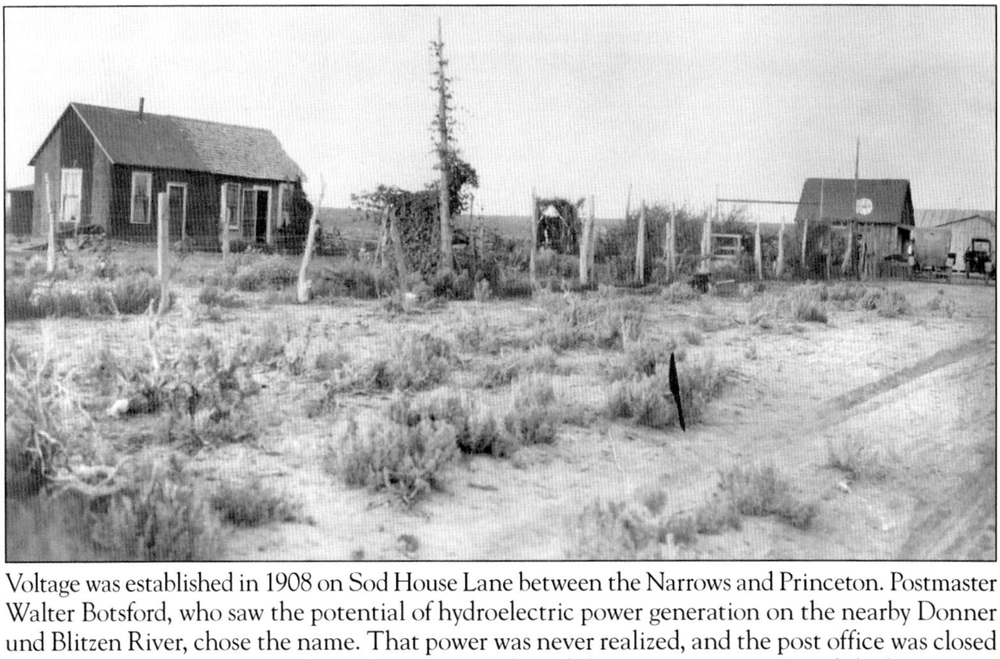

Voltage was established in 1908 on Sod House Lane between the Narrows and Princeton. Postmaster Walter Botsford, who saw the potential of hydroelectric power generation on the nearby Donner und Blitzen River, chose the name. That power was never realized, and the post office was closed in 1933. Alfred Marshall and his wife, Mary, purchased the site in 1918, occupied the homestead pictured, and ran the post office until the mid-1930s. (Courtesy Conly Marshall.)

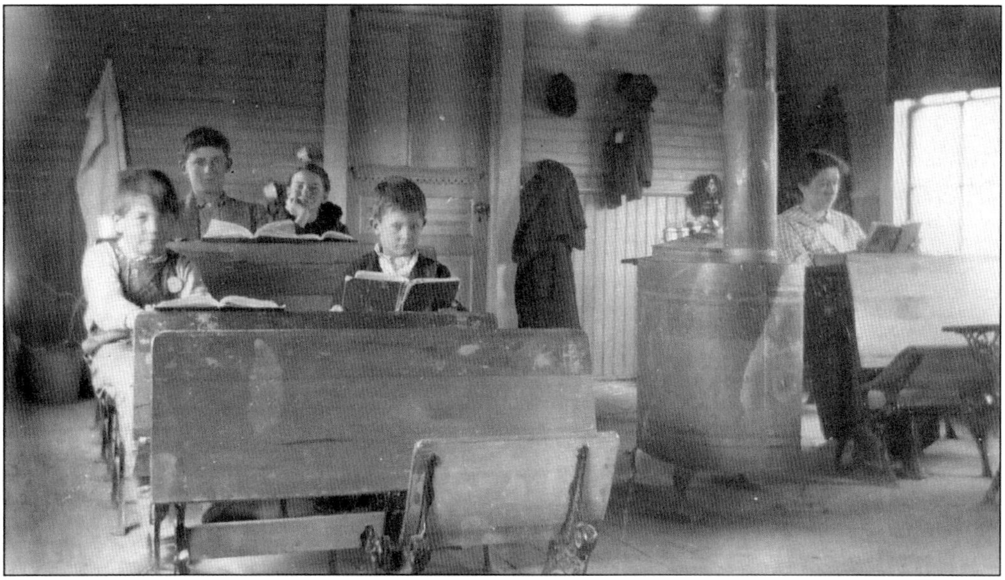

The Voltage School District was established in 1908. Georgia Cresswell taught school in 1936, earning $75 per month. Culver Marshall Jr. (seated front, left) and younger brother Conly (seated, front right with open book) were two of the pupils in her class that year. Other students in the class included Miller and Harris children. As the class size dwindled, the school was discontinued and the students were sent to Ontario. (Courtesy Conly Marshall.)

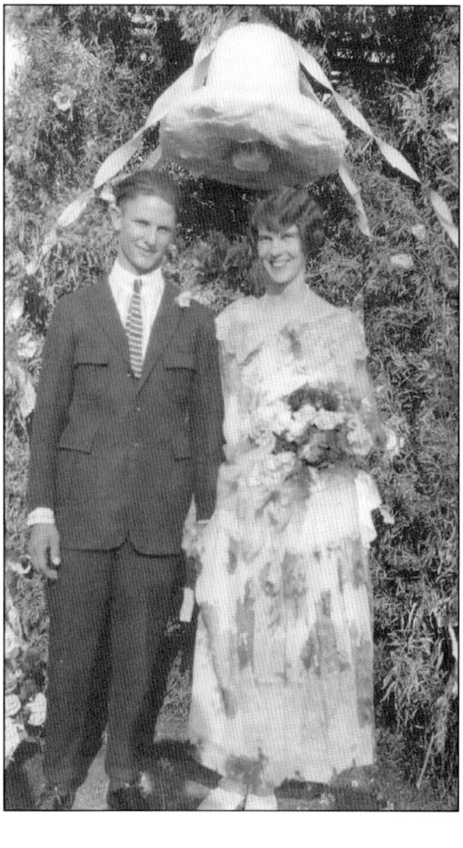

The marriage of Culver Marshall Sr. and Violet Lees on August 10, 1924, under a bower of flowers at the home of the groom's parents, Mr. and Mrs. A. L. Marshall, is believed to be the first wedding ceremony held at Voltage. The couple were to become the new schoolteachers at Wagontire and Suntex the following September. (Courtesy Conly Marshall.)

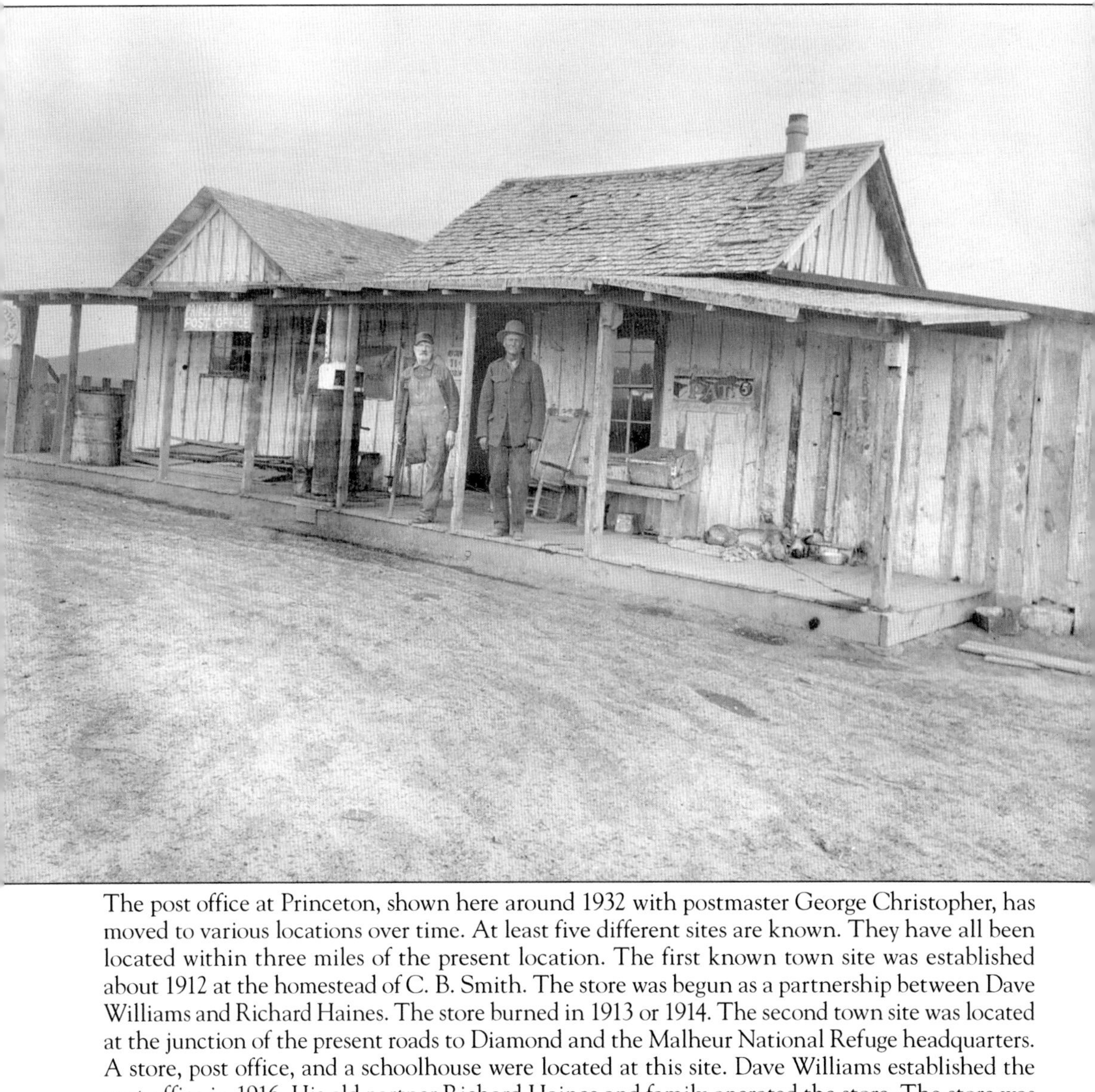

The post office at Princeton, shown here around 1932 with postmaster George Christopher, has moved to various locations over time. At least five different sites are known. They have all been located within three miles of the present location. The first known town site was established about 1912 at the homestead of C. B. Smith. The store was begun as a partnership between Dave Williams and Richard Haines. The store burned in 1913 or 1914. The second town site was located at the junction of the present roads to Diamond and the Malheur National Refuge headquarters. A store, post office, and a schoolhouse were located at this site. Dave Williams established the post office in 1916. His old partner Richard Haines and family operated the store. The store was abandoned in 1918 or 1919 but the schoolhouse remained until sometime in the 1920s. Harry Brown established the third site of Princeton but the location failed because of the lack of water. Bob and Grace Dougall established the fourth site of Princeton supporting a post office, store, and other buildings. After Bob Dougall's death in 1951, Clem Gaugler started the present Princeton town site. (Courtesy Letha Melton and Argetta Williams.)

The Princeton School District operated from 1900 to 1932. In 1918, the abandoned store of Richard Haines was converted into a one-room schoolhouse and teacherage, a building serving as a combination school and living quarters. School was held in this building until 1928 when the school was relocated about a mile to the southwest. Pictured from left to right are Princeton School students of teacher Mrs. Catterson: Ruland Officer, Dick Davies, Maurice Davies, Everett Williams, and Laverne Williams sometime in the early 1920s. (Courtesy Letha Melton and Argetta Williams.)

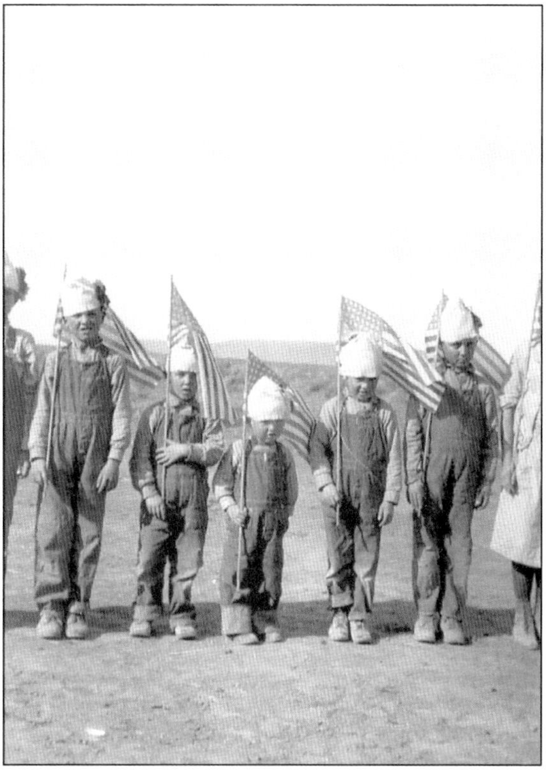

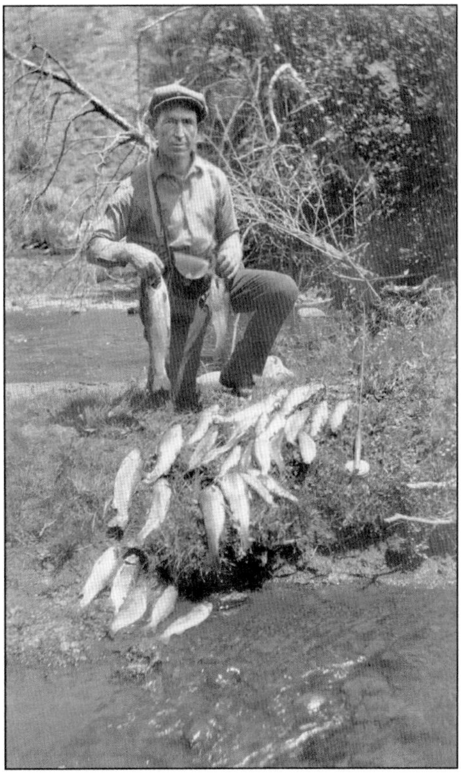

Rufus W. Heck, shown here along the Blitzen River pursuing his favorite pastime, was the most prolific photographer in the history of Harney County. He moved to Burns in 1907 and purchased the photography studio of John McMullen. Heck traveled the county recording everything imaginable during a career spanning nearly 38 years. In 1945, two months after selling his studio to Bob Lemons, R. W. Heck passed away of a heart attack.

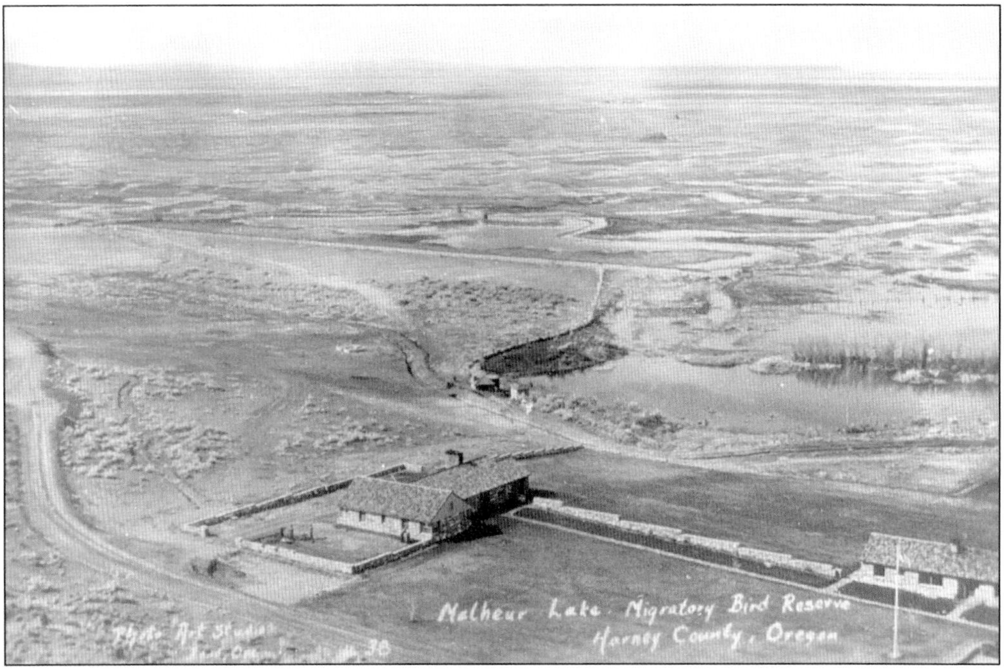

The 64,716-acre Malheur National Wildlife Refuge was established in 1935 as the Malheur Migratory Bird Refuge. The refuge lands included most of the Blitzen Valley, once the domain of the cattle empire of Peter French. Many historic sites are protected within the boundaries of the refuge. Stanley Jewett was the first refuge superintendent followed by John Scharff, who in his 35 years at the refuge pioneered the use of grazing and haying to manage the habitat. The world famous refuge attracts visitors from afar to witness the spectacular migrations that pass through the valley. (Photograph by Oregon Art Studio; courtesy Nancy Williams.)

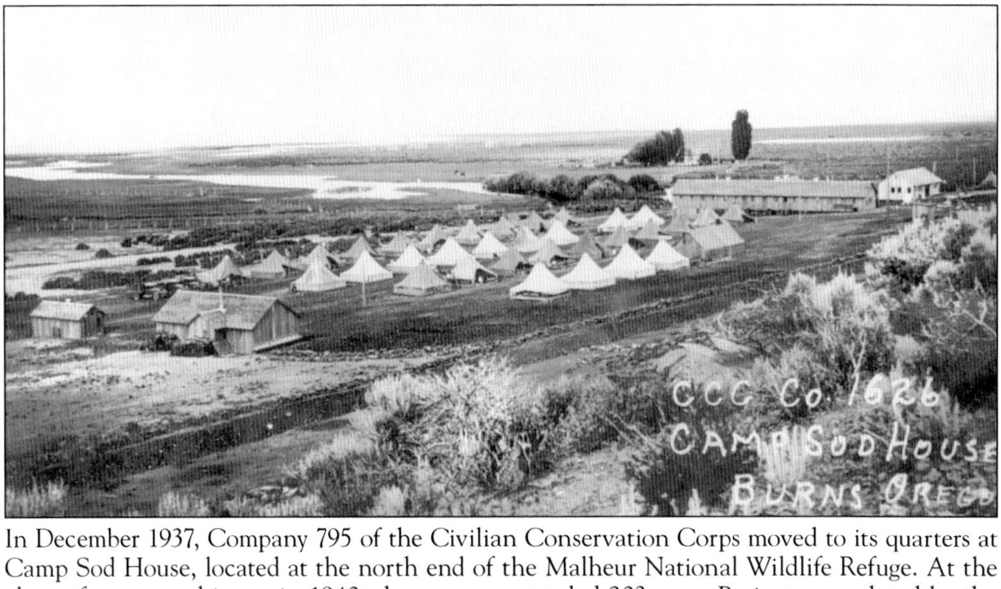

In December 1937, Company 795 of the Civilian Conservation Corps moved to its quarters at Camp Sod House, located at the north end of the Malheur National Wildlife Refuge. At the close of company history in 1940, the company totaled 203 men. Projects completed by the company included construction of dwellings, dams, fences, and trails, and excavation of canals and ditches on the refuge.

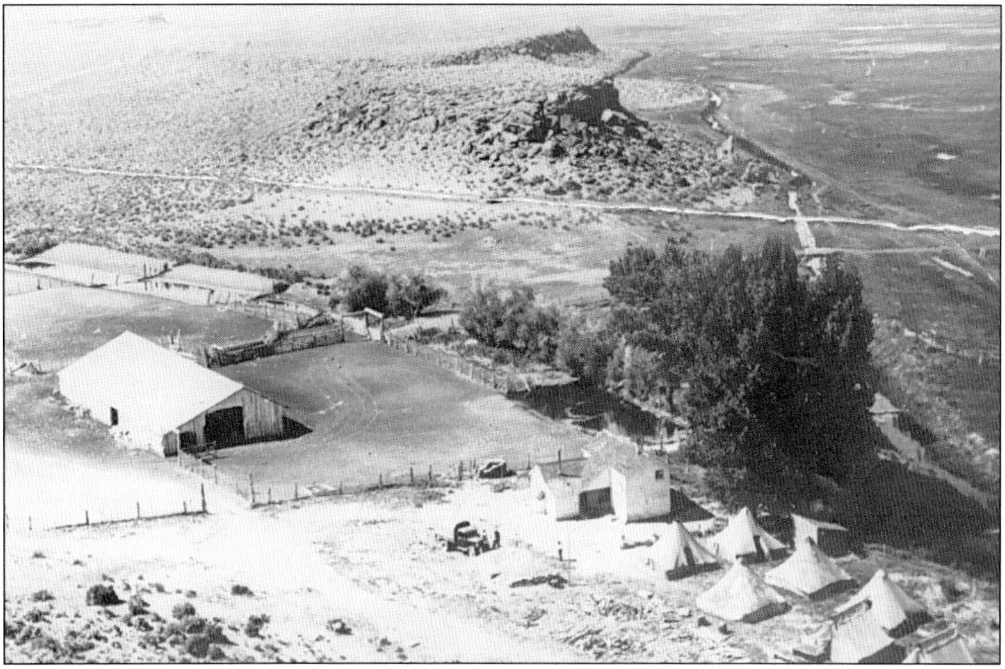

This Civilian Conservation Corps (CCC) spike camp at Buena Vista was photographed in 1935. Buildings were put up in 1937 and 1938 with CCC labor. The camp consisted of barracks, a mess hall, army personnel buildings, a recreation hall, laundry room, and a latrine. Today an overlook trail leads to the top of the point giving a beautiful view of the valley to the east.

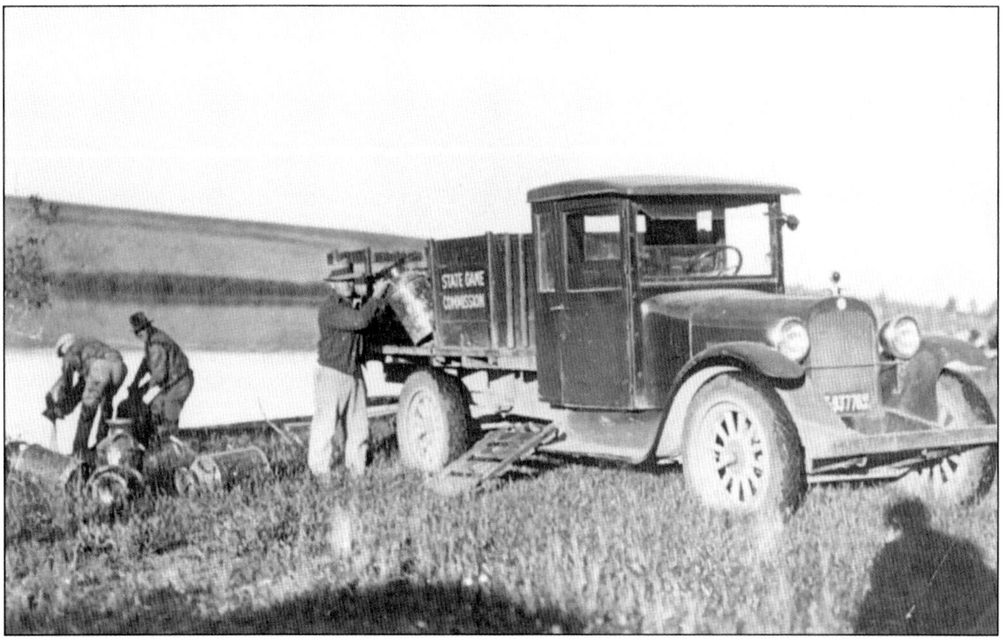

Ellis Mason began working for the Oregon Game Commission out of Burns in 1939. He was a member of the first class to graduate in the new Fish and Game Management course at Oregon State College. At the time, Mason's district included all of southeastern Oregon. Mason received an old army truck like the one shown here to use as his official vehicle.

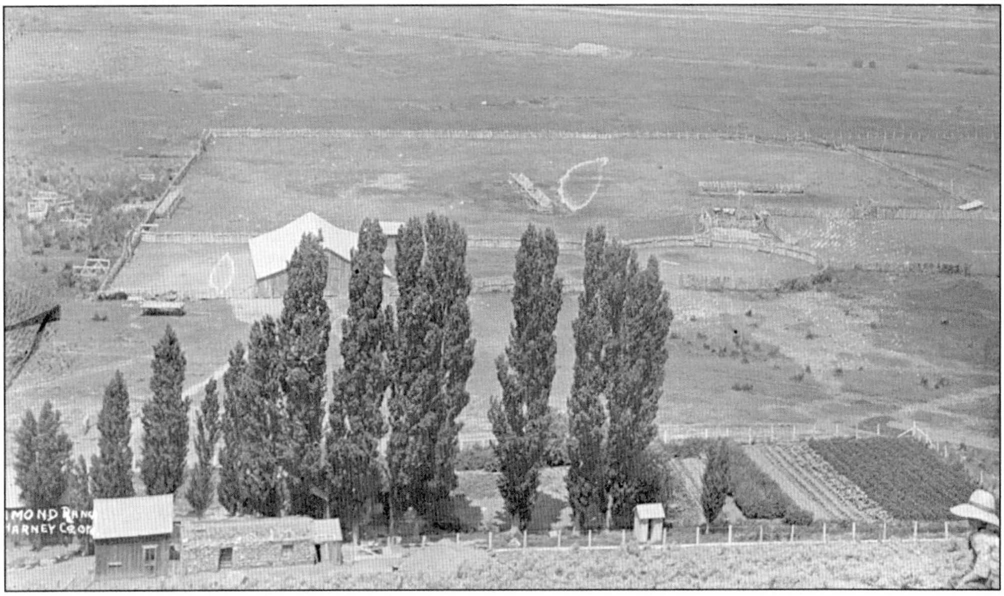

The diamond-shaped cattle brand used by early-settler Mace McCoy was the namesake for the little settlement of Diamond. The Diamond Ranch, seen here about 1913, is located in a valley on the northwest side of Steens Mountain. James Ingram is listed as the first postmaster beginning in 1887. Serving as a supply center for area farms and ranches, Diamond reached a peak population of around 50 during the heyday of cattle and sheep grazing on Steens Mountain.

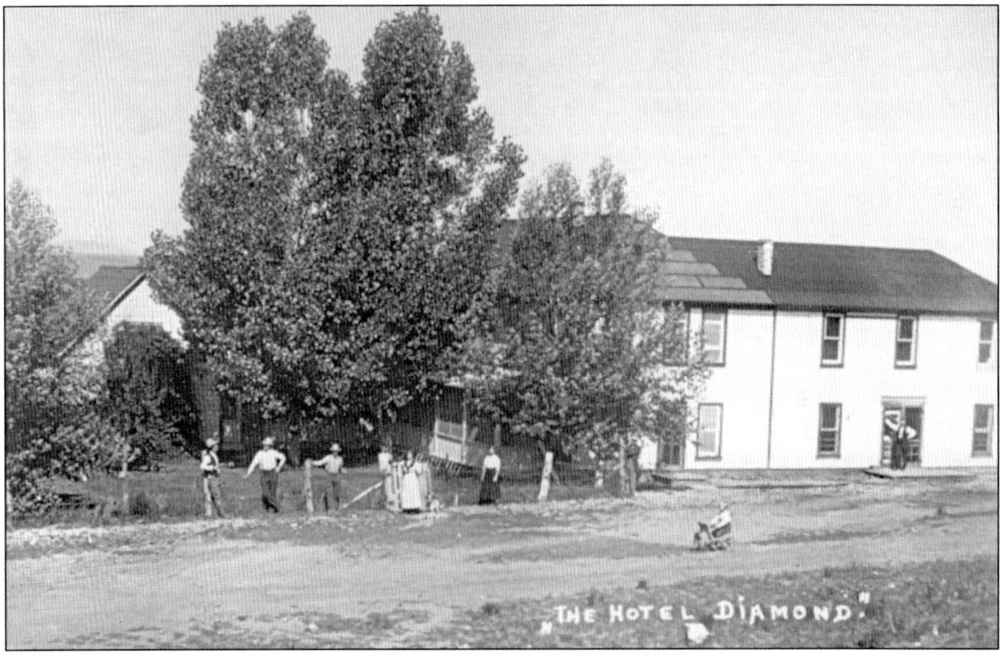

The Diamond Hotel, shown here sometime after 1913, was constructed about 1898 by Marion Horton to serve area sheepherders, stockmen, and travelers. In 1913, the hotel was sold to Sid Comegys, who added a saloon. Lodging cost $1 per night and meals could be had for 25¢ per person. The hotel is still in operation, though it has changed hands many times and undergone several renovations. The original rock cellar remains intact.

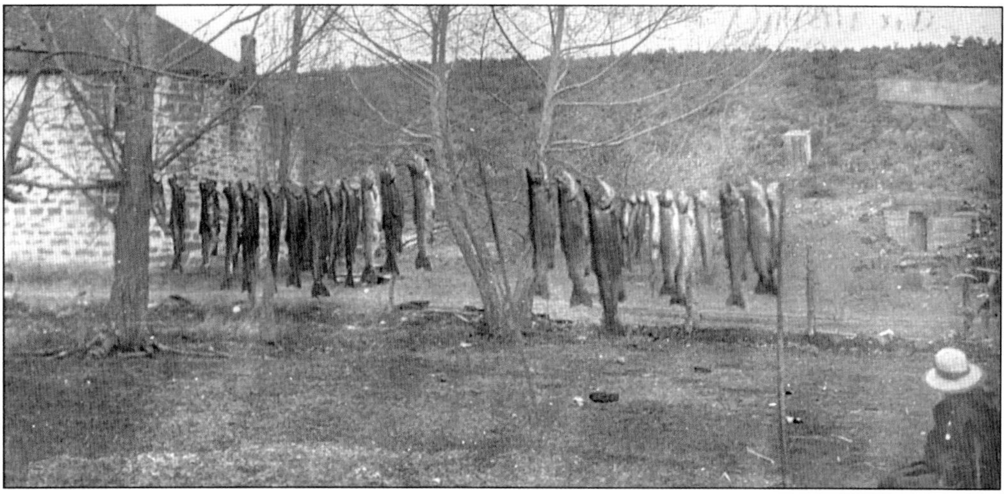

The rivers and creeks in the Blitzen Valley on the western slopes of Steens Mountain were notable for good fishing in earlier years. One family of five is said to have camped on the Little Blitzen for a week and taken over 500 fish. John Scharff, refuge manager from 1935 through 1970, remembered a time when people along all the little creeks had a fish trap in use. This photograph taken at Diamond shows off a large catch.

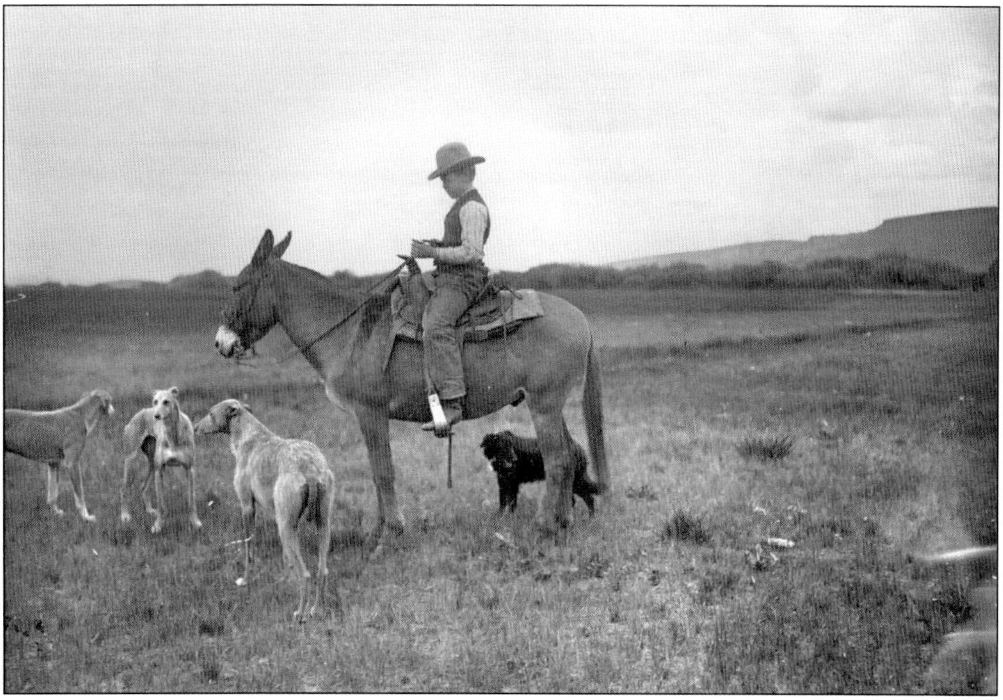

Cassie and George A. Smyth settled in Harney County in 1872 and operated a successful ranch in the Diamond area. Their son Fred W. Smyth, pictured here astride a mule, was born in 1896. He married Pearl Mahon, daughter of James F. Mahon, a noted horse and mule raiser. Smyth later purchased the family ranch and also acquired the interests of his uncle Presley. On June 14, 1878, Fred's grandfather George C. Smyth and his uncle John Smyth were killed during an Native American raid that resulted in the Smyth's house being set on fire, as told in an account of the events by Sylvester "Coon" Smith.

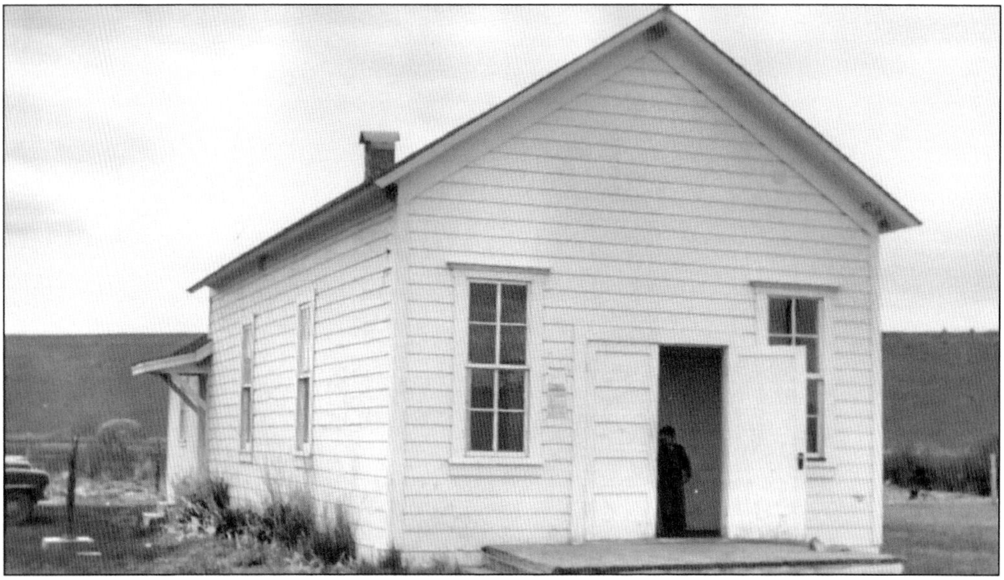

The Diamond School District was established in 1889. Miss Jackson of Baker City taught the first two terms of school in this district. An old school building was moved into town from a location two miles west of Diamond to serve as a residence in the early 1960s. The post office was located in an old school building, and Mary and Louise Moore served as postmistresses. (Courtesy Harney County ESD.)

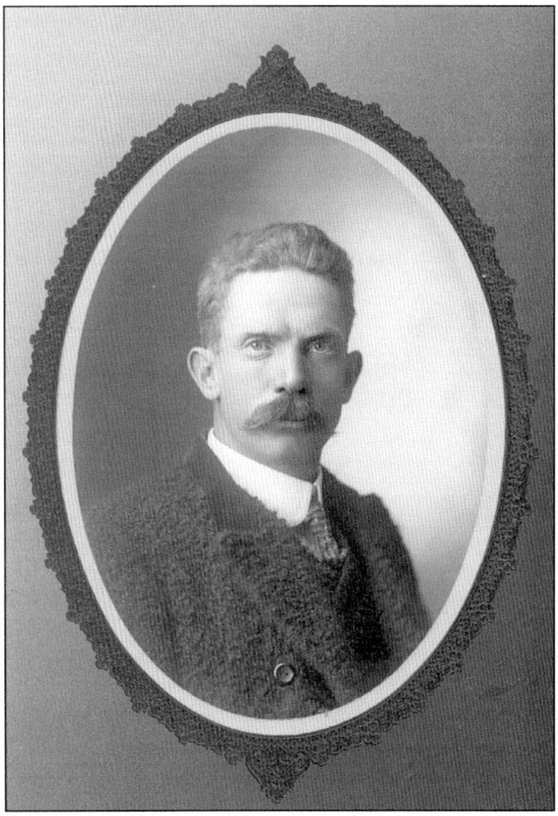

Fred Riddle, shown here in the early 1900s, was born in 1874 near the warm springs, which is near the location of the city of Hines. He was the son of Tobias Stilley Riddle, who settled in Harney County in 1872. Fred along with his brothers, Benjamin and Walter, settled near the mouth of the Little Blitzen Gorge during the early 1900s. The three brothers operated ranches together for more than 40 years, raising horses, mules, sheep, and cattle.

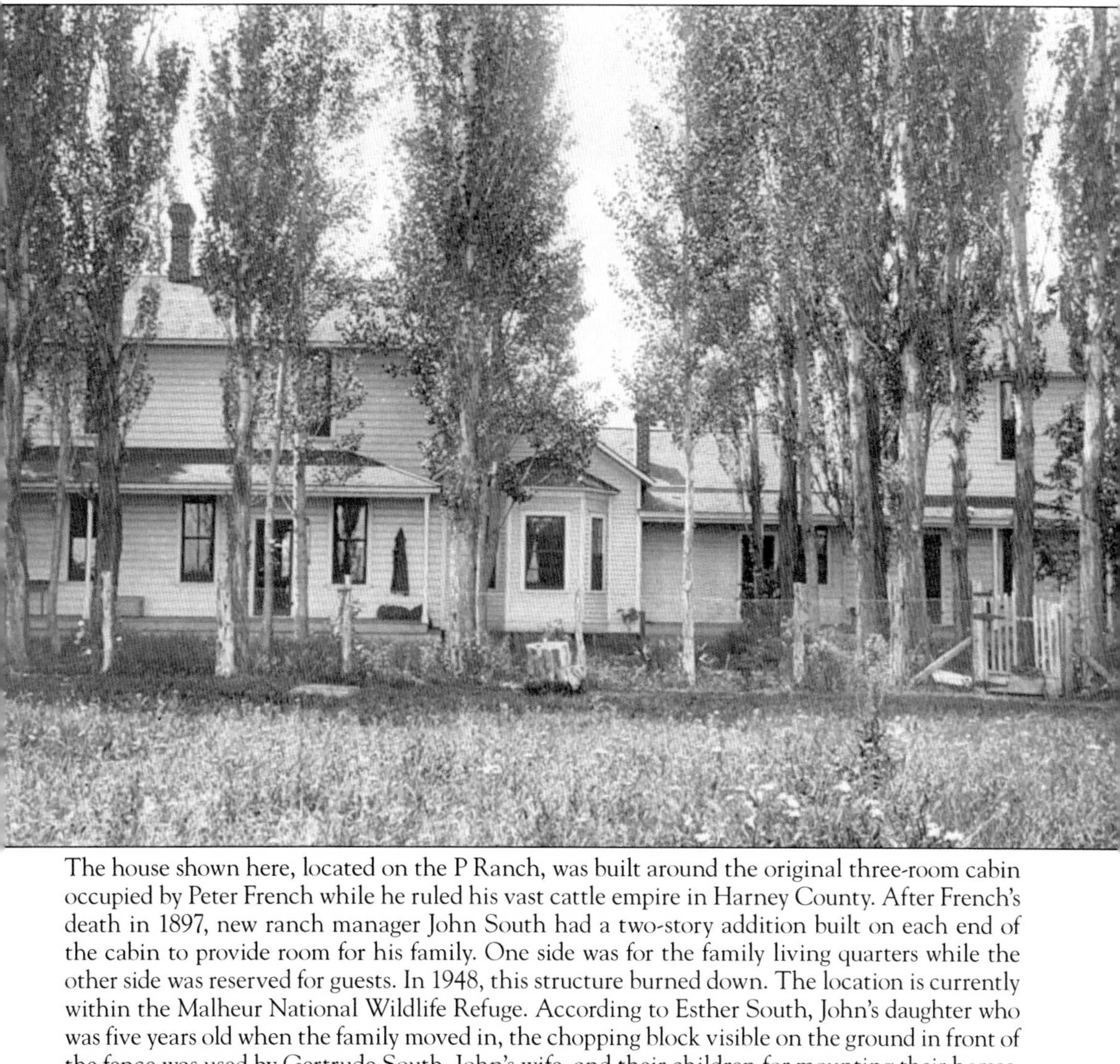

The house shown here, located on the P Ranch, was built around the original three-room cabin occupied by Peter French while he ruled his vast cattle empire in Harney County. After French's death in 1897, new ranch manager John South had a two-story addition built on each end of the cabin to provide room for his family. One side was for the family living quarters while the other side was reserved for guests. In 1948, this structure burned down. The location is currently within the Malheur National Wildlife Refuge. According to Esther South, John's daughter who was five years old when the family moved in, the chopping block visible on the ground in front of the fence was used by Gertrude South, John's wife, and their children for mounting their horses. (Photograph by R. W. Heck.)

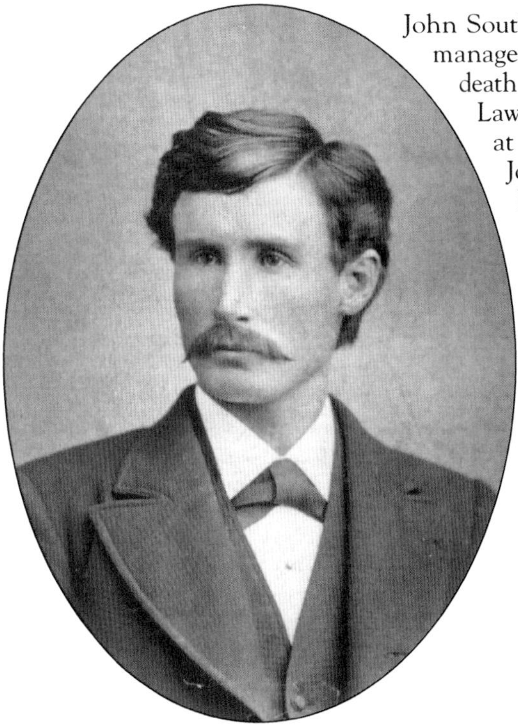

John South, shown here in the early 1890s, assumed management of the P Ranch in 1898 following the death of Peter French. With a wife and three children, Lawrence, Peter, and Esther, in tow, South settled at the P ranch for four years with the family. John's daughter said that in his younger days, Buffalo Bill tried to recruit him for his traveling shows because of his fine horse and excellent roping skills.

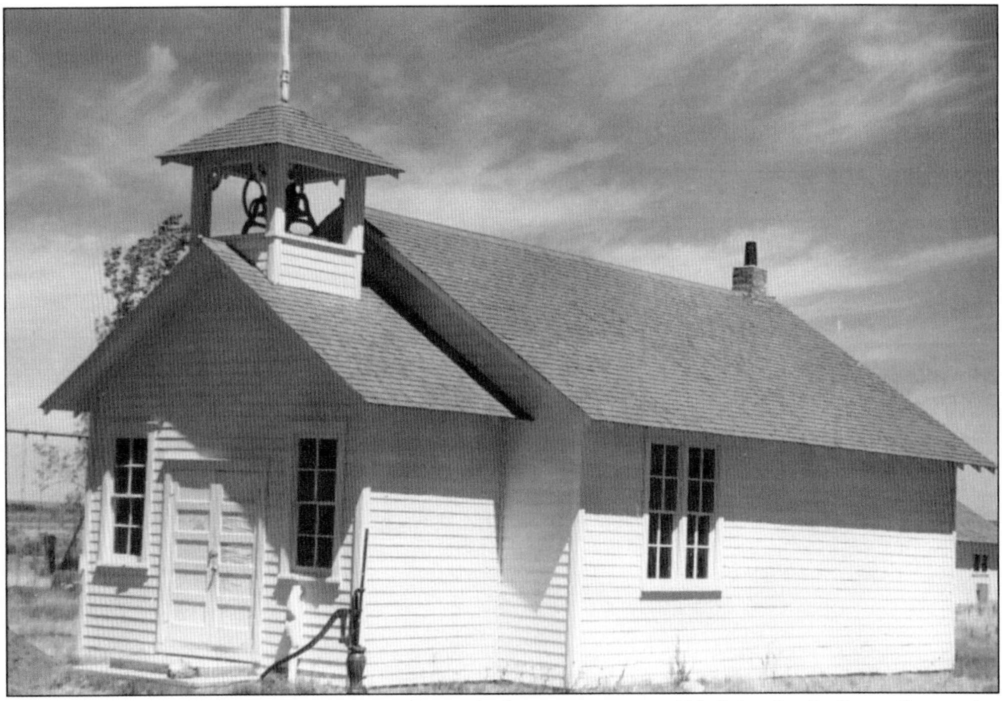

A school was organized in the town of Frenchglen in January 1927. Mrs. L. R. Barnell was the first teacher hired. The first school was replaced by the present school building located on the same site. The school is one of several one-room schoolhouses still active in Harney County. (Courtesy Harney County ESD.)

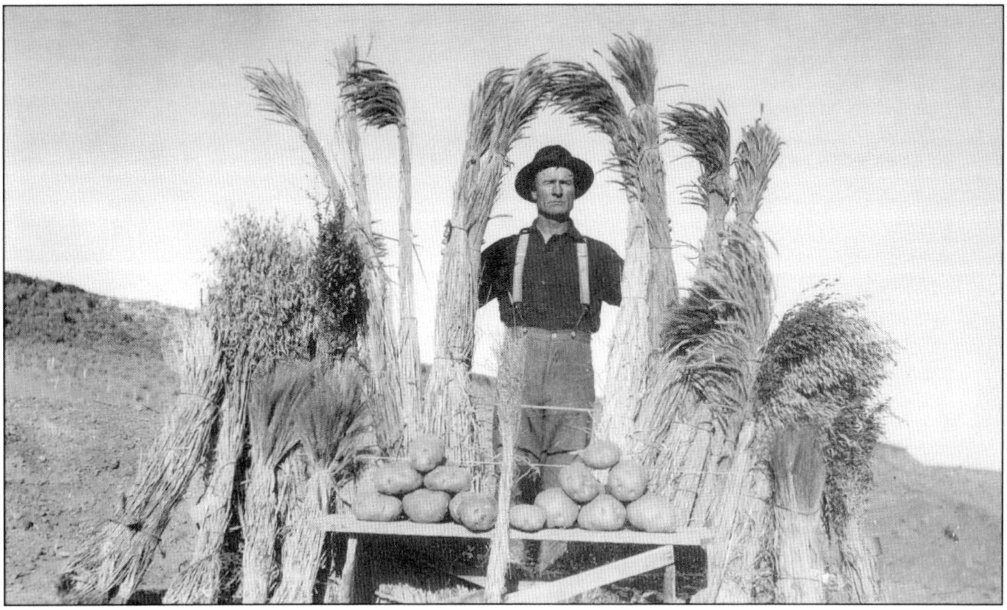

Homesteaders took great pride in the crops that were the result of their toils. For every successful farmer, there were more who could not make a living and eventually sold out. Here Charlie Downs shows off the grain and potatoes raised through dryland farming in the Catlow Valley of Harney County in 1915.

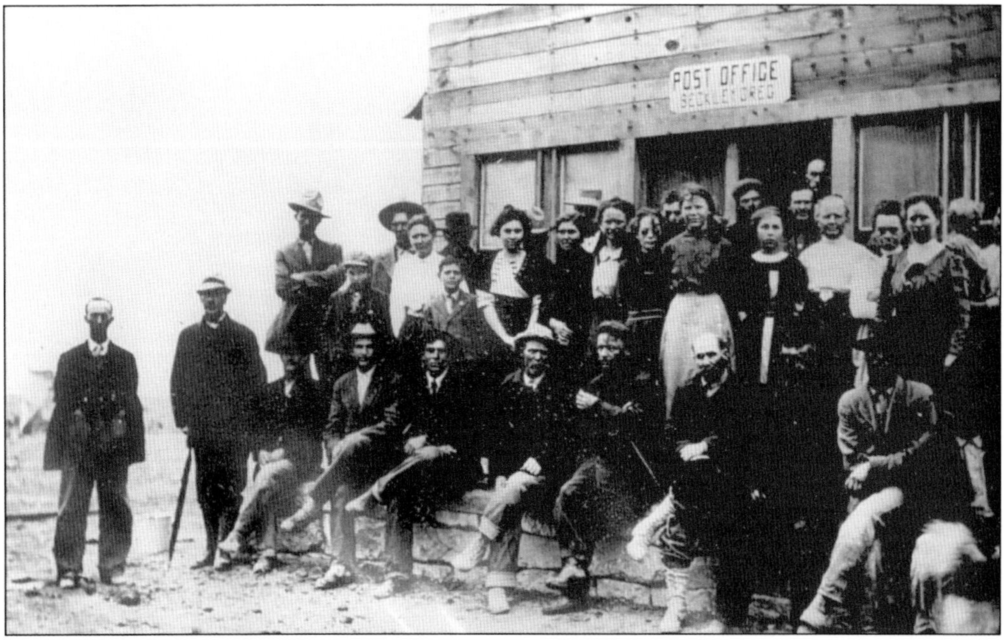

A group of settlers poses in front of the post office at Beckley, which was established in 1912 on the west side of Steens Mountain near present-day Roaring Springs Ranch. Many homesteaders in this area starved due to inhospitable farming conditions. The post office was abandoned in 1926. Virtually nothing remains of the site today.

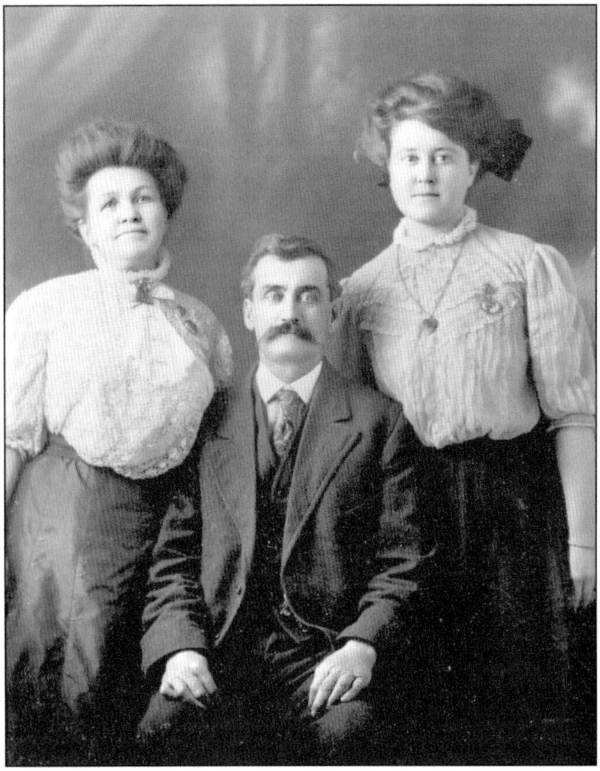

Charles M. Fields, pictured here with wife Tillie on the left and daughter Pearl on the right, homesteaded 160 acres in 1881 at the location that was later named in his honor. Fields built a hotel as a stopping place for travelers at the south end of the county. John T. Smyth, who purchased the land from Fields, named the Fields Post Office in 1913.

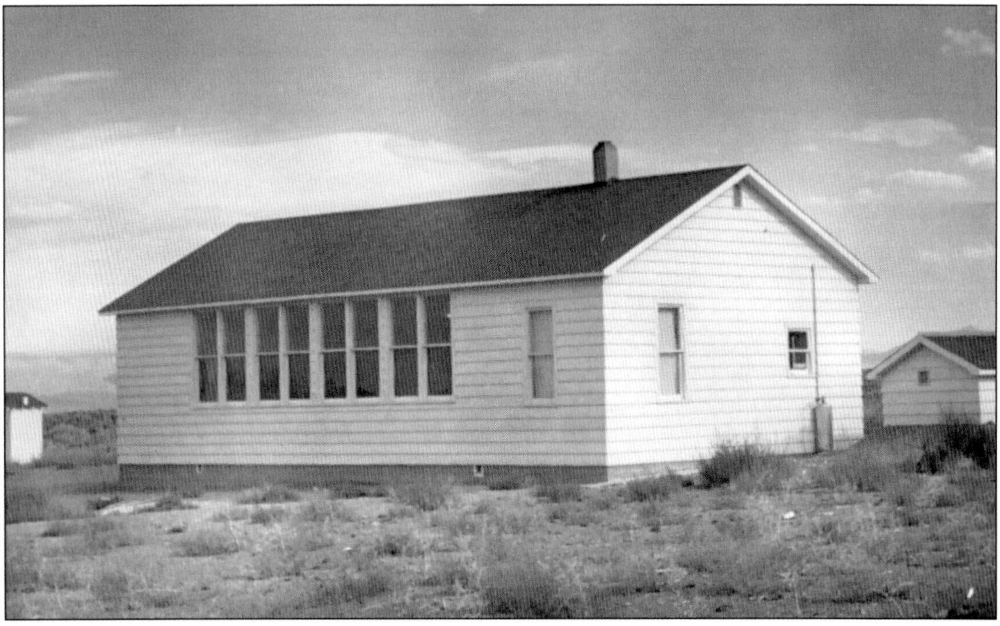

The Red Point grade school pictured here, located near Fields in southern Harney County, was first organized in 1902. Children of the Fred Holloway, Alfred Thompson, and Ed Thompson families were among the first to attend this school. Classes were suspended in 1934 when the district combined with the Fields School District. The Red Point Community Club later purchased the old schoolhouse. (Courtesy Harney County ESD.)

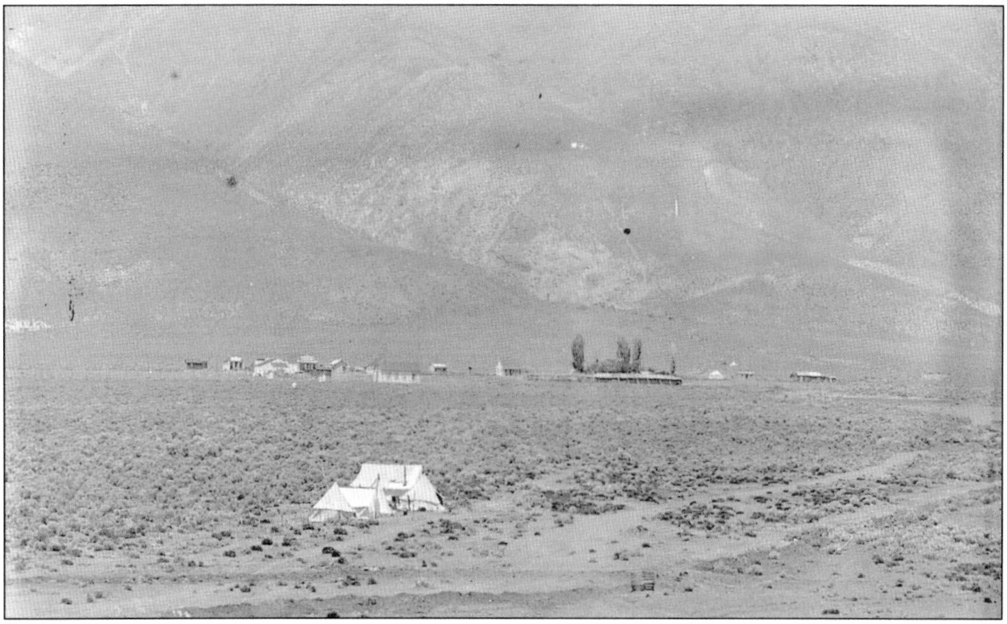

Established in 1888, the community of Denio, located 130 miles south of Burns, is shown here near the beginning of the 20th century. Early settler Aaron Denio, for whom the community is named, arrived in the area in 1885. He operated a successful stage stop and hotel. The town, which at one time straddled state lines, began in Oregon but officially relocated one mile south to Nevada.

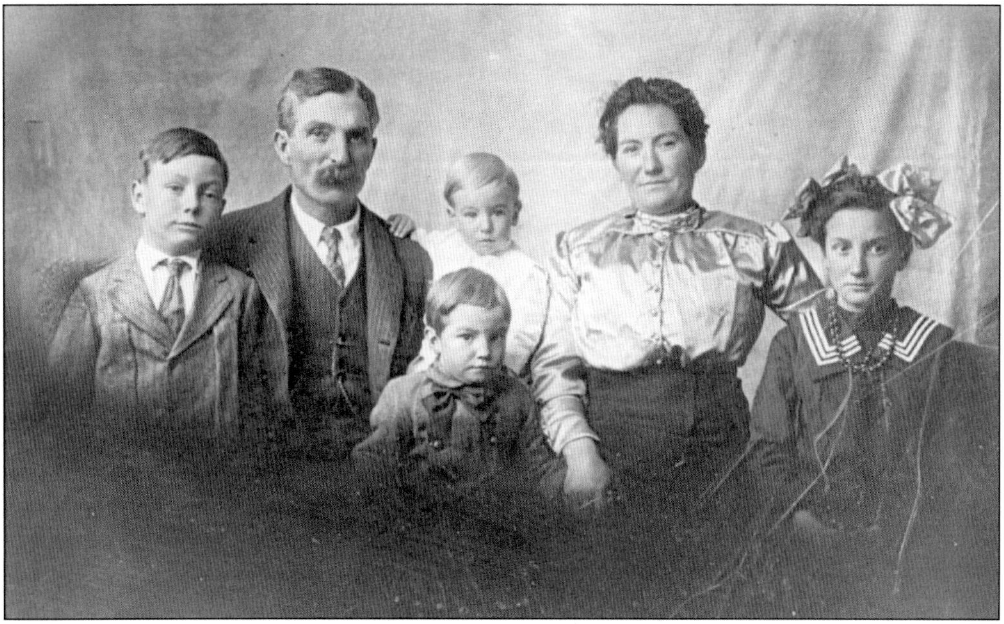

Dell Defenbaugh, pictured here c. 1914 with wife Kate and children Fred, George, Philip, and Lola, was an early Denio businessman and rancher who operated a successful merchandise business and hotel. The first school at Trout Creek was located on Defenbaugh property in the home of Bert Cameron. Defenbaugh and fellow homesteader John Beatty reportedly paid the first teacher, Ethyl Sage, out of their pockets for the first year or two.

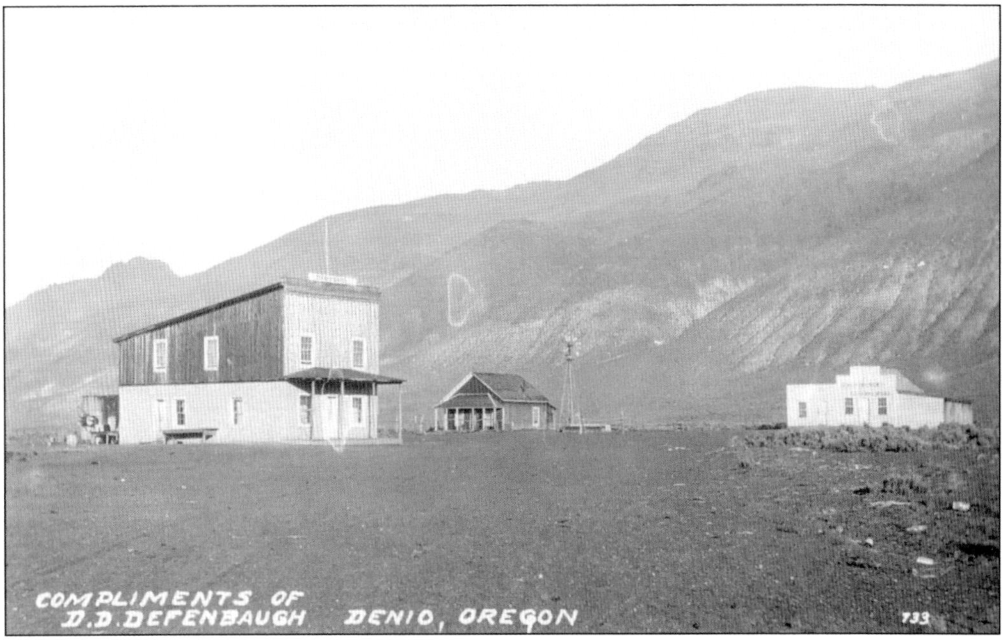

Businesses in Denio operated on both the Oregon and Nevada sides of the town. Dell Defenbaugh owned the Pueblo Hotel, pictured left. The Schubner General Merchandise Store pictured on the right was located in Nevada. Mose and Sol Schubner sold supplies to sheep men and cattle ranchers as well as to the thriving mining community in the area. Dell Defenbaugh later purchased their store and moved it near his own business in Oregon.

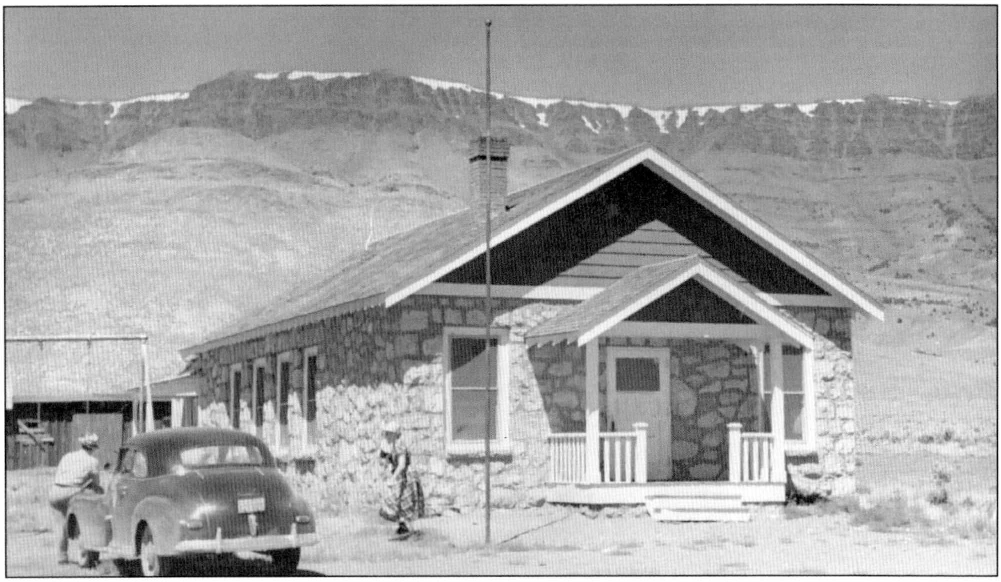

The community of Andrews was named after Peter Andrews, an early settler of the Wildhorse Valley. The post office was originally situated on Andrews's property in 1890 with Andrews as the first postmaster. Later in 1900, the post office was moved to the George A. Smyth property. The first school class at Andrews was held on October 7, 1901, in the one-room schoolhouse pictured. The last significant buildings in Andrews burned down in a 1996 fire. (Courtesy Harney County ESD.)

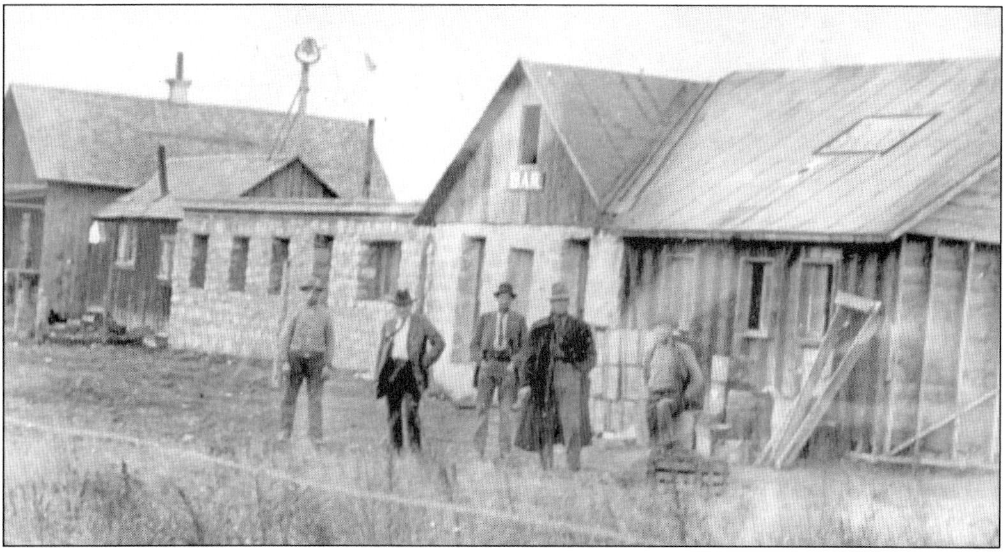

Established in September 1907 with William E. Alberson as the first of nine postmasters, the community of Alberson, located on the eastern edge of Steens Mountain, served primarily as a freight stop and supply point for area sheep men and ranchers. Several buildings, such as the saloon pictured here, were constructed of native rock and stone. Business gradually declined in the area as many sheep men found the growing community of Diamond to be closer to preferred grazing areas. The Alberson Post Office was discontinued in September 1930.

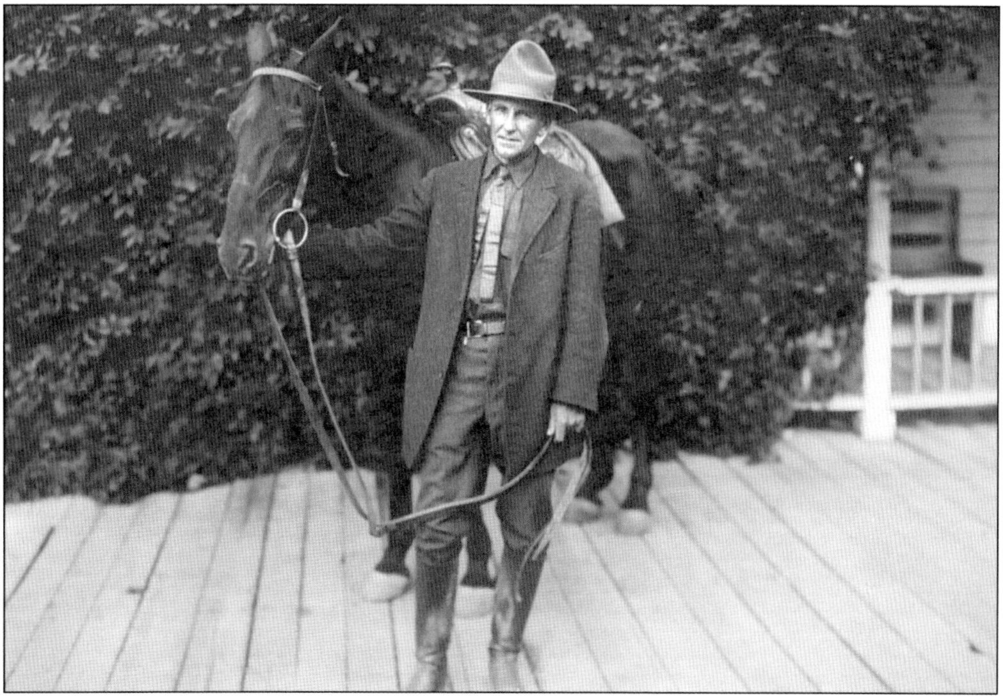

James F. Mahon, pictured here in the early 1910s, was a noted mule breeder in the Anderson Valley, which was located about 55 miles southeast of Burns. He and his wife, Lucy, established the Mule Post Office at their ranch home in 1895. Inactive from 1901 through 1903, the post office resumed services again until closing in 1906.

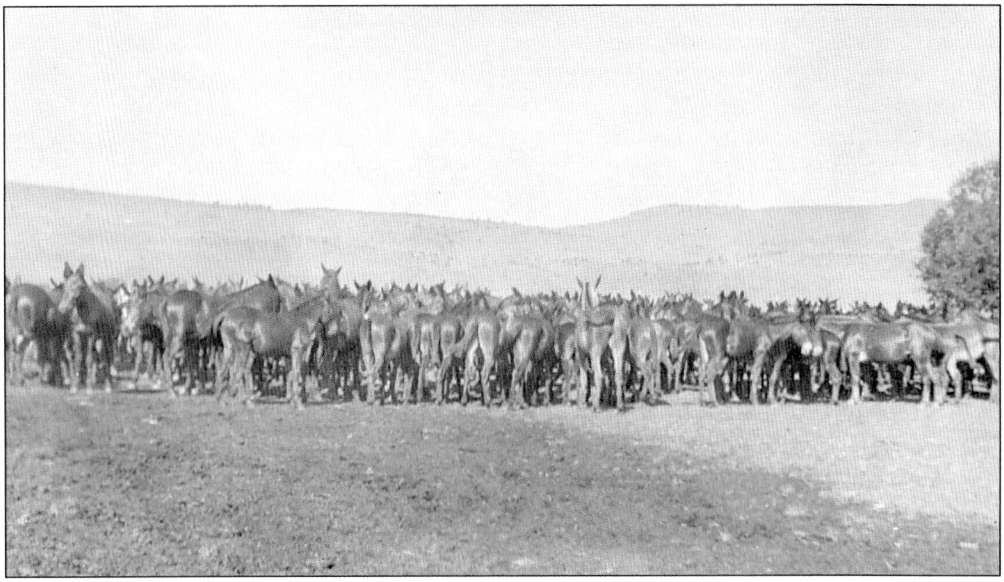

The mule herd pictured above belonged to James F. Mahon. Mules were valued for their help with the numerous freight teams that hauled supplies along the stage roads throughout Harney County. The sight of up to 20 mules hitched to two or three freight wagons was not uncommon. The U.S. Military prized mules as being good mounts for soldiers as well.

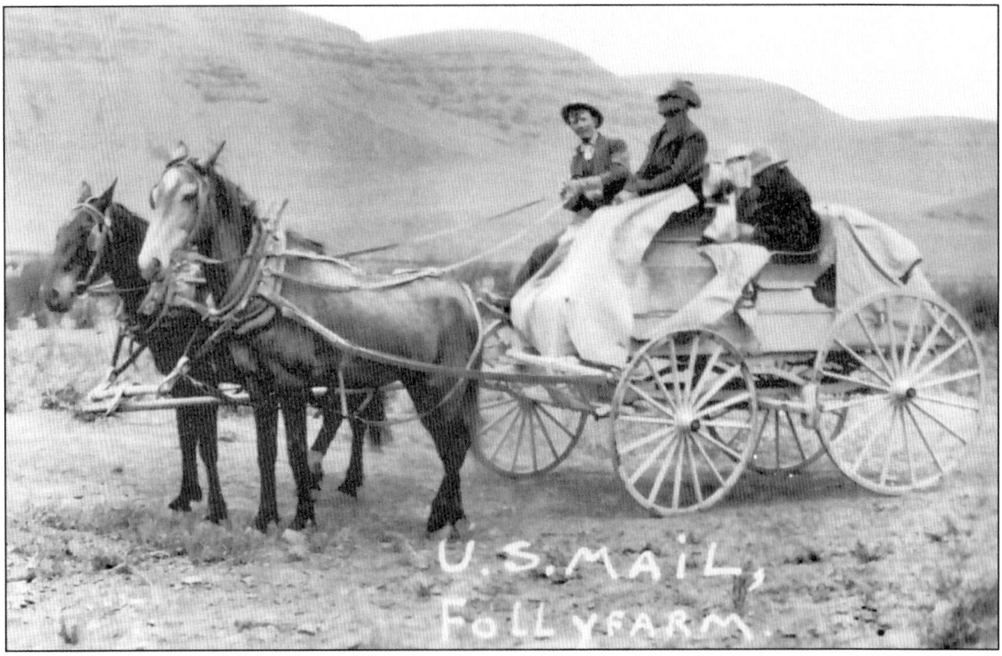

Originally named Neal's Folly, Folly Farm was established in the Happy Valley area of Harney County in 1909 when J. H. and his wife, Dorcas Neal, filed for a homestead near Smyth Creek. Dorcas Neal served as the first postmistress at the post office, which was served by the Steens Mountain mail run, shown here in 1910. After Neal built a store for freight teams in 1916, the area became a popular winter headquarters for sheep men who grazed during the summer on nearby Steens Mountain.

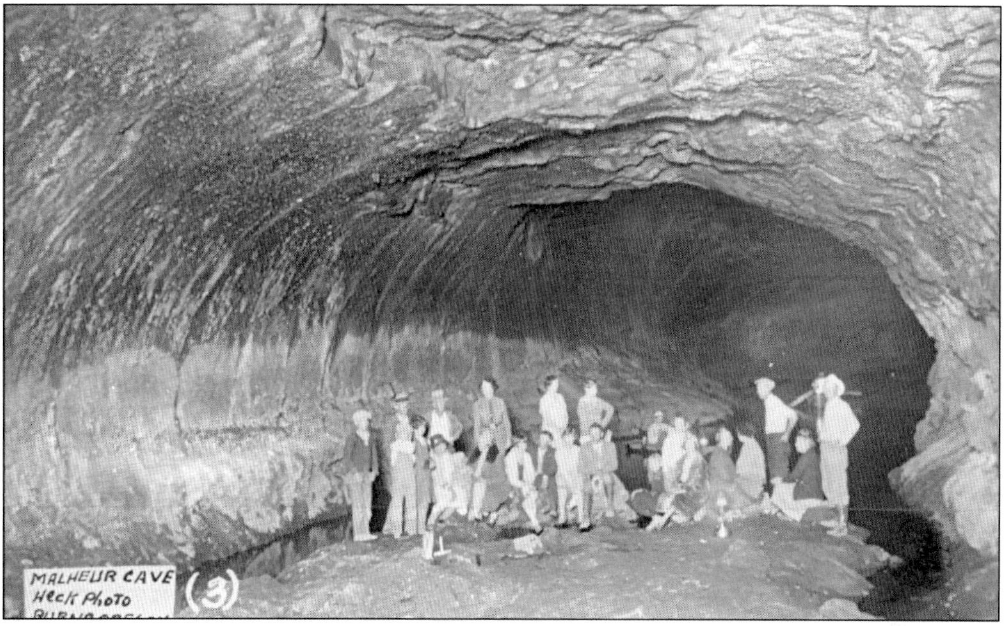

Malheur Cave is located 51 miles southeast of Burns along the South Fork of the Malheur River. The 3,000-foot-long lava tube harbors a lake in its depths. This group poses inside the cave in 1927. By 1928, the cave was a popular destination for picnics and boating. Since 1938, the Robert Burns Masonic Lodge No. 97 has held its annual meetings here. (Photograph by R. W. Heck.)

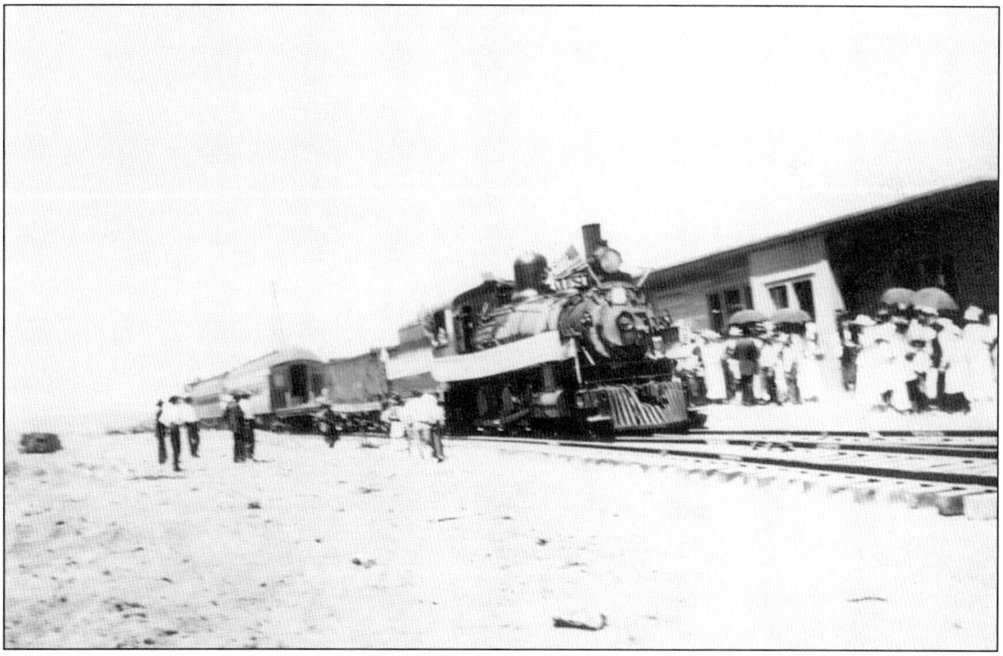

At the time the first train arrived in Crane in 1916, the town consisted of little except a pool hall and a soft drink establishment owned by Ralph Bain. A dance was held on the depot platform that continued until 5:00 a.m. An estimated 2,000 people turned out for the celebration. State officials, including Governor Withycombe, state treasurer Thomas Kay, and Secretary of State Ben Olcot, were also present. (Courtesy Holy Family Catholic Church, Burns.)

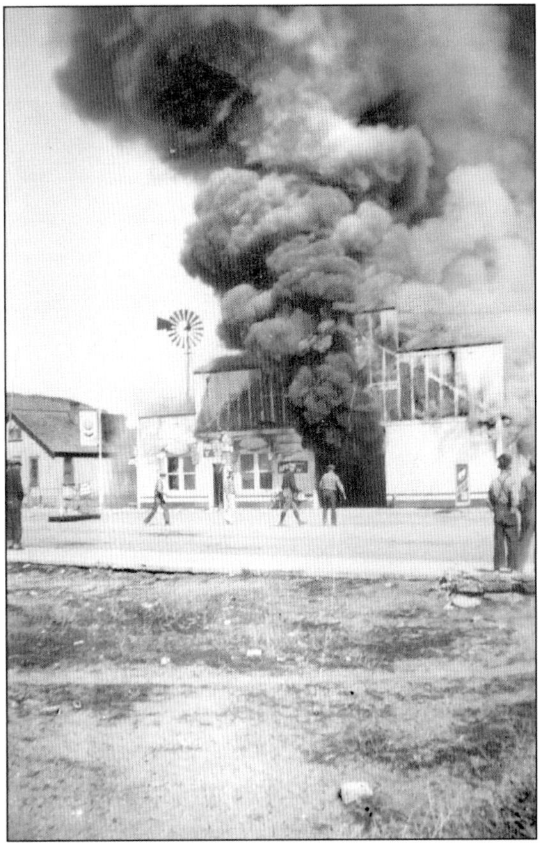

When the town of Crane reopened the post office in 1911, the town consisted of the following businesses: two general stores, a dance hall, a newspaper, a bank, a movie theater, and a Ford dealership. The extension of the railroad to Burns in 1924, coupled with a series of fires in 1938, including this one at the Ford garage, fueled the decline of the settlement of Crane. (Courtesy Letha Melton and Argetta Williams.)

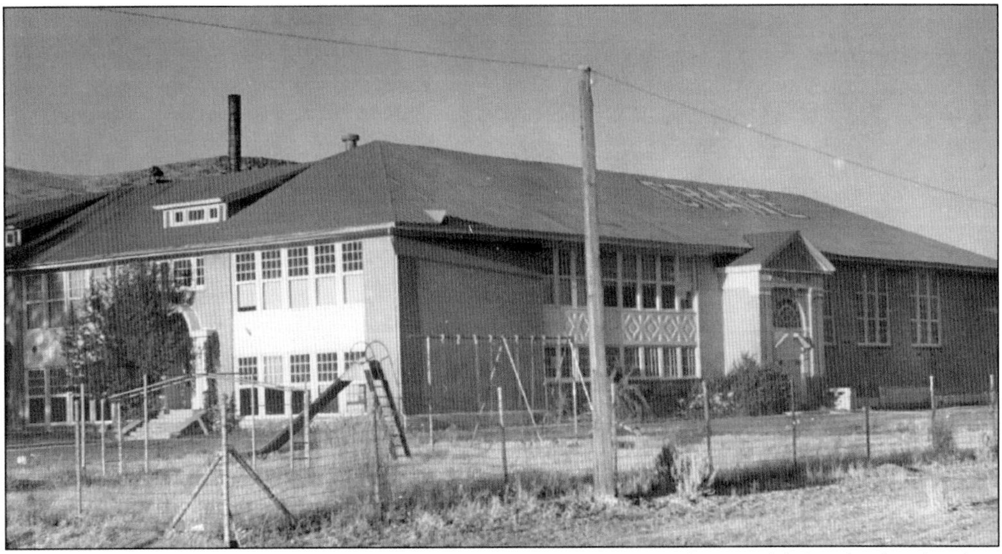

In 1920, the board of directors at Crane Grade School petitioned to establish a high school in Crane. Leroy Johnson is listed as the lone student of the first graduating class of 1922. The original boys' dormitory burned in 1921 and took the life of one student. Shown here, in this photograph taken before fire again destroyed the classrooms, kitchen and dormitories, it is believed to be the only public boarding school in the United States. (Courtesy Harney County ESD.)

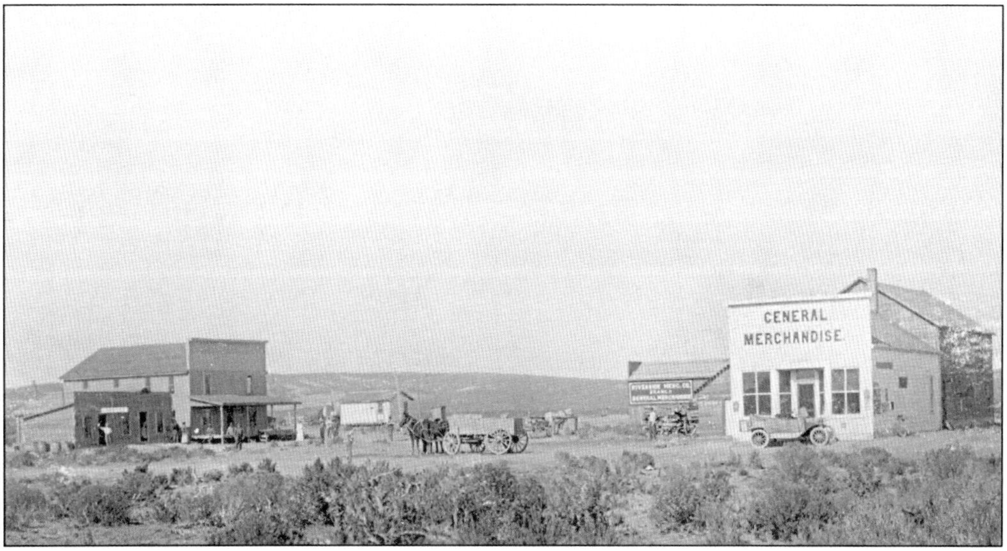

The Harriman Post Office was established in 1907. Bertha Denman served as the first postmistress. After the railroad reached Crane, several of the buildings from Harriman were relocated to Crane to take advantage of the growing population there. By 1916, the post office was closed and much of the population had drifted away. Nothing remains of the site today. (Photograph by Browning.)

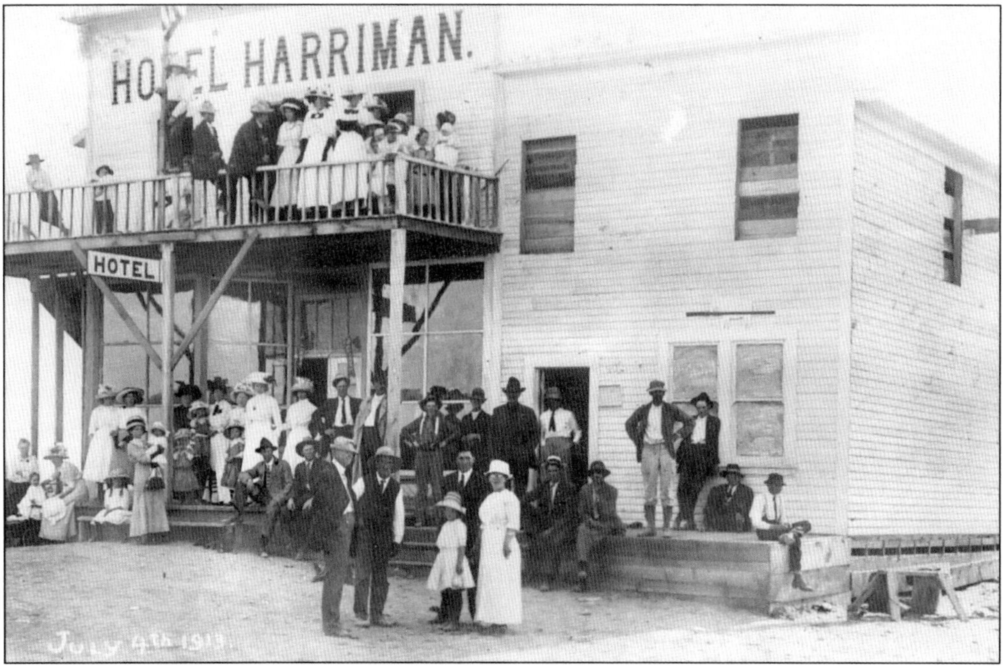

Advertisements hoping to attract new settlers and investments to Harriman boasted of exceptional opportunities for making a good city. The Oregon-Eastern Railway upon completion, however, missed Harriman by a mere three-fourths of a mile. Doctor Denman had a home there and an office in the Denman Hotel, which was moved to Crane in 1917. There is said to have been another hotel here that was burned from a fire started with a match by the owner, so that she could collect insurance money and rebuild. (Courtesy Nancy Williams.)

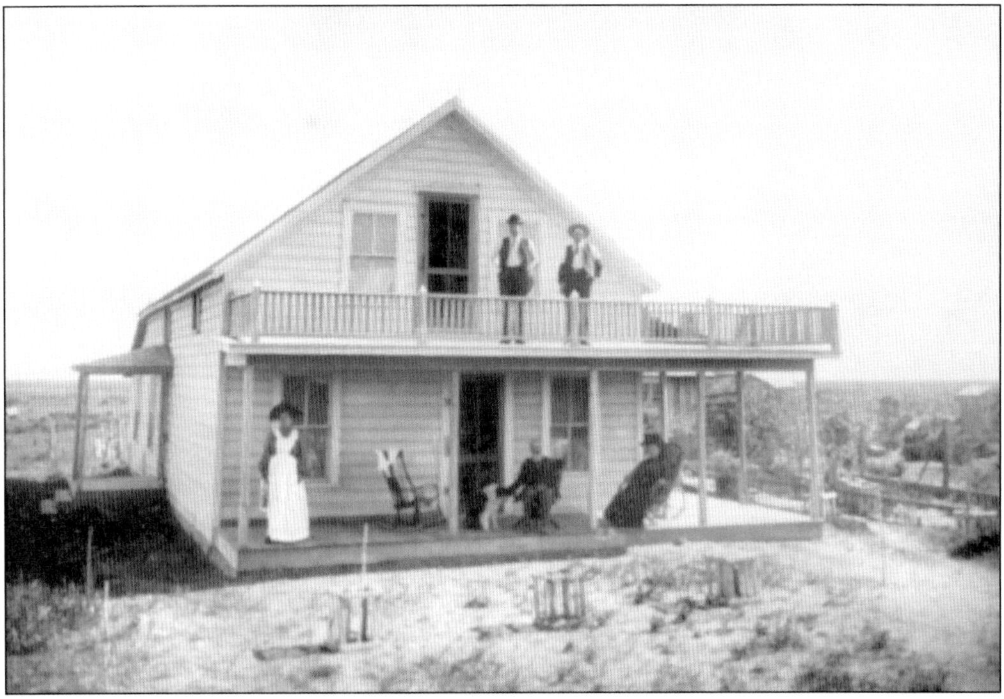

Named after local settler Henry Lauen, the platted community of Lawen, located on the north side of Malheur Lake, was established in the first decade of the 1900s. The 1900 U.S. Census Bureau reported 27 persons in the town; however, the post office was established much earlier, in 1891. P. H. Gray and his family built the first hotel (shown here) and also ran a general merchandise business. (Courtesy Frank Catterson.)

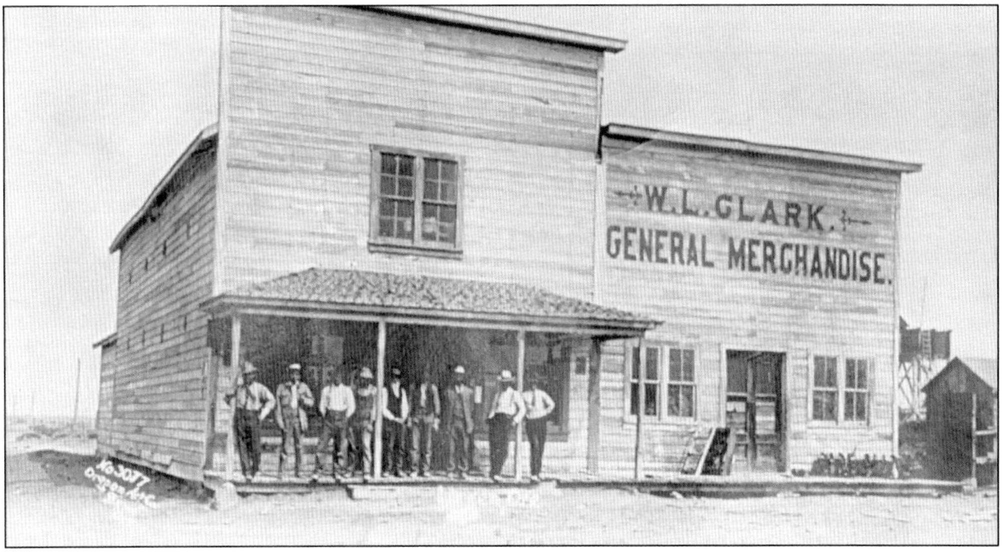

At the peak of its population of about 100, Lawen boasted a saloon and dance hall, a livery stable, drugstore, blacksmith shop, hotel, doctor's office, and a schoolhouse. The W. L. Clark General Merchandise store, built around 1896, was one of two stores. When the road to Crane was rerouted in 1920, the population of Lawen declined. In 1929, this store was moved to its present location along Highway 78, seventeen miles east of Burns. (Photograph by Oregon Art Company.)

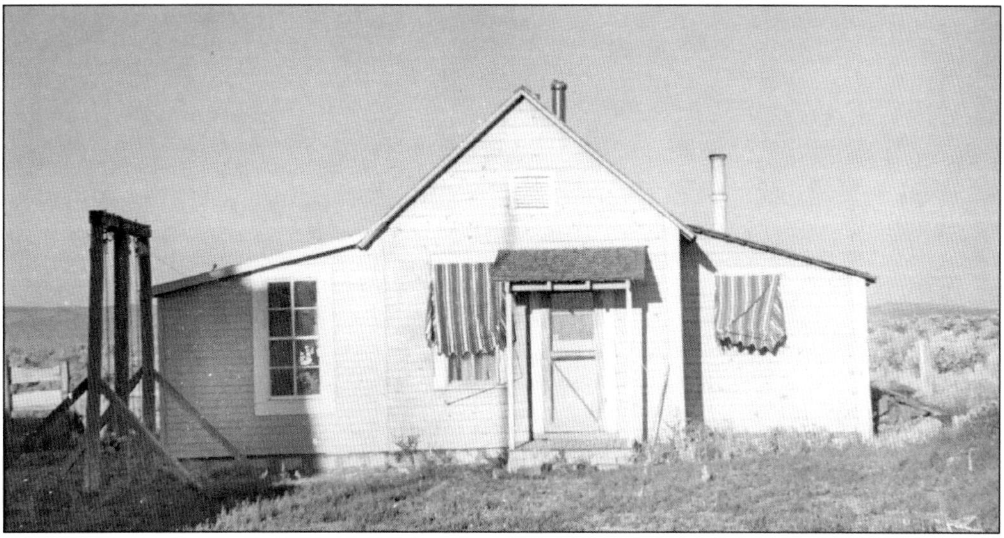

In 1898, 45 students were reported to have attended Lawen School. The building was moved 21.5 miles north of its original location and has endured numerous alterations through the years. Today the school building stands abandoned as a result of Malheur Lake flooding in the 1980s. The schoolhouse bell was donated to the Harney County Historical Museum. (Courtesy Harney County ESD.)

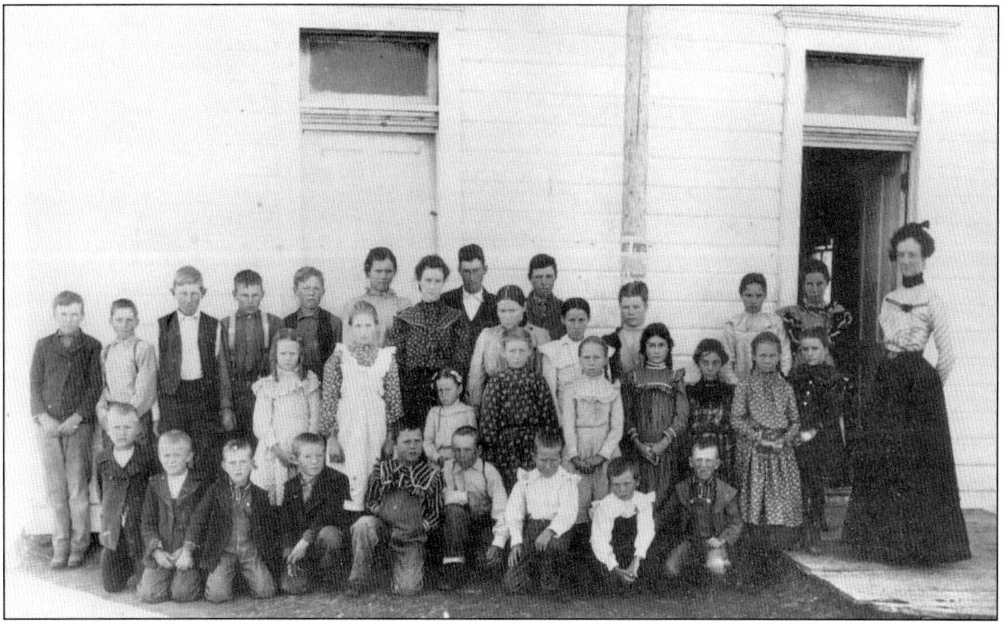

The class of 1900 at Lawen poses for a photograph in front of the school. Ella Thompson (standing at the far right) was the teacher. The students pictured are, from left to right, (first row) Alpha Oard, Charles Oard, Willie King, Arthur Jordan, McKinley Thompson, Dick Otley, Albert Swain, and Sammy King; (second row) Bessie Swain, Alice Parker, Annie Otley, Ethel Thompson, Ella Johnson, Florence Thompson, Willie Hawthorn, Emma Johnson, and Lizzie Turner; (third row) Pete Oard, Henry Otley, Ralph Catterson, Arthur Pope, Ray Catterson, Helene Swain, Floy Thompson, Frank Thompson, Mary Otley, Ed Turner, Ina Hartness, Rachel Turner, Bertha Parker, and Lizza Parker. (Courtesy Ron and Linda Whiting.)

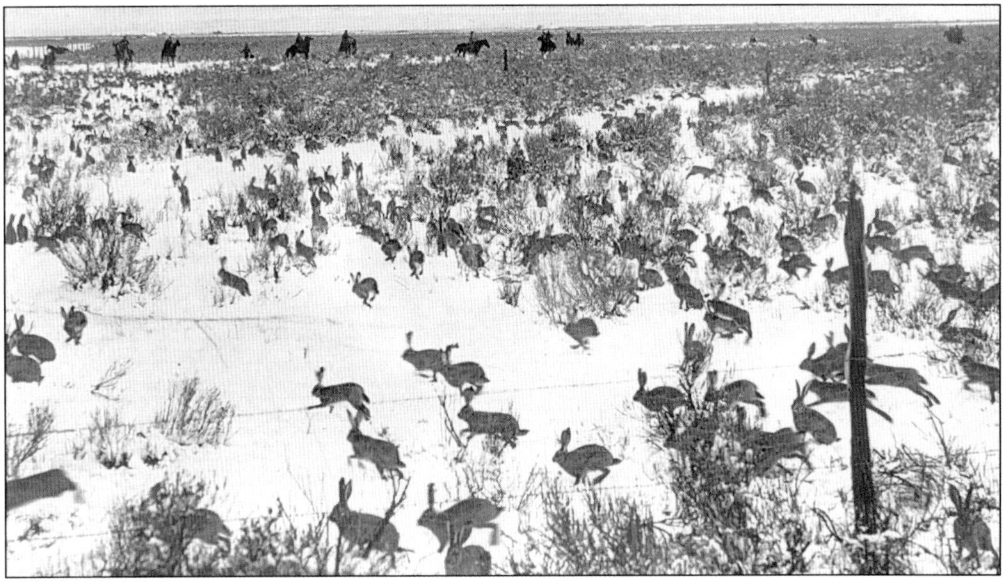

Jackrabbits became a plague to county homesteaders in the early 1910s. Pictured is a jackrabbit roundup that occurred in the winter of 1912. A low fence was constructed to funnel the rabbits as people fanned out to drive the animals into the trap. A bounty of 5¢ per pair of ears was waged. Some merchants took rabbit ears in trade for supplies. During the year of 1926, bounty was paid on 350,000 jackrabbits.

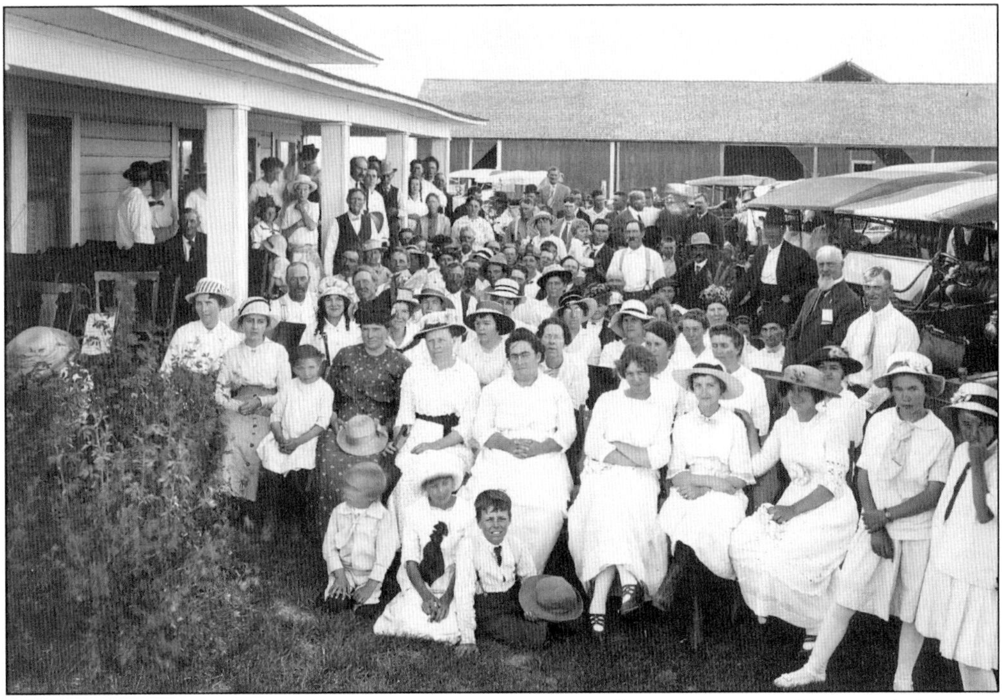

The Harney County Branch Experiment Farm was located six miles east of Burns. A field day was held each year when crops were at their best. A field tour in the morning was followed by speeches from local dignitaries and professors from Oregon State College in the afternoon. The noon potluck meal was a highlight. One such gathering in 1911 is pictured here.

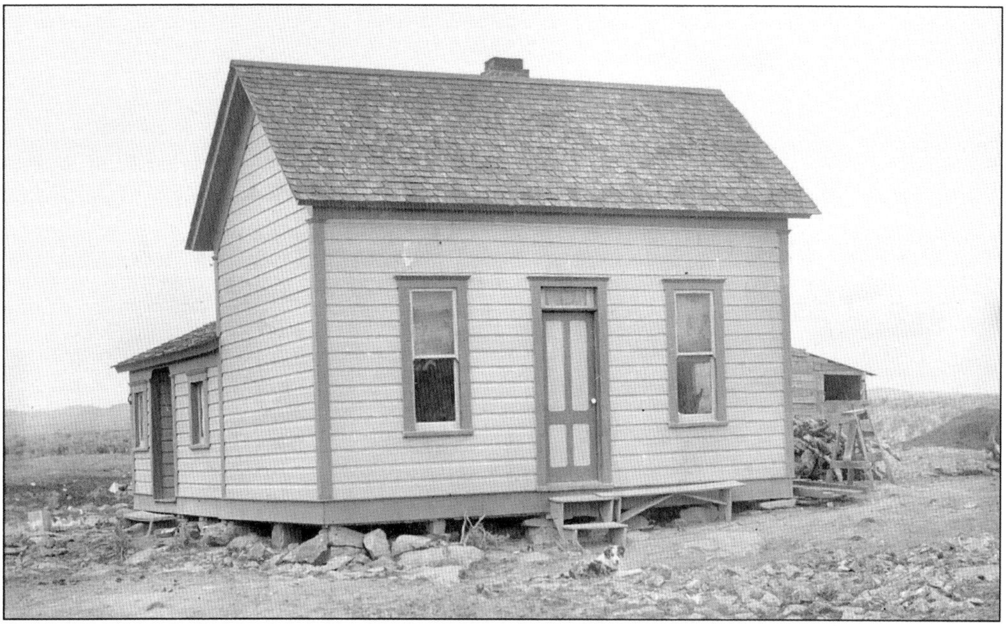

Thomas Whiting and his wife, Ione McClintock Whiting, arrived in Harney County on October 12, 1874, with children Lizzie, Skip "Schuyler," George, and Frank. He built this house in 1875 from logs that floated down the Silvies River from Emigrant Creek. Thomas died on October 17, 1891, from blood poisoning received by injuries to his left foot, which got caught in the spokes of a wagon wheel while trying to stop a runaway horse team. (Courtesy Ron and Linda Whiting.)

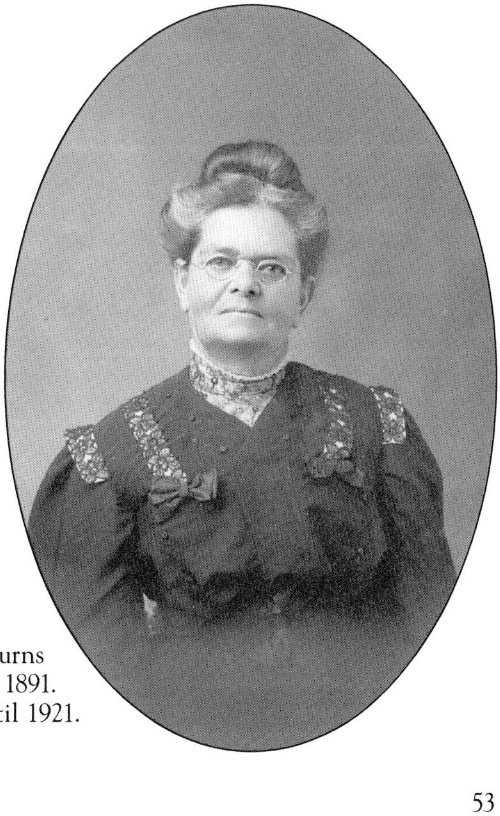

Ione McClintock Whiting continued to live in Burns following the death of her husband, Thomas, in 1891. She served as postmistress and stage agent until 1921. (Courtesy Ron and Linda Whiting.)

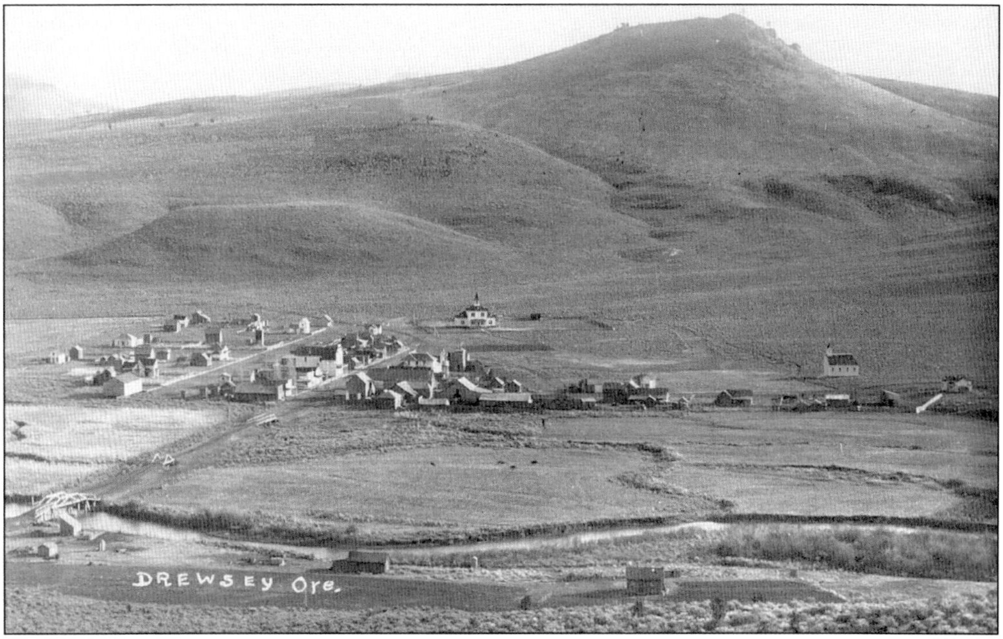

The area around the town of Drewsey was settled in 1883 after the U.S. government opened the land to homesteaders after the dissolution of the Malheur Indian Reservation. Located along the Middle Fork of the Malheur River about 40 miles northeast of Burns, Drewsey acquired a post office in 1883 with Mrs. Tom Howard serving as postmistress. The little settlement is reported to have had a population of 40 in 1889 but grew to 200 by 1907. Most of the commerce in the area was related to sheep and wool production with some cattle ranching as well.

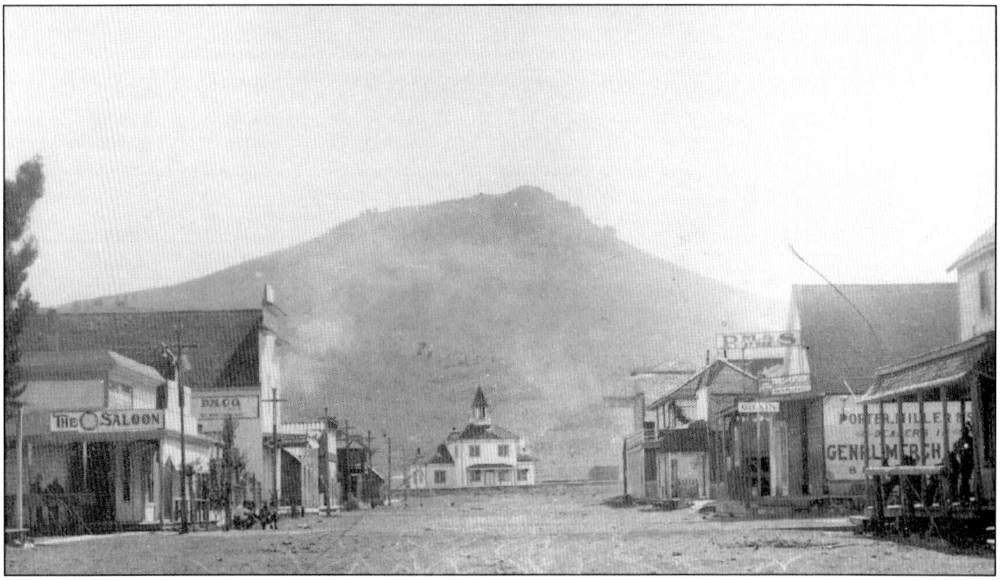

In 1883, Abner Robbins established a 10-foot-by-12-foot box frame mercantile business. After a three-month trip from The Dalles, the first load of goods arrived. By 1907, the population of the town had increased to 200. Businesses included two general stores, two hotels, at least three saloons, a dentist, a doctor, a sawmill, and a daily stage to Burns and Ontario. This photograph shows Main Street as it appeared around 1900. (Courtesy Paul Cronin.)

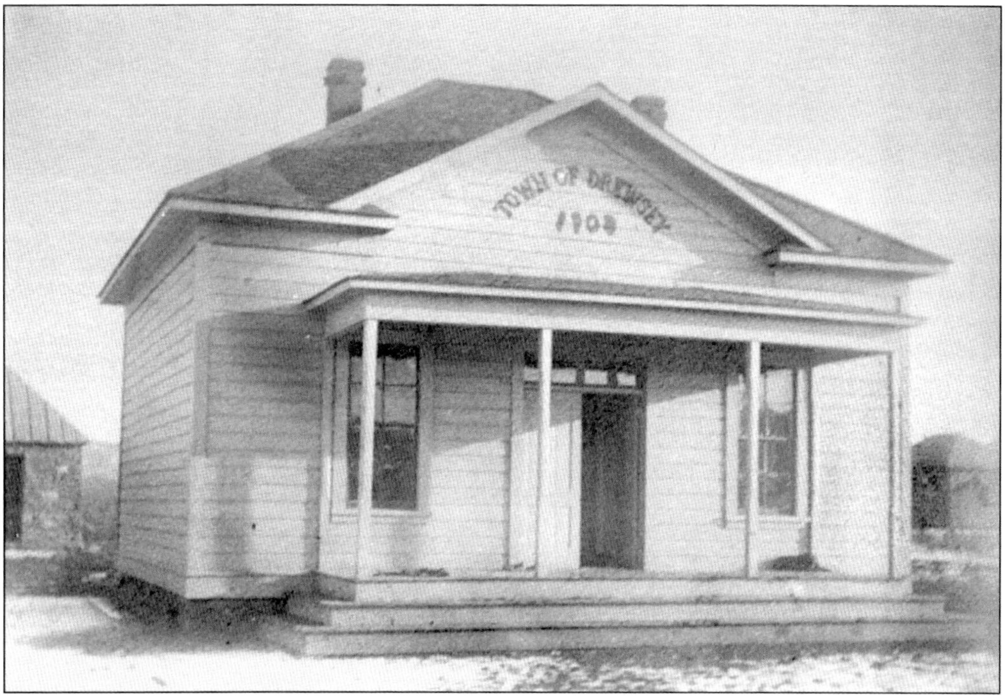

Drewsey City Hall, shown here, was constructed around 1902 during a time when the community was beginning to prosper from the increasing livestock market. During this time, Drewsey was one of the largest settlements in Harney County and rivaled Burns and Harney City.

This schoolhouse in Drewsey was built around 1900. It was located on the end of town set back from the surrounding buildings. The Drewsey School District was established in 1880s. Mrs. Tom Howard was the first teacher. During the 1889–1890 school year, it was reported that 28 students were present in the district. As the community prospered during the early part of the 1900s, as many as three teachers were employed here. (Courtesy Paul Cronin.)

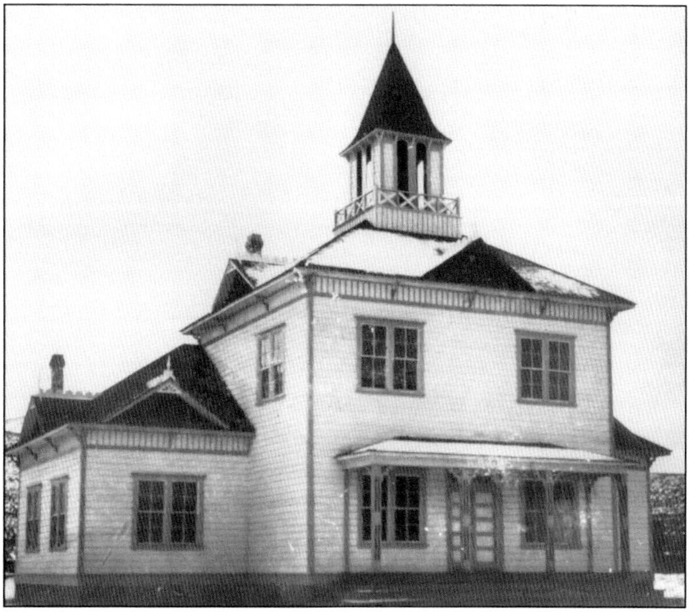

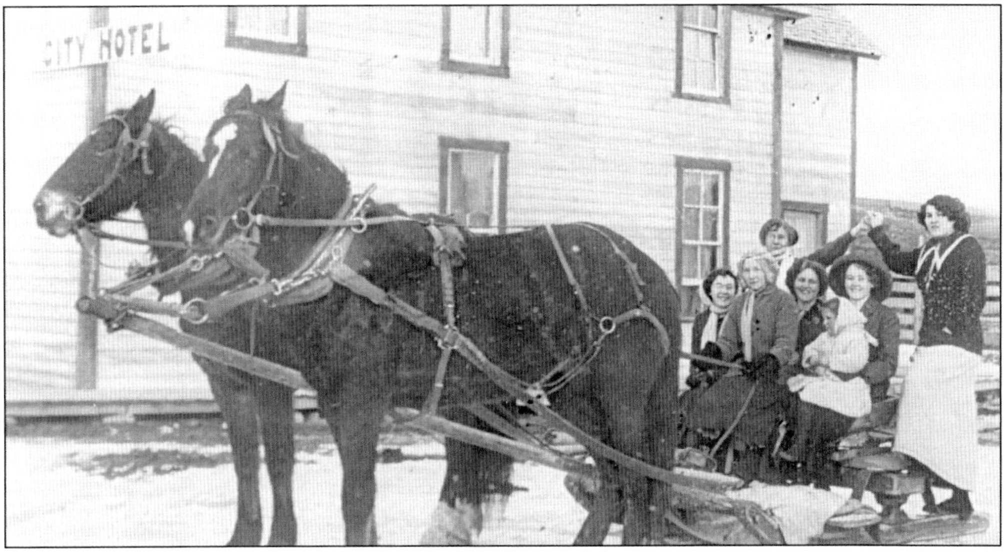

This group of unidentified travelers is posed in front of the City Hotel in Drewsey in the early 1900s. Travel was done frequently by horse and bobsled during the winter due to heavy snows and poor roads. Freight and mail were also moved by sleds when the higher mountain stage roads were impassable.

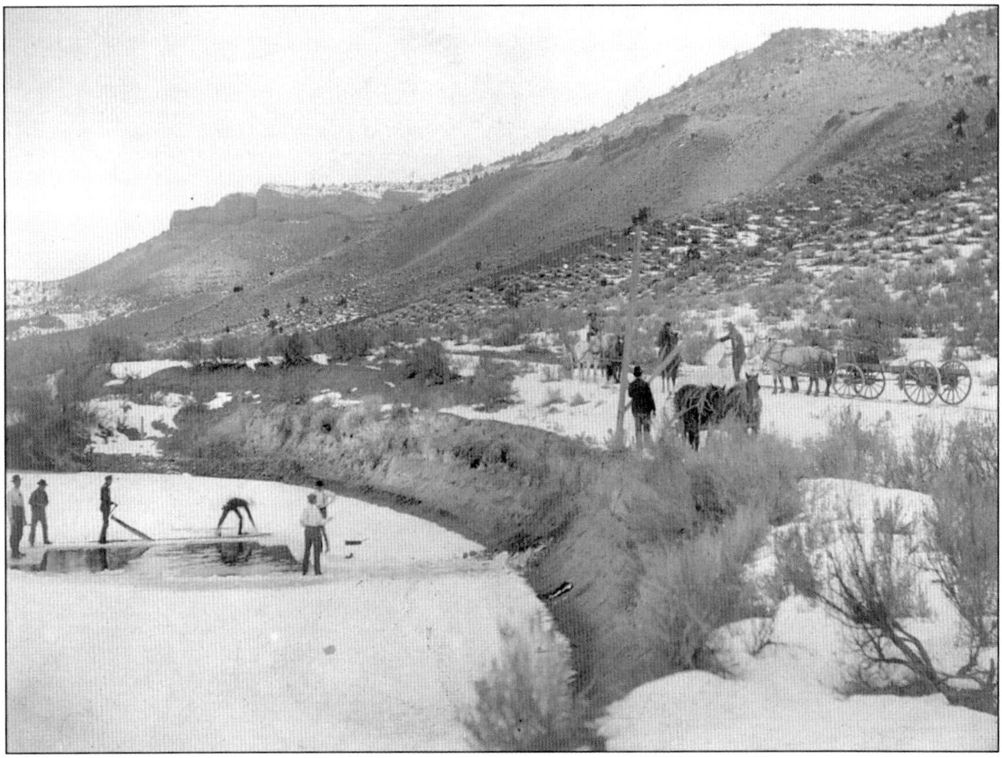

Winter was a time to stock up on ice supplies for the coming warmer months. This group of men cuts blocks of ice from the Middle Fork of the Malheur River near Drewsey. Ice was stored in thick-walled outbuildings and covered in sawdust. Ice stored this way would keep cold for many months. Ice cream for picnics and celebrations were often made from ice cut the previous winter.

Dr. William L. Marsden began his Harney County practice in the settlement of Drewsey after graduating from the Kentucky School of Medicine and obtaining his Oregon license to practice in 1891. Marsden married Clara Bryan of Canyon City. The doctor was a champion for the health of the local Paiute population. By 1889, Dr. Marsden had moved to Burns and continued his practice there. According to one source, Marsden related, "The wealthy who can afford it, pay me enough so I can live and care for these poor people who must somehow be taken care of."

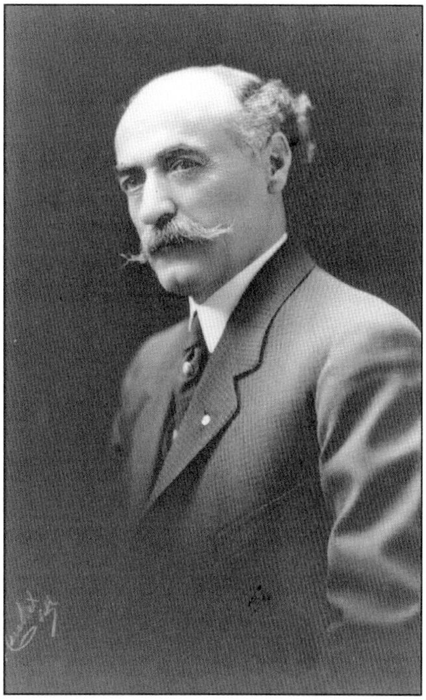

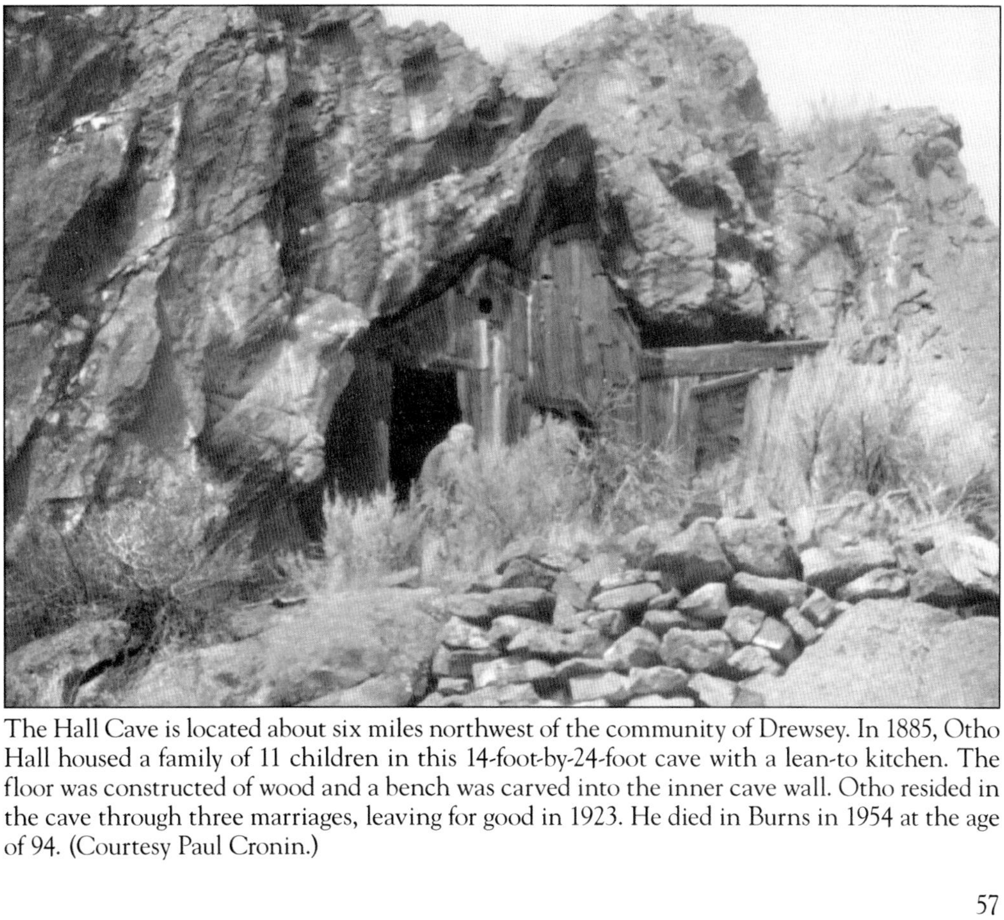

The Hall Cave is located about six miles northwest of the community of Drewsey. In 1885, Otho Hall housed a family of 11 children in this 14-foot-by-24-foot cave with a lean-to kitchen. The floor was constructed of wood and a bench was carved into the inner cave wall. Otho resided in the cave through three marriages, leaving for good in 1923. He died in Burns in 1954 at the age of 94. (Courtesy Paul Cronin.)

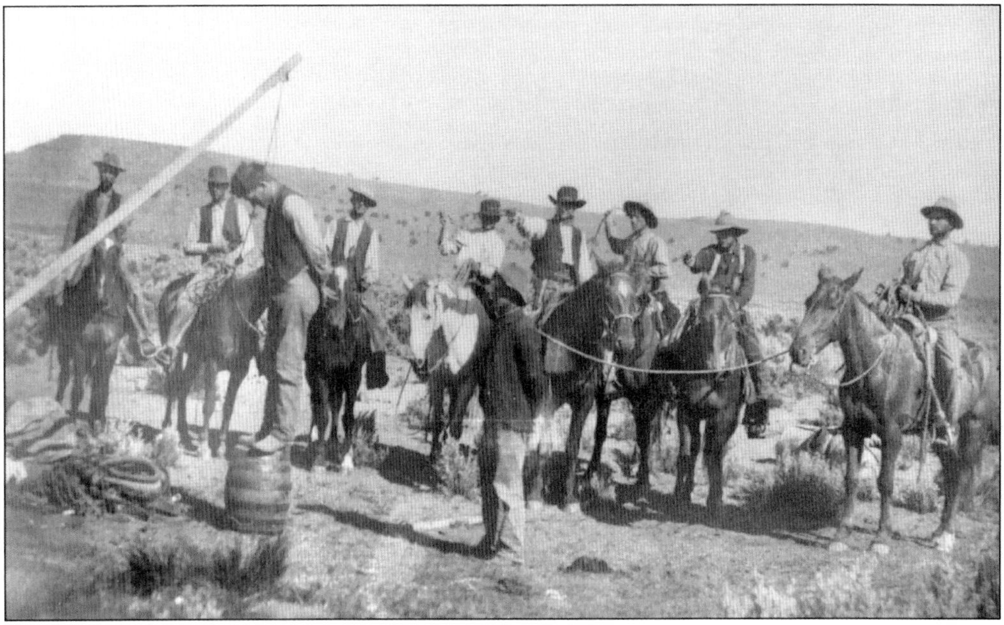

Drewsey was said to be a rough-and-tumble town during its heyday. The true story behind this photograph remains a mystery but this group of unidentified men appears to be staging a hanging. While documented hangings in the county are rare, justice on the frontier could be swift and severe. (Courtesy Nancy Williams.)

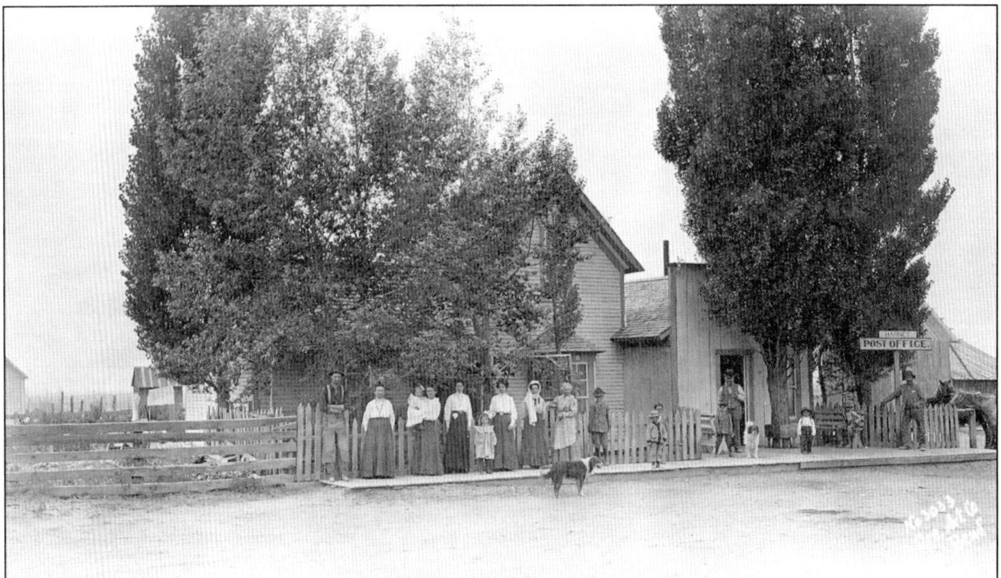

The Oregon, Washington, and Idaho Gazetteer and Business Directory of 1889–1890 attributes the population of Harney City as 300. After Burns was designated county seat in 1889, the settlement of Harney City declined. By 1919, the post office was abandoned and mail service went through Burns. By 1925, the population of Harney City had declined to 23 while the population of nearby Burns had jumped to over 1,000. (Photograph by Oregon Art Company.)

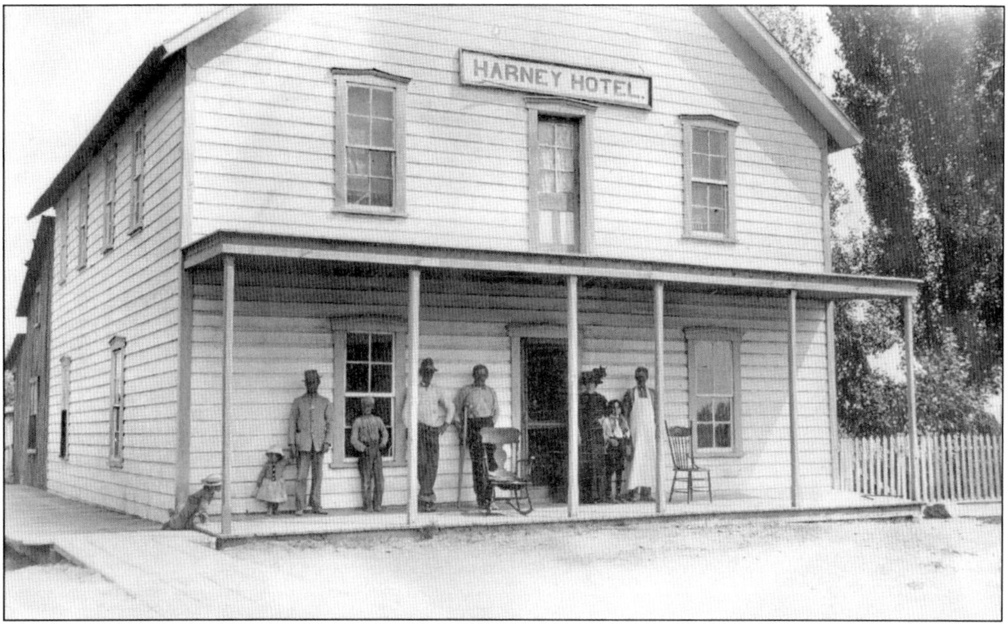

The Harney Hotel, pictured here around 1890, was located in Harney City approximately one to two miles south of the location of the old Camp Harney. Harney City was established in 1885 and rivaled in size the city of Burns. By 1888, Harney had businesses, including a hotel, a saloon, two blacksmith shops, a sawmill, an attorney, a justice of the peace, a physician, a public school, and a post office.

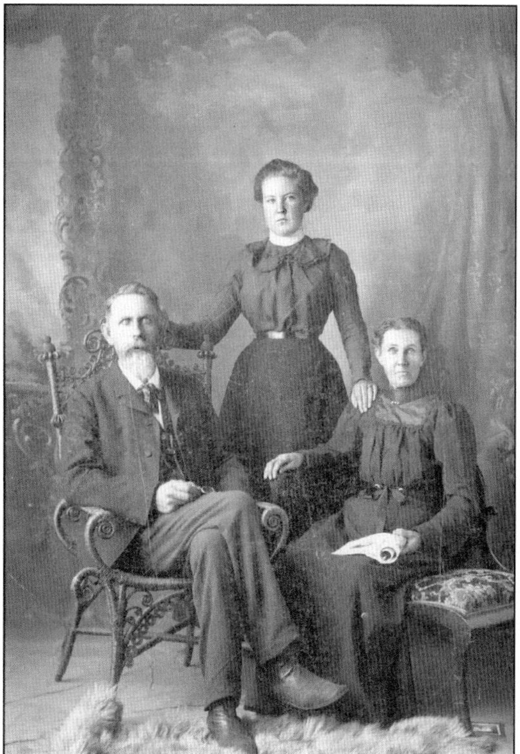

In this c. 1910 photograph, David N. Catterson and his wife, Rebecca, shown here with daughter Grace Cochran, settled in Harney County after moving from LaGrande. The family first settled near Harney City then later homesteaded near Lawen. Catterson was originally from Pennsylvania, where he served during the Civil War. (Courtesy Frank Catterson.)

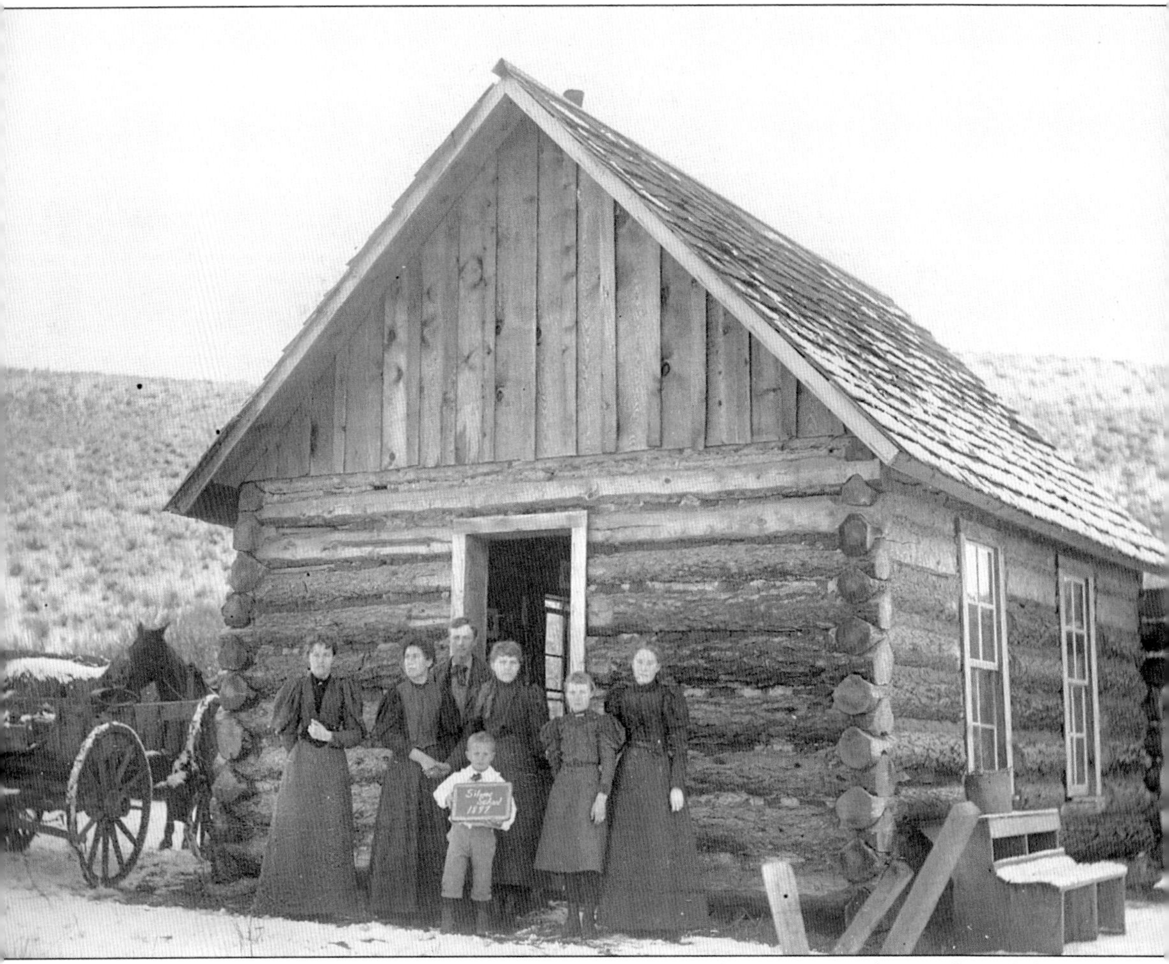

This little log cabin schoolhouse was located between the Trout Creek Ranch and the old Melvin Purdy Ranch about 25 miles north of Burns. Mrs. Jack Dorris is the teacher. Albert Cross is holding the slate dated 1897. Albert's father, Walter, homesteaded near Trout Creek. (Courtesy Grant Gunderson.)

Two

Ranching

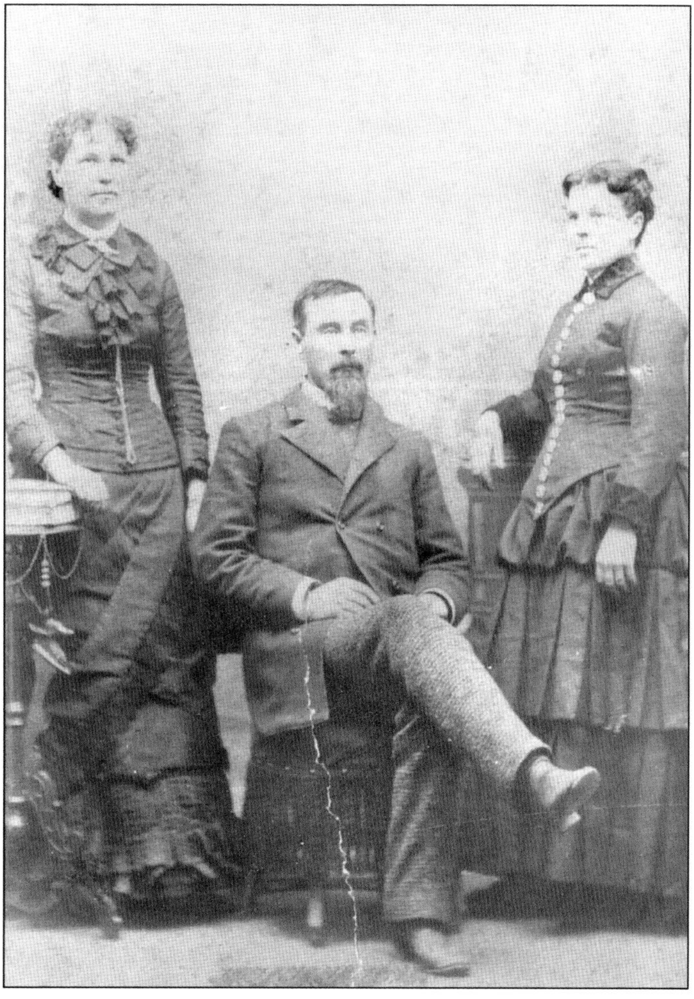

John Devine arrived in Harney County about 1868 with a herd of 2,500 cattle. Along with partner W. B. Todhunter, he established the first major ranch in the area, which became known as the White Horse Ranch. Through shrewd management, Devine acquired large holdings throughout Harney County but was nearly wiped out during the hard winter of 1889–1890. The Pacific Livestock Company purchased most of Devine's holdings but allowed Devine to reside at his Alvord ranch until his death in 1901. John Devine is pictured here with his second wife, Jennie, and sister Frankie Shultz.

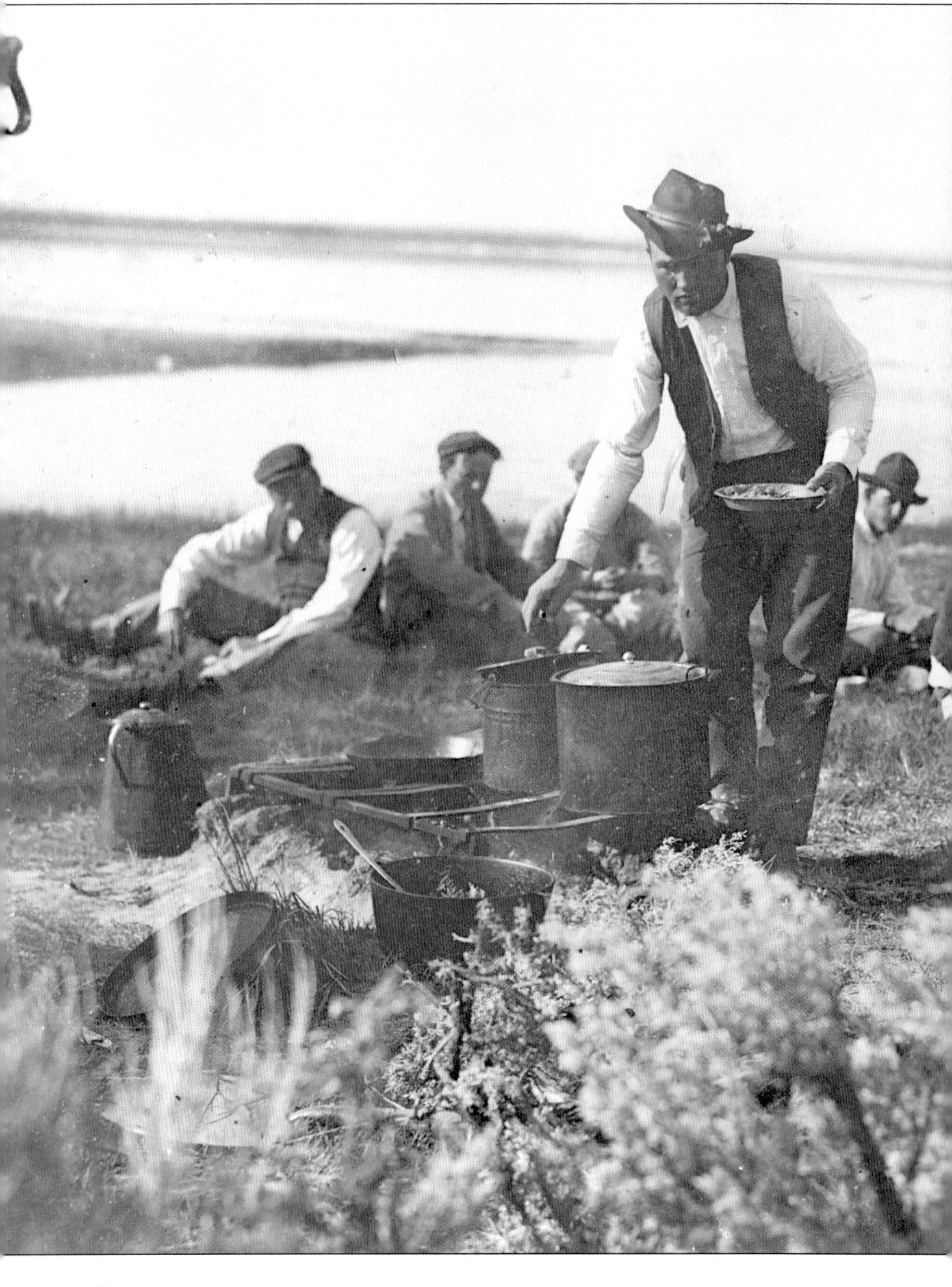

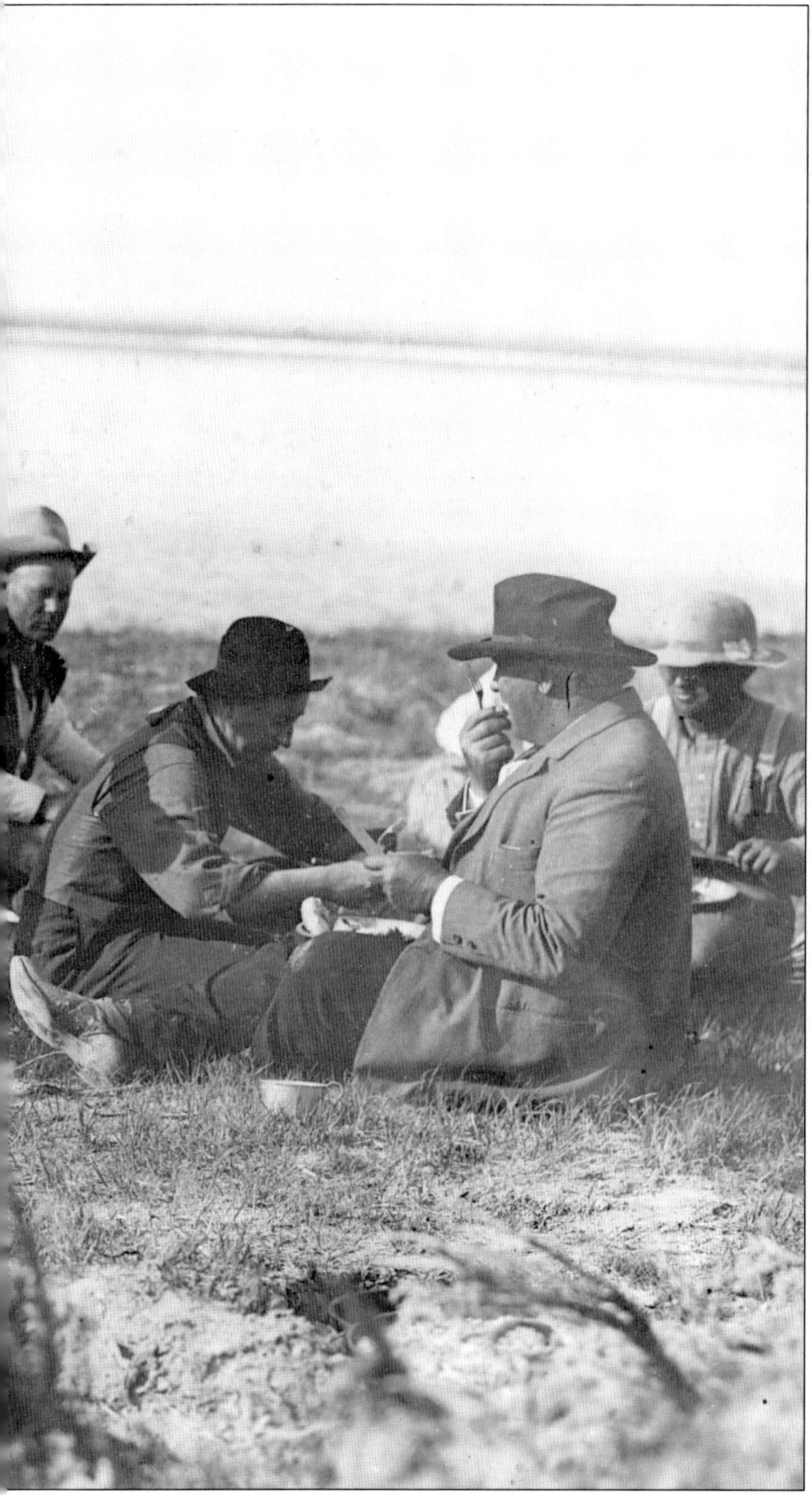

Arriving in Harney County about 1872 with a small herd of cattle brought from Jacksonville, Oregon, William Hanley ushered in the era of local cattle baron to replace the large livestock operations that traced their roots to California. Hanley is pictured here (seated foreground and far right) in his later years eating with some of the buckaroos in his employ. His properties included the Bell-A Ranch, Double O Ranch, and for a time, a managing interest in the P Ranch. In ill health for the last several years of his life, Hanley died September 15, 1933, at the age of 74, the day after having attended "Hanley Day" held in his honor at the Pendleton Roundup.

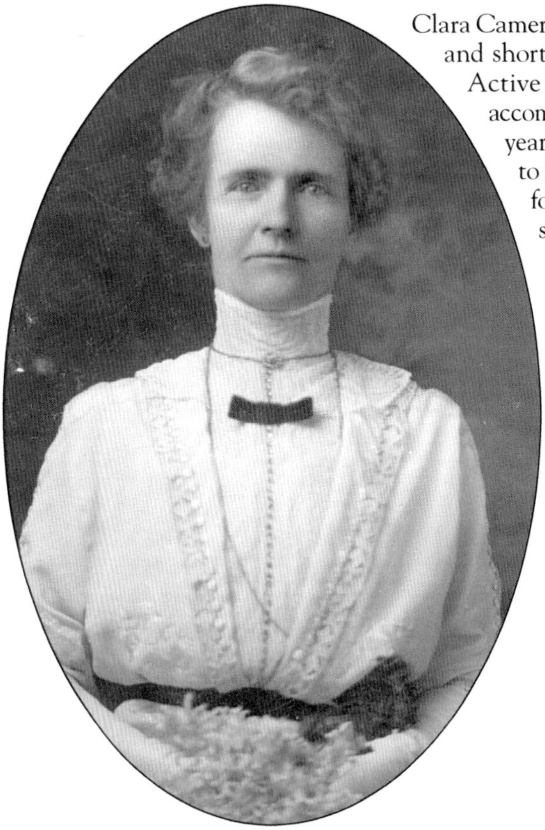

Clara Cameron married William Hanley on July 6, 1892, and shortly thereafter, settled at the Bell-A Ranch. Active in ranch activities, Clara could be found accompanying cattle herds on several trail drives per year. Upon her husband's death, Clara continued to manage the Hanley holdings until ill health forced her to relinquish control. In 1941, Clara sold over 14,000 acres of the Double O Ranch to the federal government for inclusion in the Malheur National Wildlife Refuge.

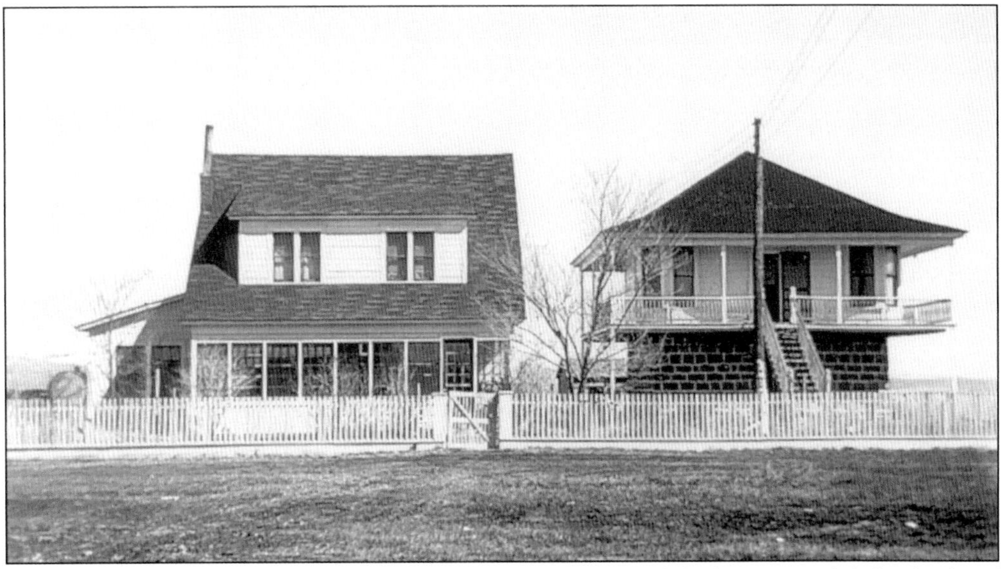

Clara Hanley had the distinctive main house on the Bell-A Ranch built in 1911 while her husband William Hanley was away selling cattle in Omaha, Nebraska. This house served as the main headquarters of the Hanley cattle operation. Clara entertained frequently and kept 12 beds for guests. The outward appearance of the house, shown here as it appeared in the 1950s, has changed little over the years. (Courtesy Letha Melton and Argetta Williams.)

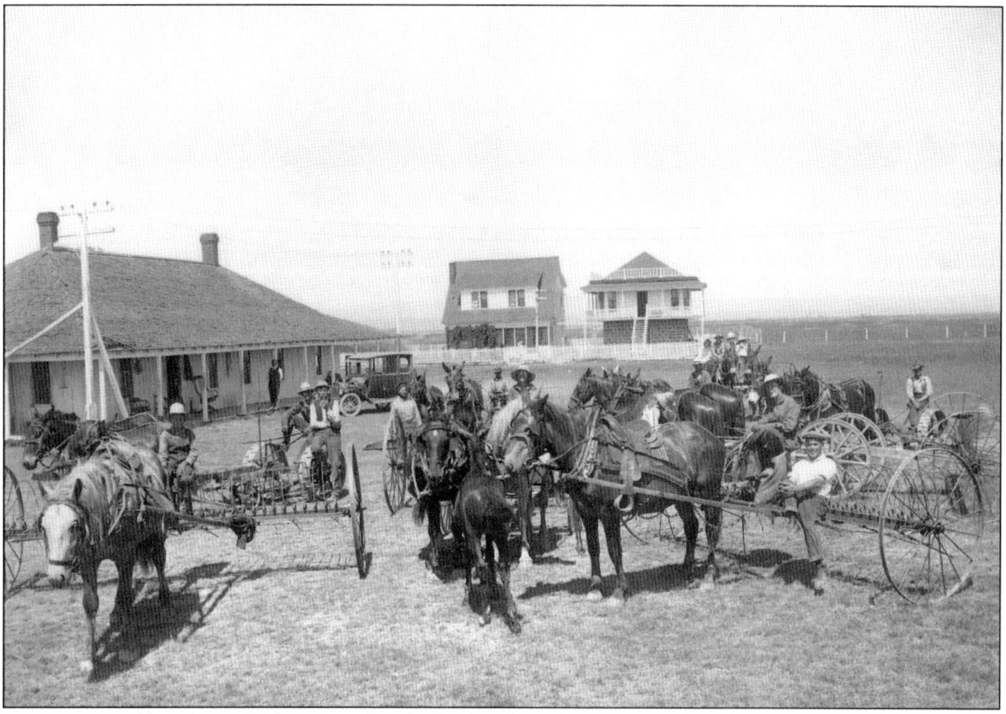

Partners and brothers William and Ed Hanley bought up parcels of land adjoining their own along the East Fork of the Silvies River and built up the Bell-A Ranch to 1,200 acres by 1890 and to over 4,000 acres by 1898. They went from running 300 head of cattle to over 1,000 by 1898. Pictured is a haying crew in front of the Bell-A bunkhouse and main house.

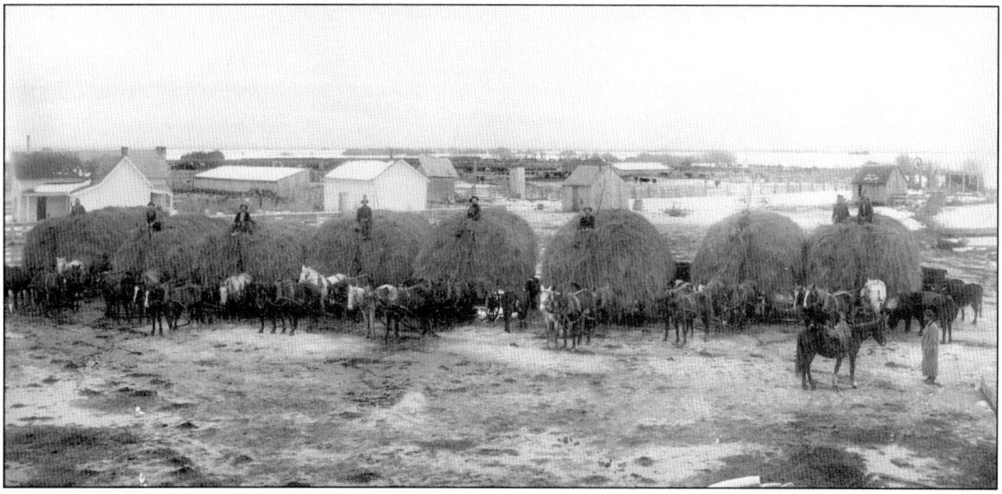

In older days, 8 to 10 men staffed the Bell-A Ranch, jumping to 75 during the busy haying season. As machinery replaced hand labor, Bill Hanley was able to put up over 120 tons of field hay in a day. Seventy horses and mules worked on the ranches. Loaded hay wagons are pictured here during wintertime on the ranch.

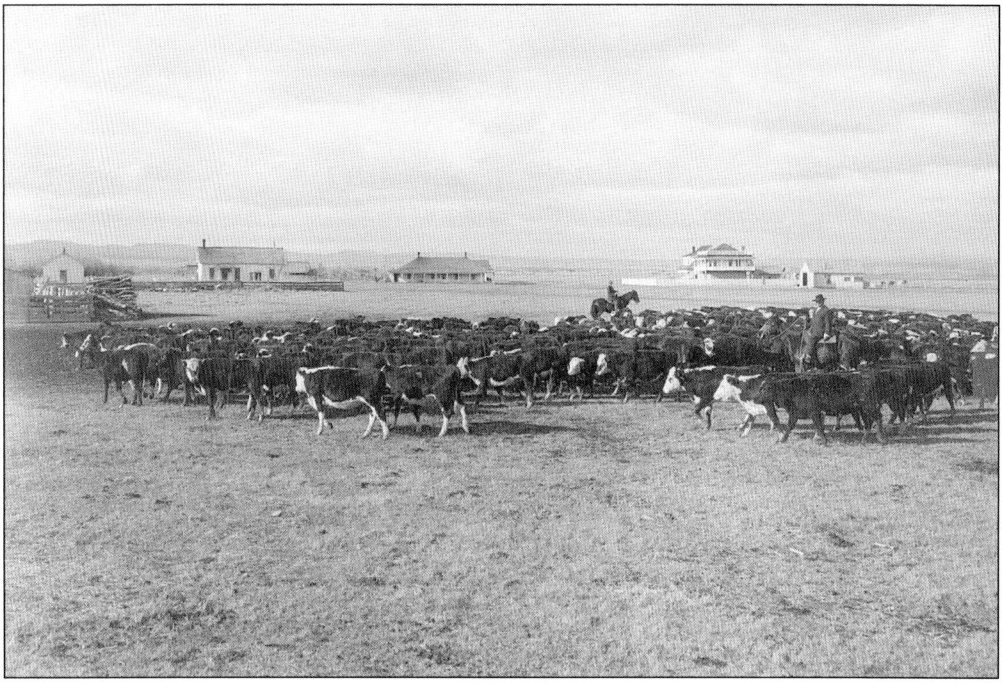

Around 1898, William Hanley bought out his brother Ed's interest in Bell-A, and during the same period, was appointed manager of the P Ranch following the death of Peter French. Hanley was now the controller of the second-largest ranch in the county (P Ranch) and the owner of the fourth largest (Bell-A). Combined, Hanley controlled over 195,000 acres of private land in Harney County, or about 31 percent of the total.

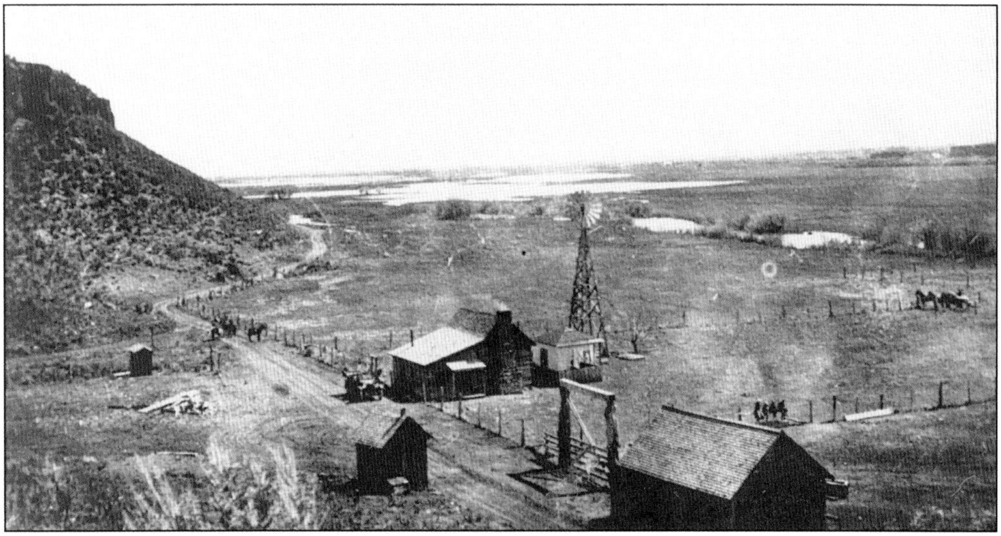

In about 1875, Amos W. Riley along with partners Col. James A. Hardin and John Taylor originally founded the Double O Ranch, located in the Warm Springs Valley northwest of Harney Lake. By 1880, the ranch holdings supported 8,000 head of cattle, making it third largest among Harney County cattle operations at the time. During the severe winters of 1889–1890, the Double O lost nearly 1,000 of its 3,500 head of stock. William Hanley purchased the Double O Ranch in 1903.

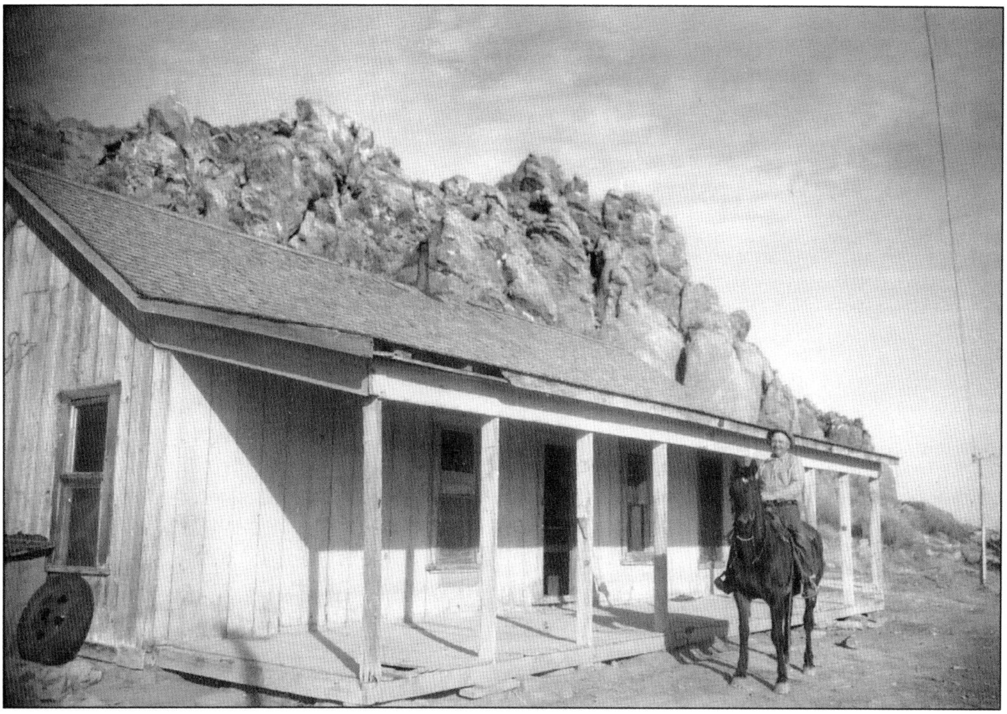

Longtime P Ranch foreman Judd Wise poses in front of the white house nestled along the rimrock at the Double O Ranch during the 1950s. This dwelling was used by William Hanley to lodge guests who were invited to the ranch. Few original structures remain today. The location currently serves as a maintenance and residential facility for the Malheur National Wildlife Refuge.

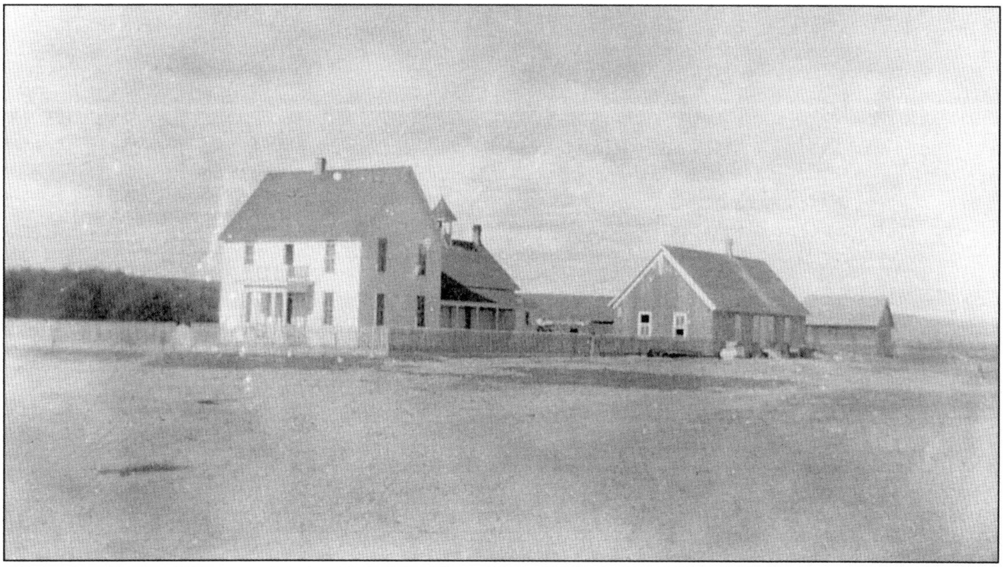

The Island Ranch was established between branches of the Silvies River, creating a natural "island" within the valley. The ranch served as the headquarters for the Pacific Livestock Company following the death of owner Henry Miller in 1916. Located 16 miles south of Burns, the buildings of the ranch consisted of a main house, foreman's house, bunkhouse, storeroom and cellar, icehouse, horse barn, blacksmith shed, well house, and as corrals.

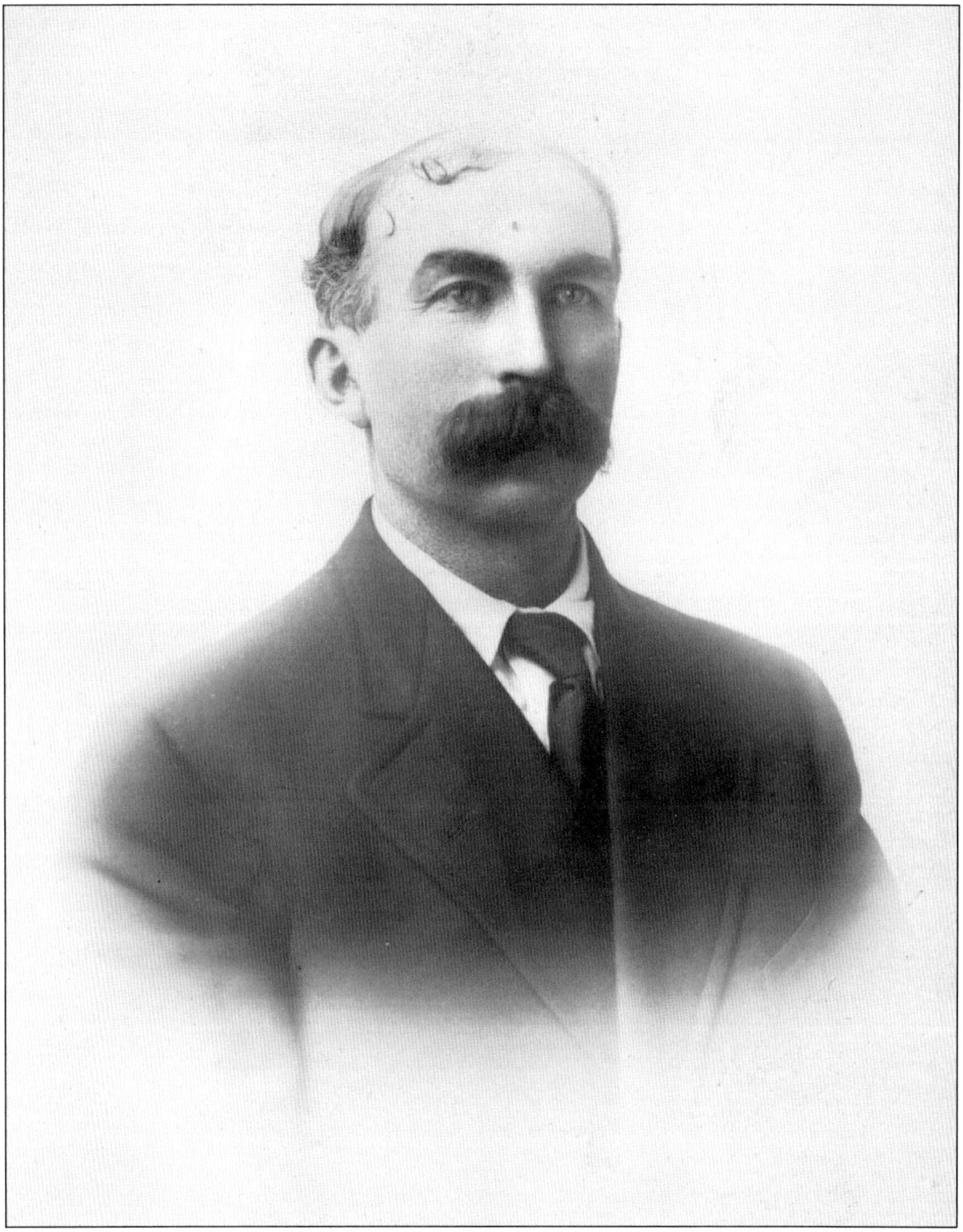

The Pacific Livestock Company began in Harney County as Overfelt and Company. It was run by cattlemen from California seeking new grazing lands for expanding herds in the early 1880s. Upon Overfelt's accidental death in 1885, his business partners Henry Miller, Charles Lux, and N. H. Mason purchased his interest in the company from his widow, thus becoming Miller and Lux, one of the largest cattle operations in the world. Charles Cronin (pictured) served as superintendent for the Miller and Lux ranch operations in Harney County. In a letter dated October 9, 1893, Henry Miller states that Charles Cronin is to work for $30 per month until haying time. Later he was superintendent of the Whitehorse Ranch, another ranch owned by the Pacific Livestock Company under the control of Henry Miller and Charles Lux. (Courtesy Paul Cronin.)

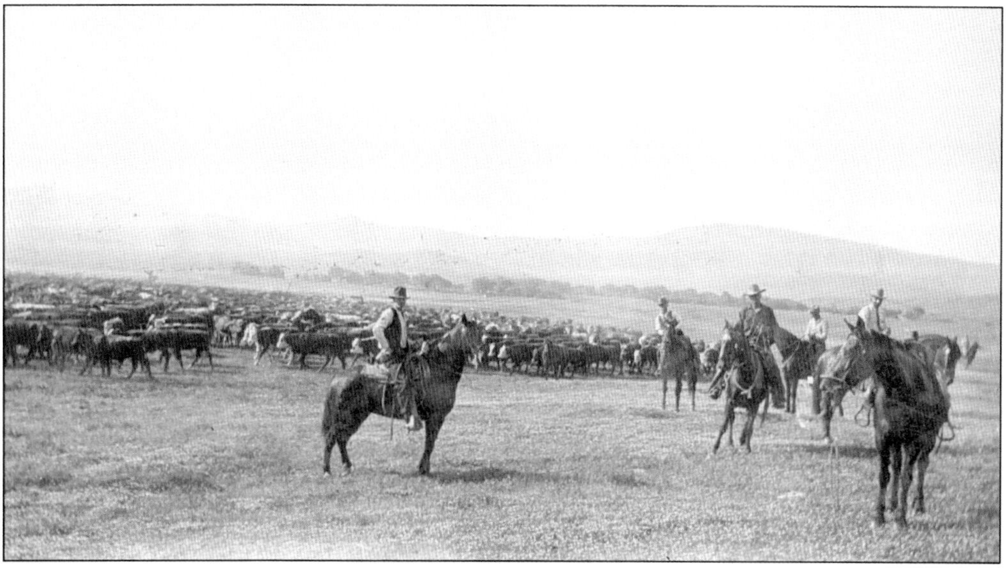

Herds of cattle such as this one belonging to the Pacific Livestock Company photographed in the early 1900s were gathered for long trail drives. Cattle marketed in California were shipped by rail from Winnemucca, Nevada, while cattle bound for eastern markets were shipped from railheads in Ontario, Oregon. Drives commonly traversed only 10 miles per day. (Courtesy Bonnie Smith.)

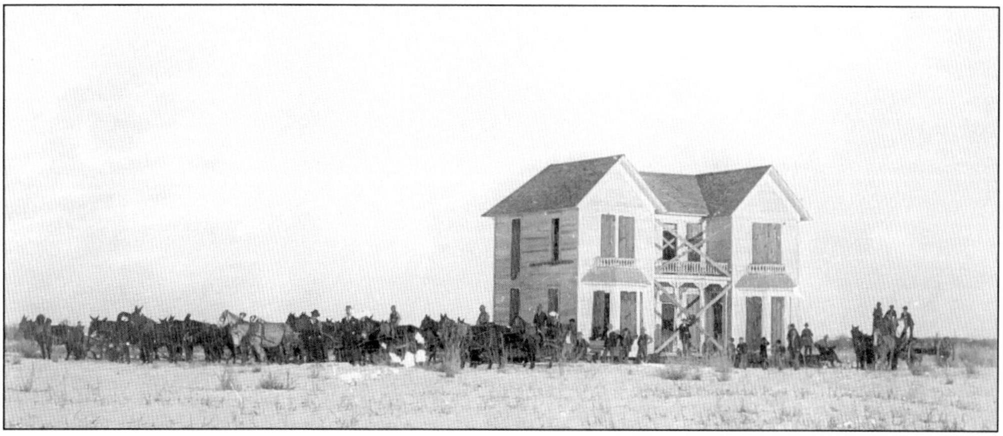

This house, known locally as the Holland House, was constructed in Harney City and used as a headquarters for the Pacific Livestock Company. In the winter of 1897–1898, the company moved the building from Harney City to Burns with the aid of at least 40 horses and mules. The house sat at the edge of the Silvies River until it was frozen solid enough to cross then moved to its present location on the corner of Buena Vista Avenue and B Street with rollers and a capstan.

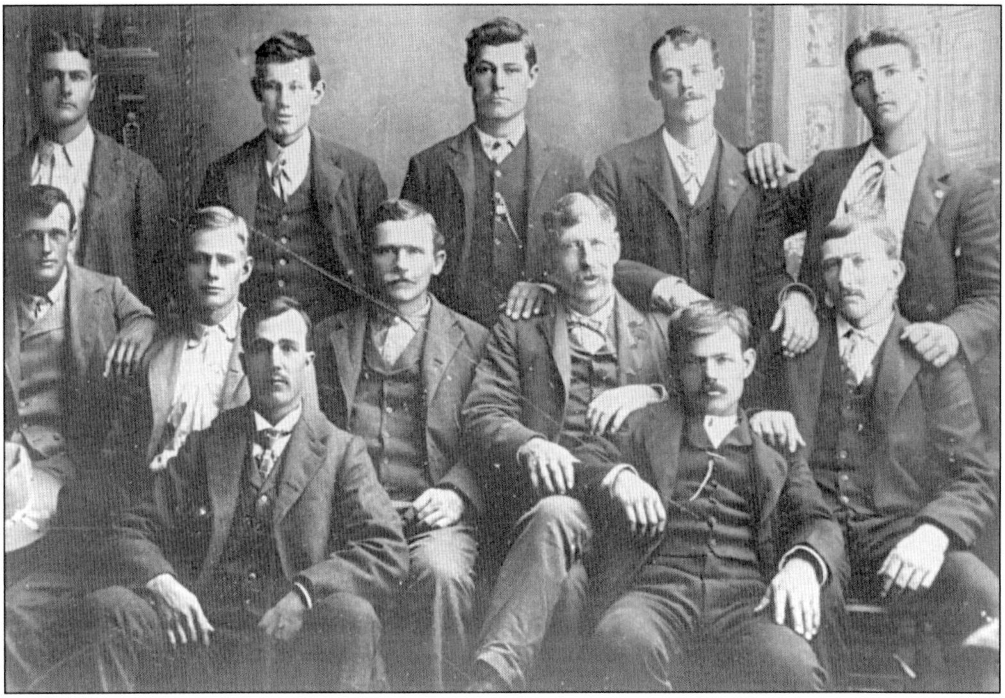

Miller and Lux hired local rancher John Gilcrest to superintend the Oregon ranches. Gilcrest hired many locals. The company quickly became the area's largest employer. The local company payroll went from $36,610 in 1888 to over $208,000 in 1891. Buckaroos employed by the Pacific Livestock Company pose for a c. 1898 group photograph. Members identified include the following: (first row) George Franklin and unidentified; (second row) Dave Cox, Joe Fine, unidentified, Bob Baker, and Dennis O'Brion; (back row, fourth from left) Fred Fine.

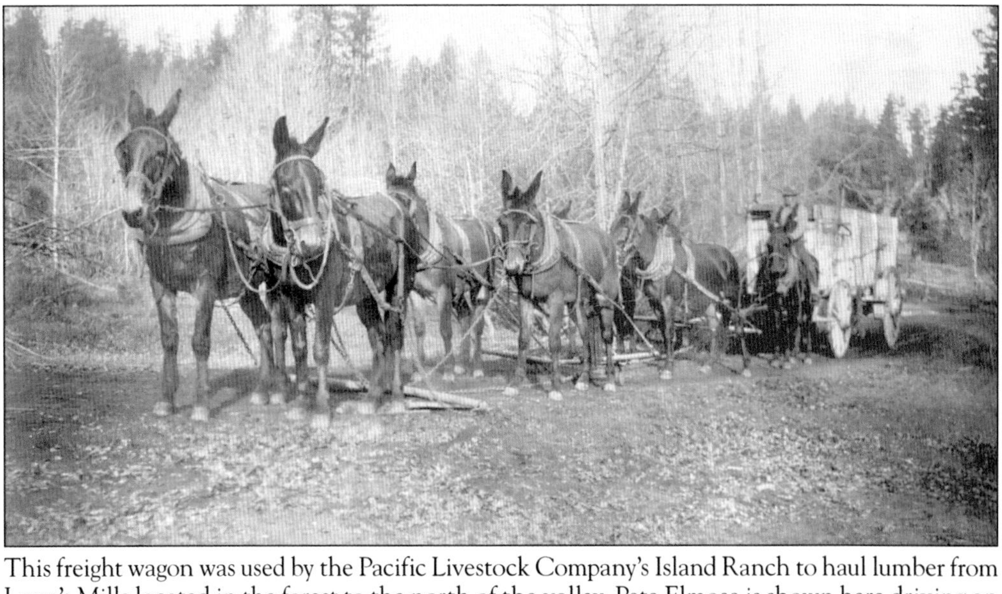

This freight wagon was used by the Pacific Livestock Company's Island Ranch to haul lumber from Lowe's Mills located in the forest to the north of the valley. Pete Elmose is shown here driving an eight-mule team making the three-day round trip for lumber. The trip took one day to complete each way with a full day allotted for loading the supplies. (Courtesy Bonnie Smith.)

A group of buckaroos working for Island Ranch—owned by the Pacific Livestock Company—pose for this photograph taken around 1900. Identified are Emil Baker (first row, sitting) and Charles Brittingham (center, sitting). Jim Brandon and Charles Lewis are also pictured.

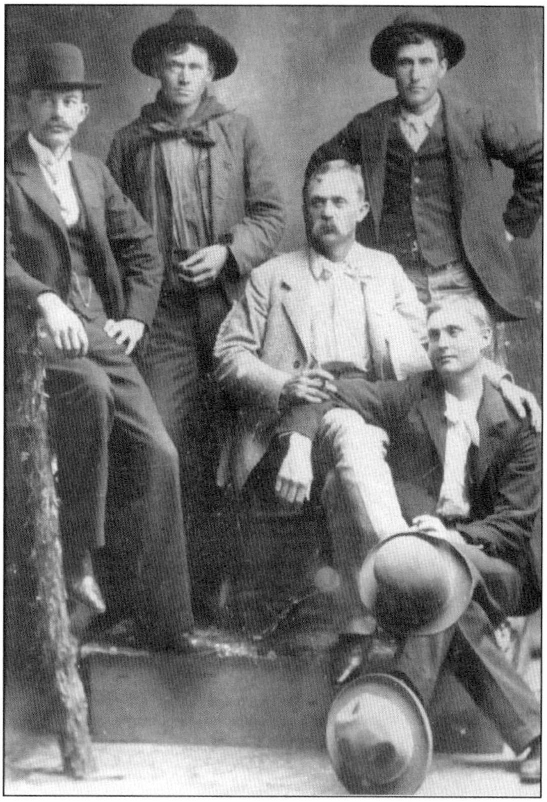

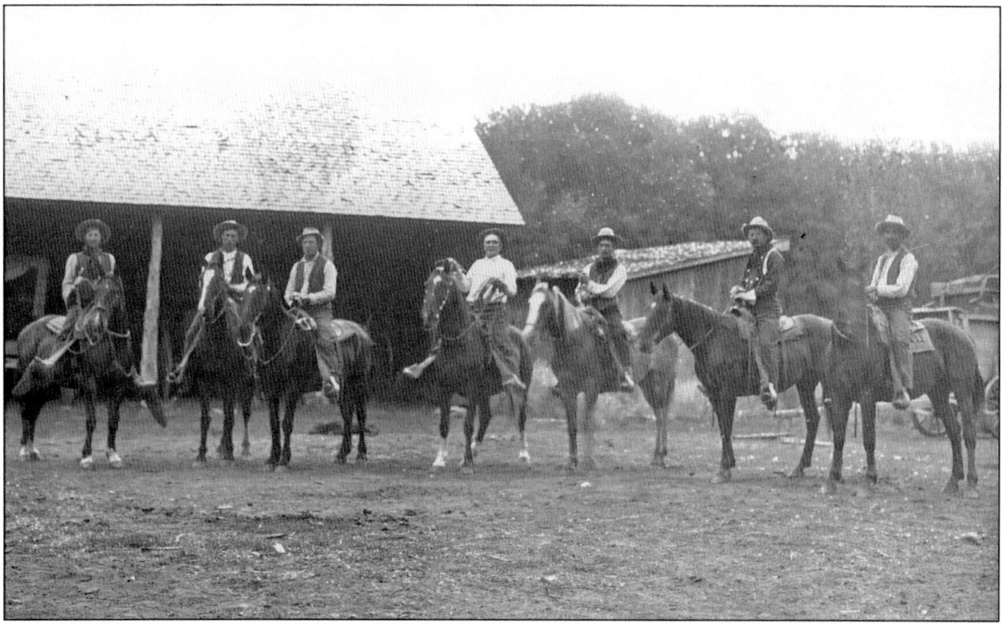

This group of buckaroos for the P Ranch in the 1890s includes Prim Ortega, far right, who came to the Harney Valley from California with Peter French. Also known as Tebo, Ortega was well known for telling tall tales and performing a variety of card tricks and feats of strength. Peter French was so fond of Ortega that he promised him a job for the rest of his life.

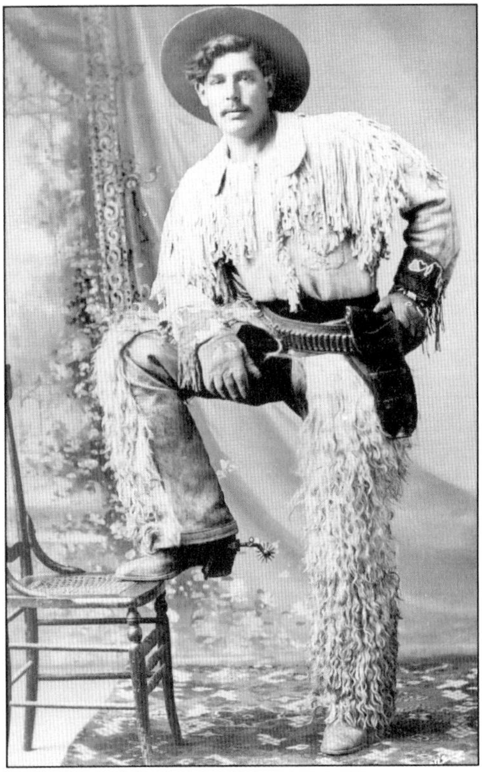

An unidentified Harney County buckaroo poses for a studio photograph in the late 1800s wearing traditional vaquero garb of wooly chaps and gauntlets. In a letter written by Henry Miller in 1894, he states that, "Ordinary buckaroos—vaqueros as he calls them here—shall work for us this winter for $25 a month, and boys and inexperienced men accordingly. If this is not satisfactory to the above, they can quit."

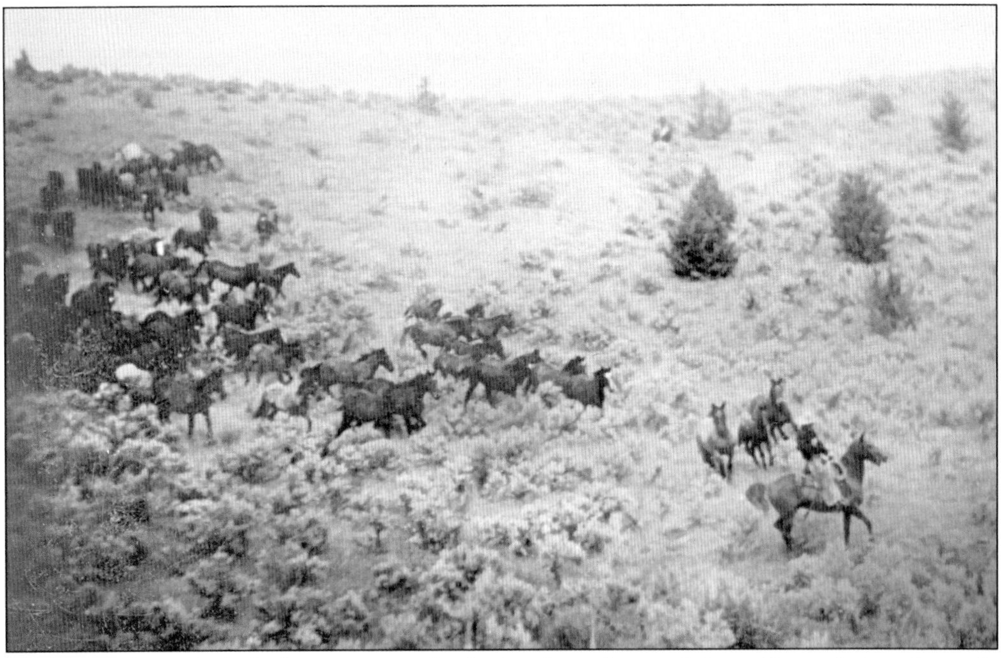

The demand was high for horses to supply the local ranches and the military during the early 1900s. In later years, horses were also supplied for rodeos. Horses were left on the open range, then rounded up when needed. Jiggs Catterson leads a band of horses in the Little Stinkingwater area in the northeastern part of Harney County around 1945. (Courtesy Frank Catterson.)

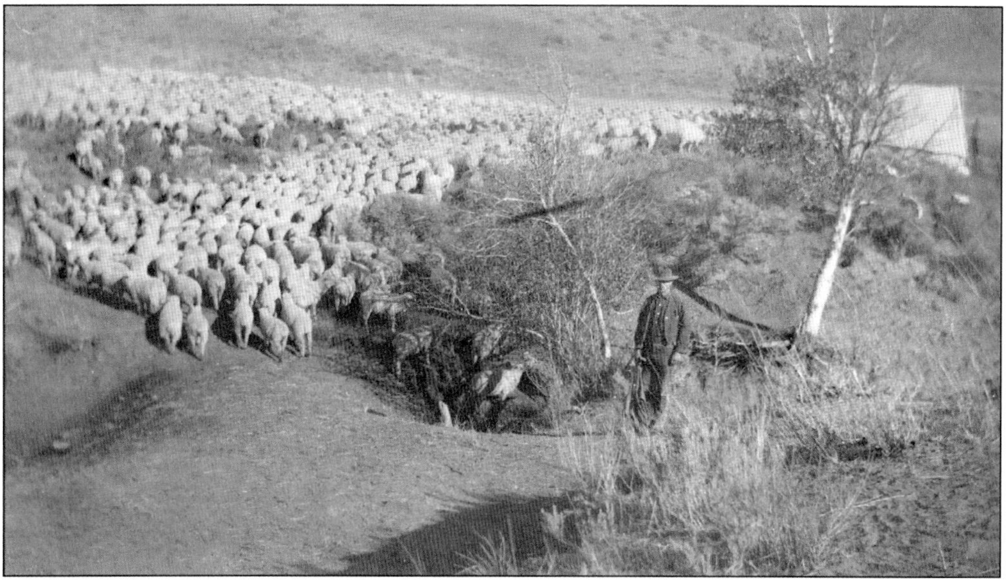

Culver Marshall Sr. is shown here with a band of sheep at Burnt Flat near Riddle Mountain in the early 1930s. Sheep were often trailed to the railheads in Crane or Riverside in the fall. It could take two to three weeks to move the herds along established stock trails. The Taylor Grazing Act enacted in 1934 put an end to the itinerant sheep operations dependent upon seasonal movements across these newly regulated lands. (Courtesy Conly Marshall.)

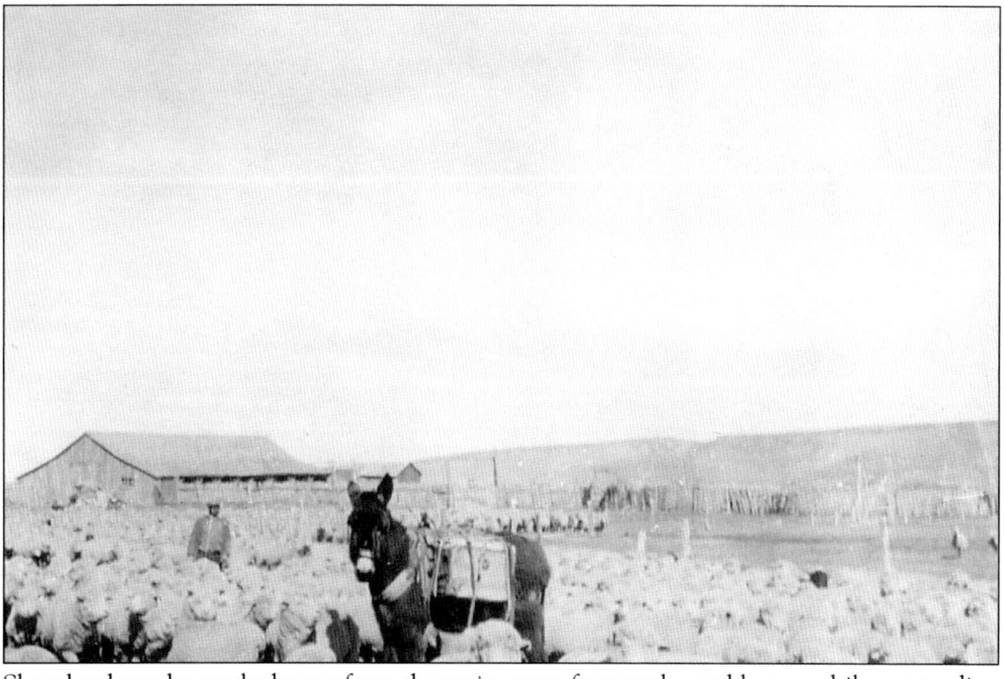

Sheepherders who worked away from the main camp frequently used burros while out tending the flocks. The burro was loaded with a sleeping shelter, a bedroll, clothes, and a small supply of food. This band of 2,000 sheep from the Diamond Ranch is headed for summer pasture on Steens Mountain. (Courtesy Dick Jenkins.)

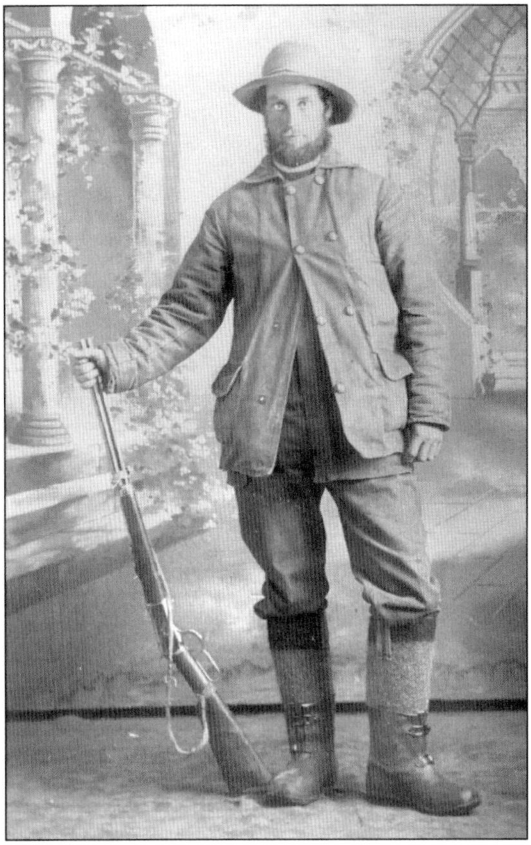

Sheepherders of several nationalities tended the flocks that roamed Harney County. Frank Herington, pictured here about the late 1890s, was of Irish descent. Scotch, Welsh, and Basque herders were also prevalent. Many came to work for several years until they could save enough money to purchase an outfit of their own.

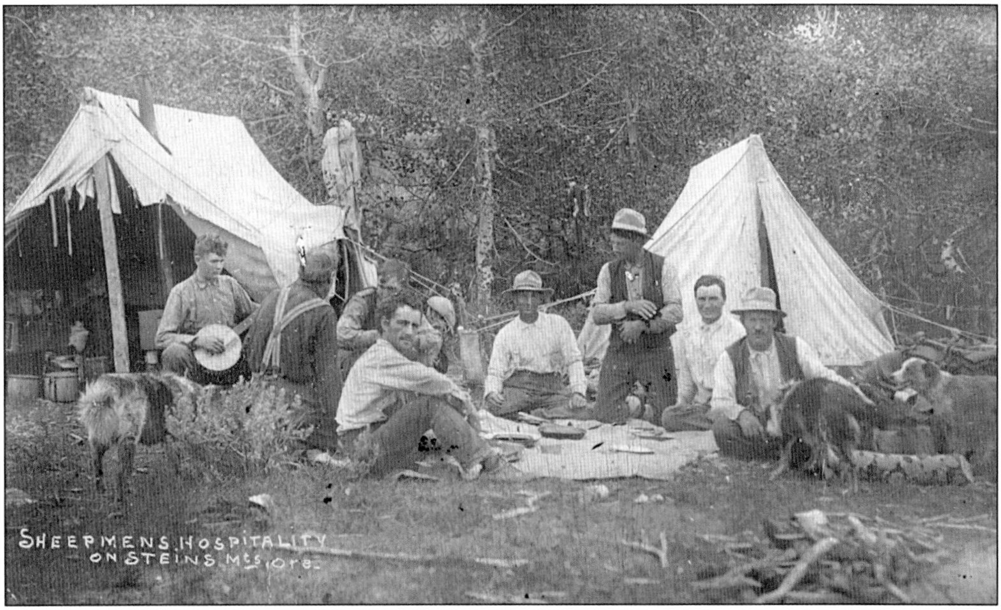

A group of unidentified sheep tenders is pictured at about the early 1900s at a typical sheep camp on Steens Mountain. The life of a herder left little time for relaxation; however, the man on the far left provides a little banjo music. (Courtesy Frank Catterson.)

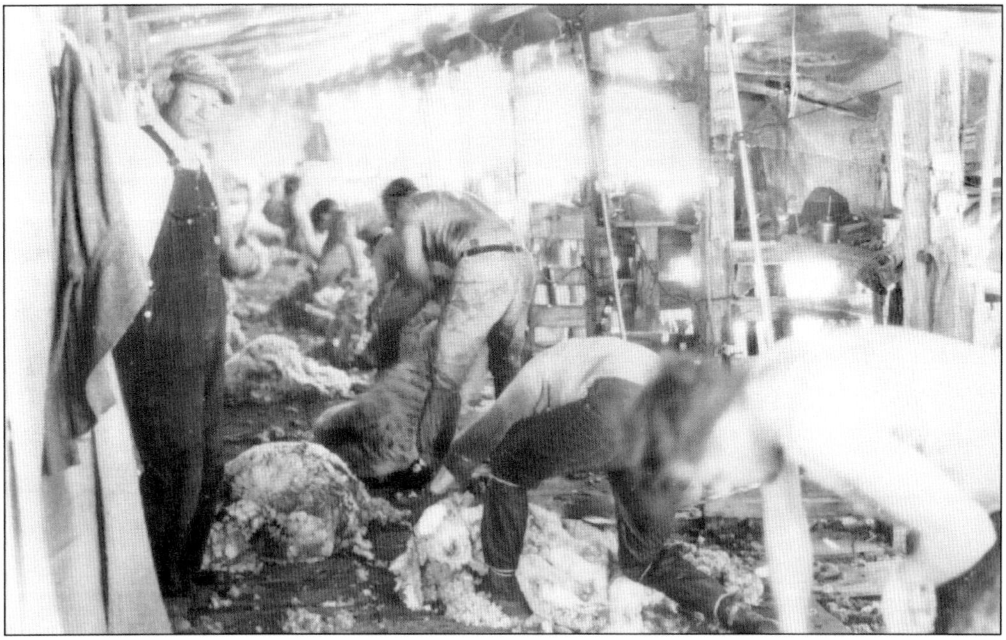

Dewey Quier poses with his sheep-shearing outfit sometime in the 1920s. Quier ran a crew of 12 shearers, some wool tiers, and hazers. He used an old gas plant to run shears using belts, pulleys, and a drive shaft. He would travel throughout the county stopping at places such as Andrews, Folly Farm, and Alberson Station. The outfit would shear sheep for several months, spending a week to 10 days at each location then moving on.

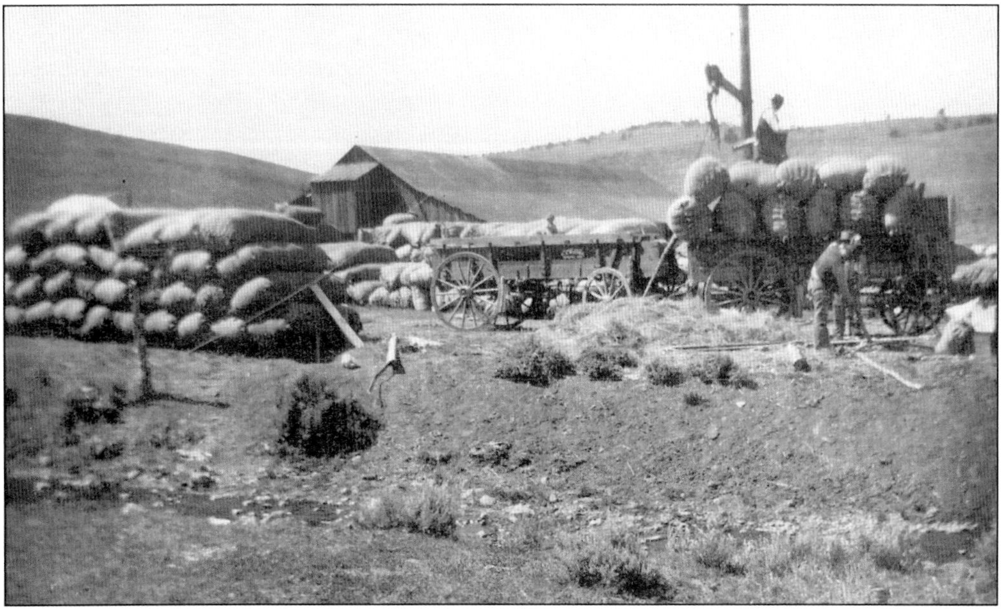

From the shearing plant, wool bales weighing upwards of 10 pounds each were packed into large sacks then loaded onto freight wagons for the long trip to the nearest railhead for shipment. The woolsacks, each weighing 400 pounds, were loaded aboard the wagons using a cable attached to a derrick, such as the one shown here on the East Riddle Mountain operation of J. R. Jenkins and Sons. (Courtesy Dick Jenkins.)

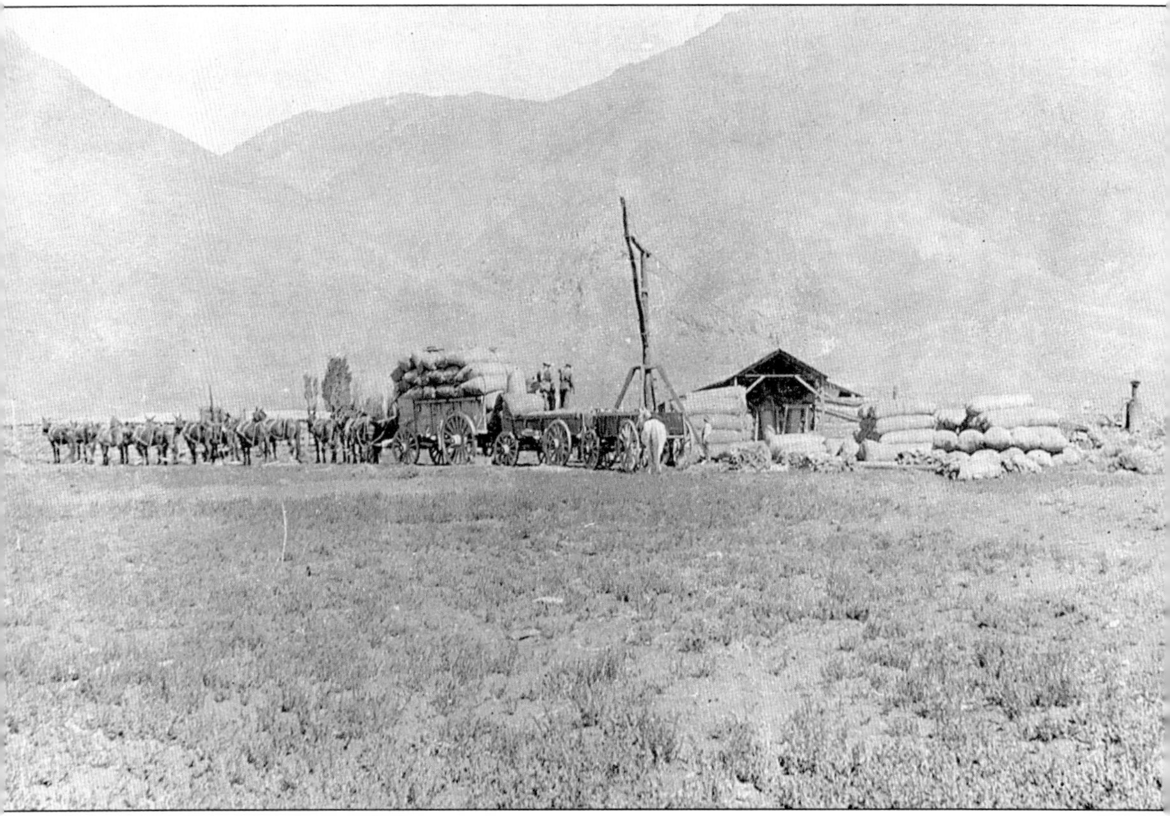

After the woolsacks were loaded at the shearing plant (pictured here), the freight wagons faced a long haul to the nearest railhead at West Fall, Ontario, or Vale. The journey could sometimes be as far as 200 miles. These long trips could take up to a month to complete. The haul grew shorter as the railroad advanced into Harney County.

Three

Logging and Timber

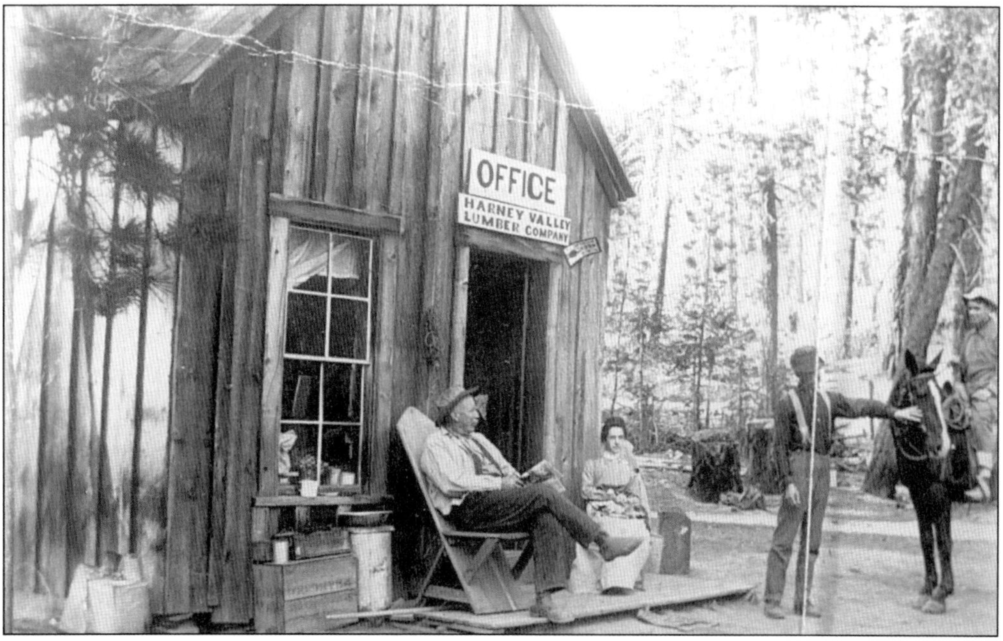

One of the earliest sawmills in Harney County was the Harney Valley Lumber Company, established in 1887 by Charles F. McKinney, who located a mill on the Main Fork of Mill or Soldier Creek about 20 miles northeast of Burns. He sold the interests in the company to his son-in-law Elmore E. Purrington in 1908. Purrington later operated another mill on Prather Creek, which eventually was bought by Dickenson and moved north to Trout Creek.

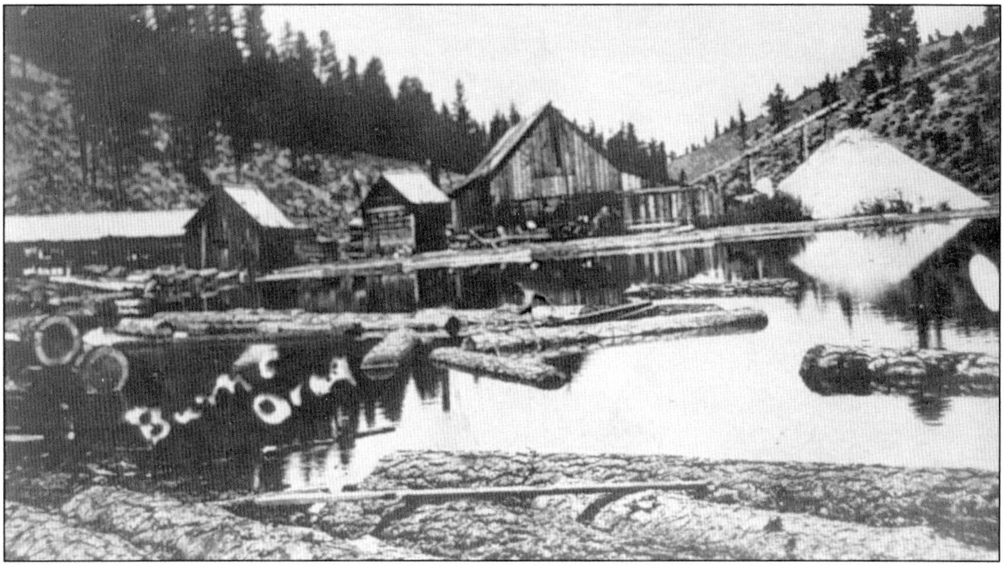

Samuel C. Dore and John W. Sayer operated the Sayer and Dore sawmill as early as 1887. This mill was located along the Silvies River near the town of Burns. Logs were floated down the Silvies River to supply the mill. In 1900, this mill burned. Sayer purchased the Horton Mill, which had been located on Cricket Creek, and moved the operation to Burns.

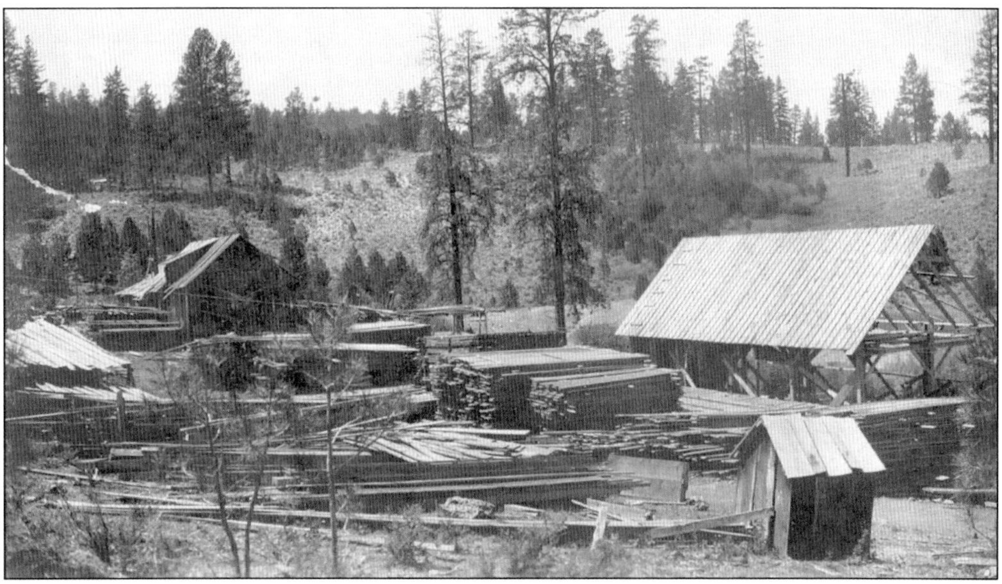

Many small lumber mills operated in the ponderosa pine forests located in the northern portion of Harney County. A. H. Robie is believed to have started the first sawmill in 1865 on land near Coffeepot Creek. This sawmill is identified on the back of the photograph as Smith's Mill: "A little sawmill where lumber was manufactured for building little towns and ranch houses in Harney County, Ore."

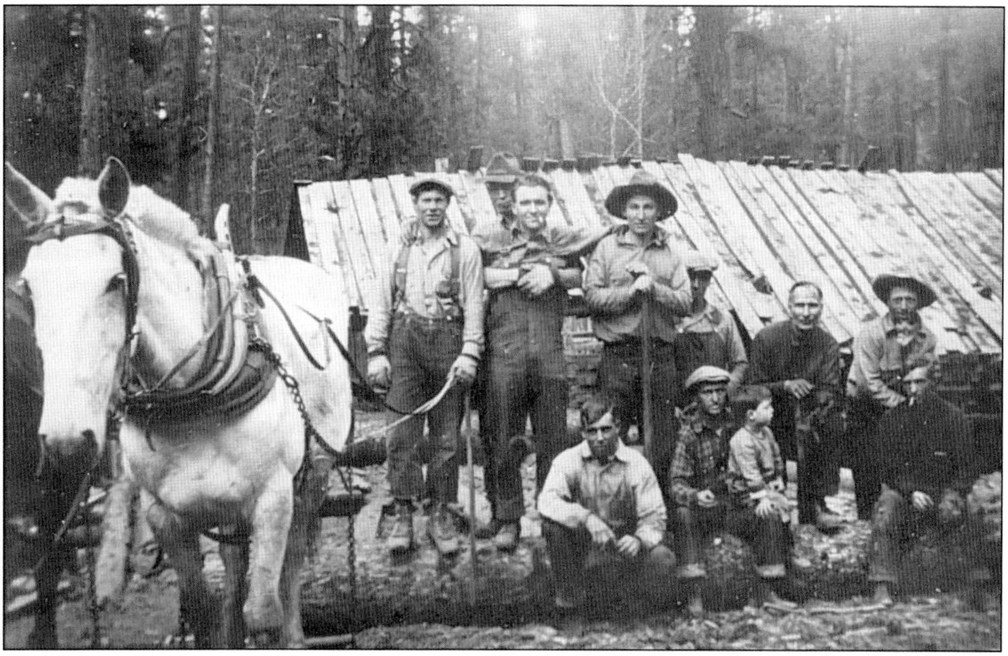

Paul Weil's sawmill, located on Bridge Creek north of Burns, is shown here in 1926. The sawmill cut trees in order to be transported by railroad to Seneca. Pictured along the bottom row from left to right are Paul Weil, Floyd Jones, and Floyd's son Darrel. Bob Hawkins is leaning on the pole behind Weil. (Courtesy Merle Weil.)

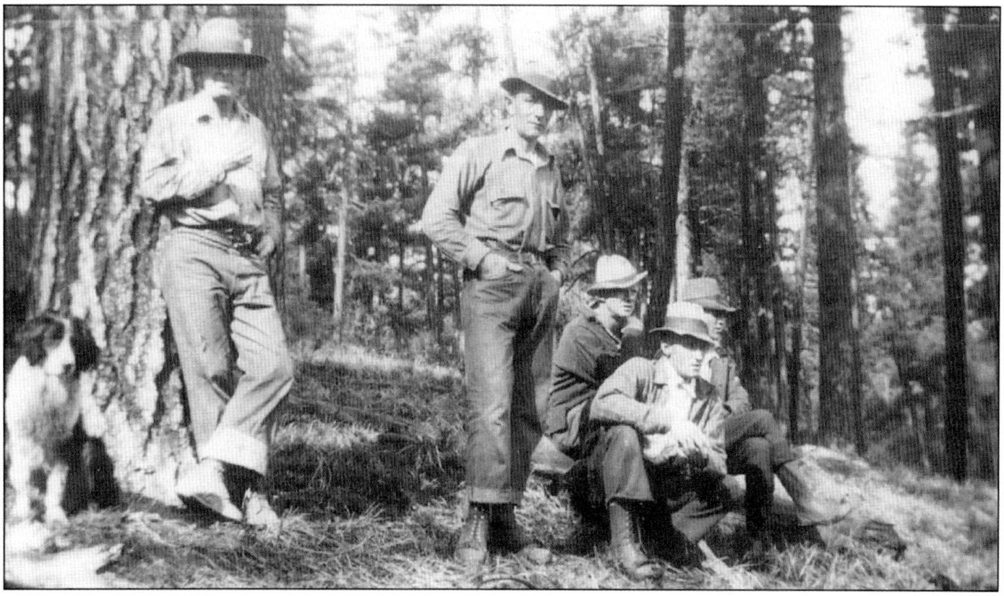

A lumber mill built in 1912 by John Farns, Elmer Drewett, and Bob Moffet was located at Moffet Springs in the Malheur National Forest, about 20 miles north of Drewsey. There were houses, a cook shack, spring shed, and a sheepherder's house as well as the mill. Bob Moffet sold the mill to Elmer Drewett but financial troubles caused the ownership to revert back to Bob Moffet. He gave the mill to his son William Perry (Bummer) Moffet, who with partner Jim Capps eventually let the mill become idle. (Courtesy Paul Cronin.)

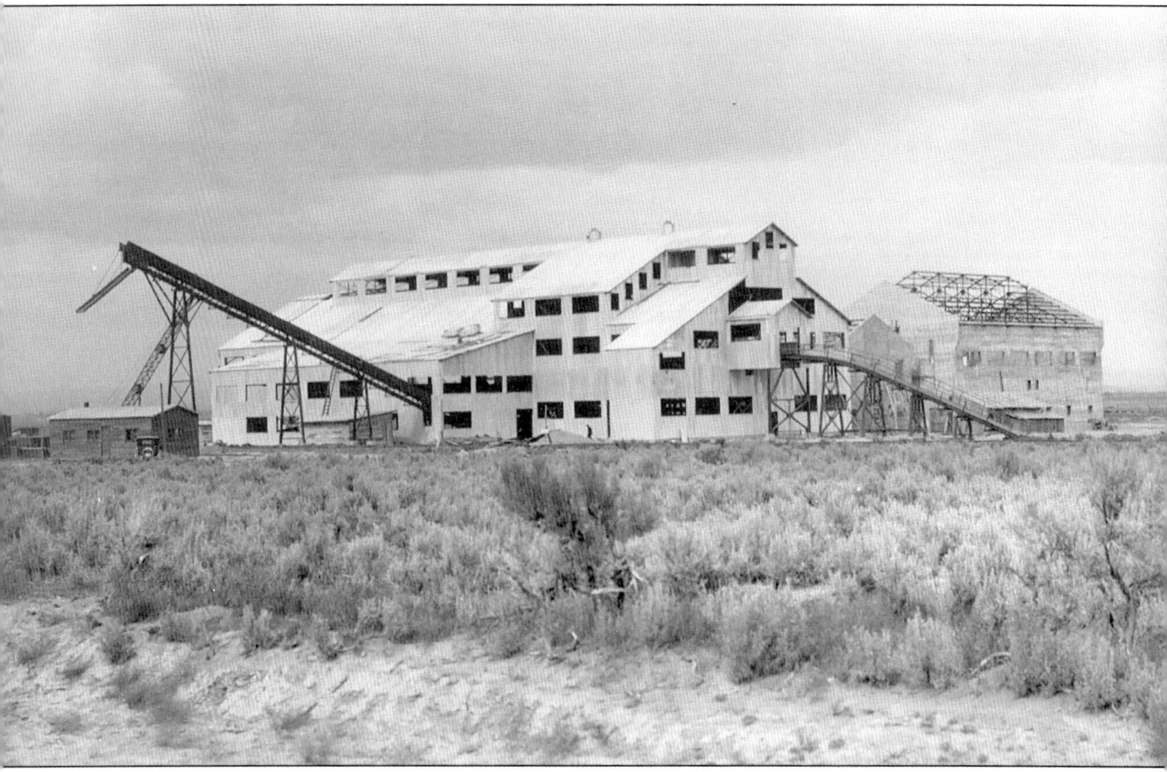

The Edward Hines Lumber Mill has long been a fixture of Harney County. The mill began as a venture by Fred Herrick, who purchased 890 million board feet of timber from the newly created Malheur National Forest in 1923. It was the largest block of timber offered for sale in the Pacific Northwest. The Forest Service planned to manage the unit for a continuous yield of 68 million board feet per year indefinitely. A stipulation of the contract was that the purchaser build approximately 100 miles of standard-gauge railroad from Crane to Burns and into the forest. After investing a considerable sum in the construction of a sawmill, powerhouse, and generator, along with over 50 miles of railroad, Herrick's finances dried up. The uncompleted mill is pictured. The Edward Hines Lumber Company purchased the entire operation from Herrick for the sum of $750,000.

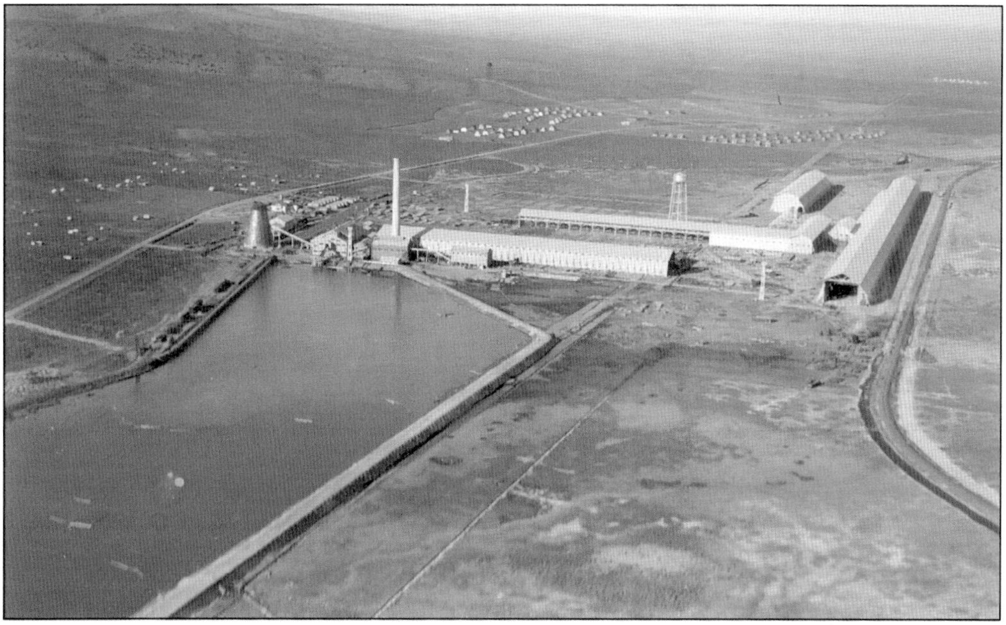

The Edward Hines Lumber Mill, completed in 1929, billed itself as one of the most modern sawmills of its time. The company boasted that once a log entered the facility, the product remained under cover through the time that it was loaded on railcars for shipping. A prominent feature of the mill was a nearly half-mile-long storage shed, where railcars could pass for loading.

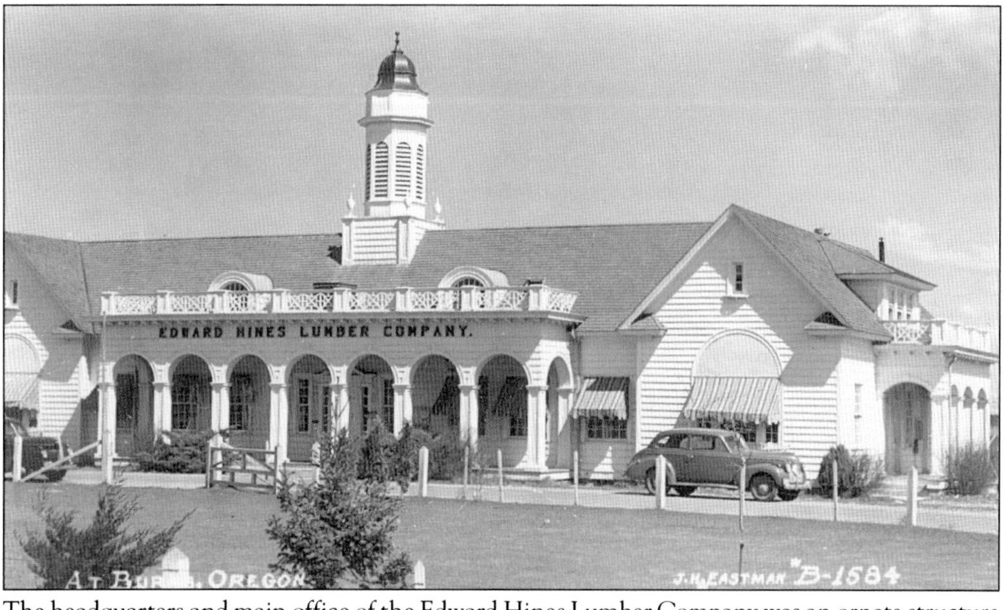

The headquarters and main office of the Edward Hines Lumber Company was an ornate structure built south of the community of Hines. It appears here in the heyday of the mill operations. The building continues to grace the old mill grounds, though it is now used for other purposes. (Photograph by J. H. Eastman; courtesy Grant Gunderson.)

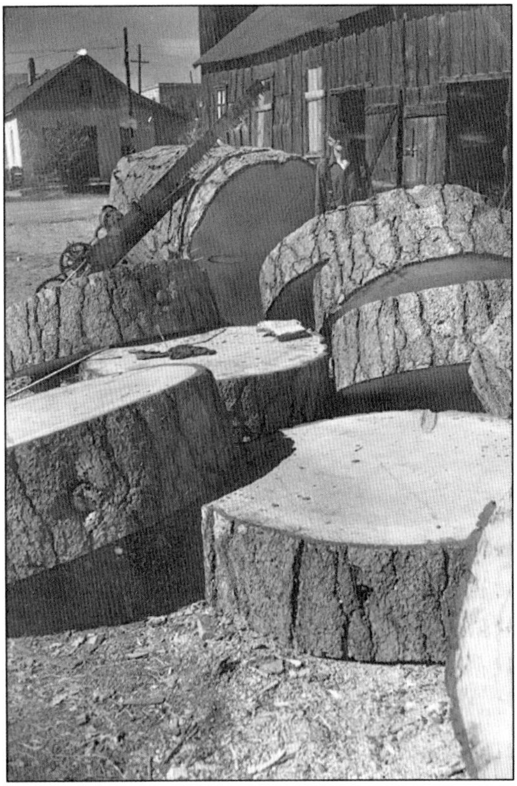

Frank Short is posing with a drag saw used to cut these oversize logs that were too large for the Edward Hines Lumber Mill to process. A seven-foot-long saw blade was required to buck the logs, which measured six feet in diameter. Short was paid in half the volume of the wood.

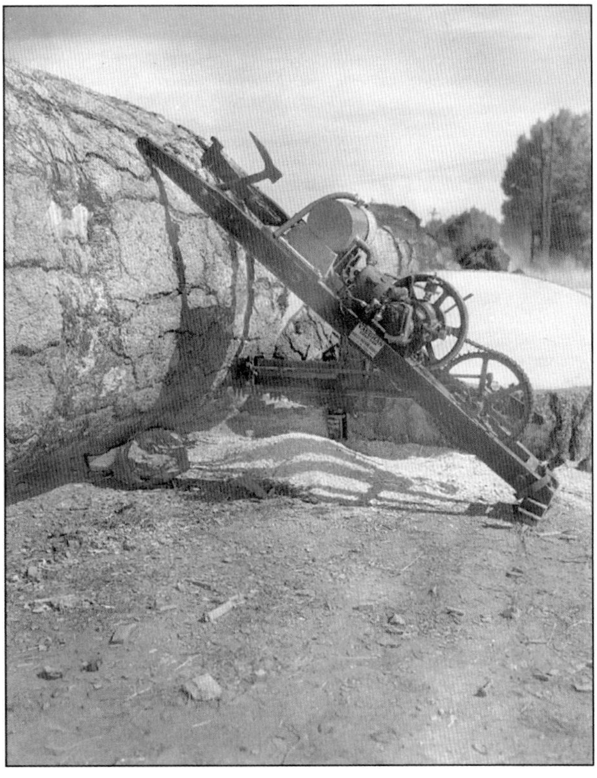

The drag saw with a seven-foot blade used to cut oversize logs is shown here. Frank Short, who rigged up the saw, owned a blacksmith shop in Burns.

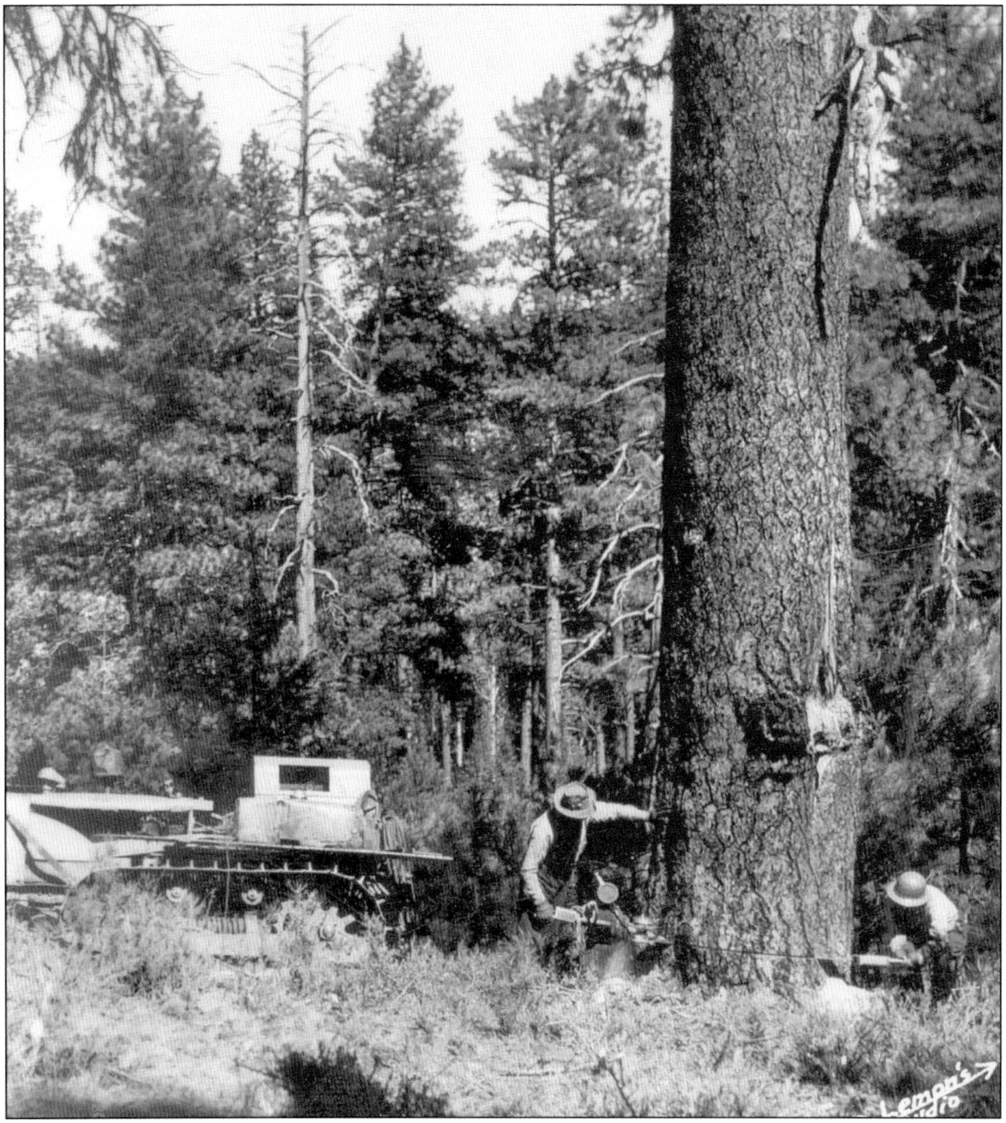

Prior to the creation of the Blue Mountain Forest Reserve in 1905 and the Malheur National Forest in 1908, lumber operations were supplied by timber that was not purchased or owned by the companies. In 1923, Fred Herrick was awarded a contract by the Forest Service to cut 890 million board feet of lumber for the sum of $2 per thousand board feet. Unable to finance the completion of his lumber mill and a railroad spur line through to Seneca, Herrick sold out to the Edward Hines Lumber Company, which began operation in 1930. These timber cutters are felling ponderosa pine with electric saws near Seneca, Oregon, for shipment to the Edward Hines Lumber Mill sometime in the 1940s. (Photograph by Lemons Studio.)

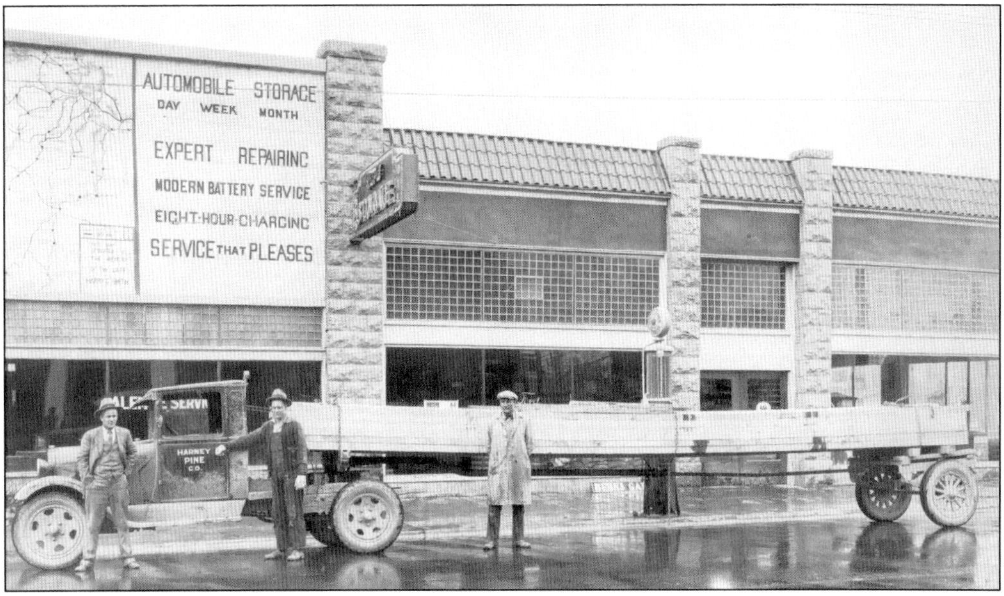

The Harney Pine Company operated by Everett G. LeRoy was one of several small independent lumber companies doing business in Harney County during the early 1930s. This loaded truck is shown parked in front of the Burns Ford Garage around 1930. Other local lumberyards included the Central Lumber Company and the Burns Lumber Company.

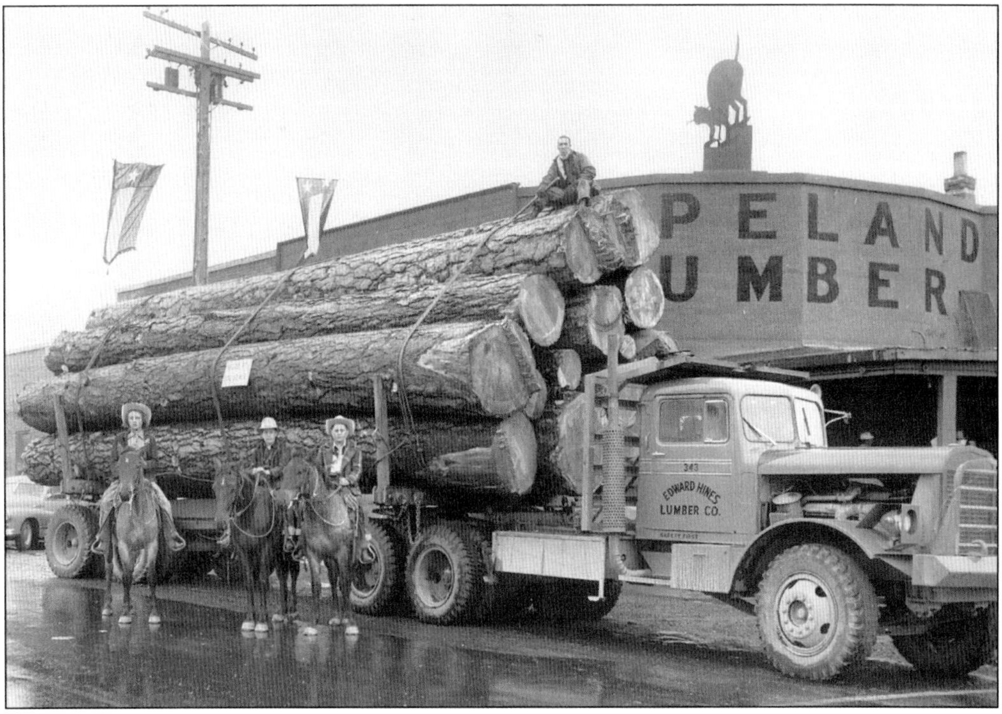

A trio of mounted horsemen pose with a loaded Edward Hines Lumber Company log truck, likely during the Harney County fair parade in Burns. Log trucks gradually began to replace the rail line due to their greater flexibility in moving from site to site as timber was cut farther from the existing spur lines. Note the Copeland Lumber Company building in the background.

Four

Transportation

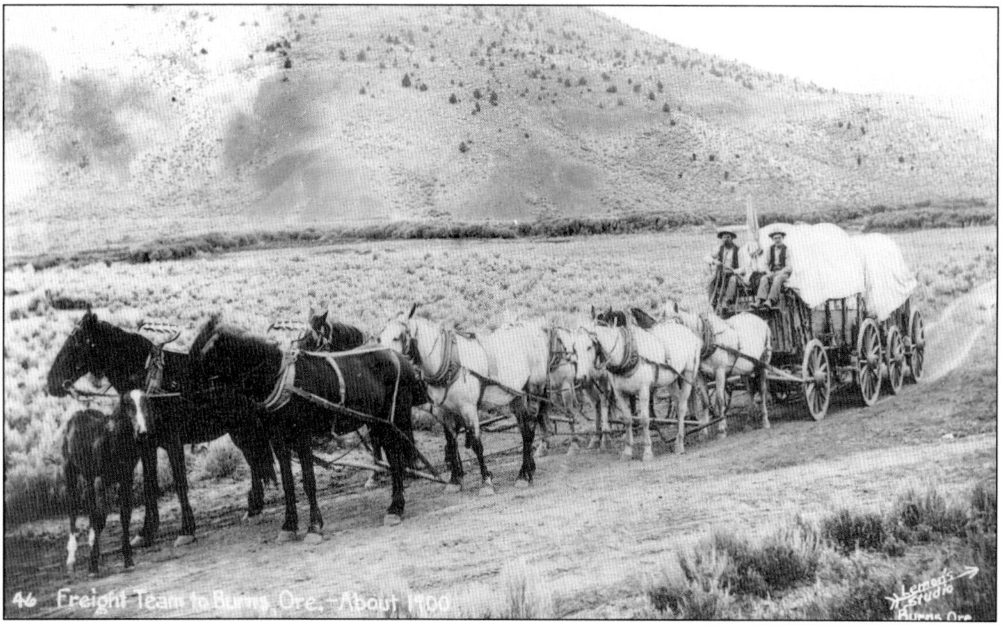

Freight wagons were used to transport just about everything. As many as three wagons could be hitched together at one time. Eight to 20 mules were commonly used to pull the wagons. Each pair of mules within the team was trained to perform specific maneuvers to guide the wagons along the sometimes narrow and winding freight roads. This freight wagon is pictured near Drewsey about 1900.

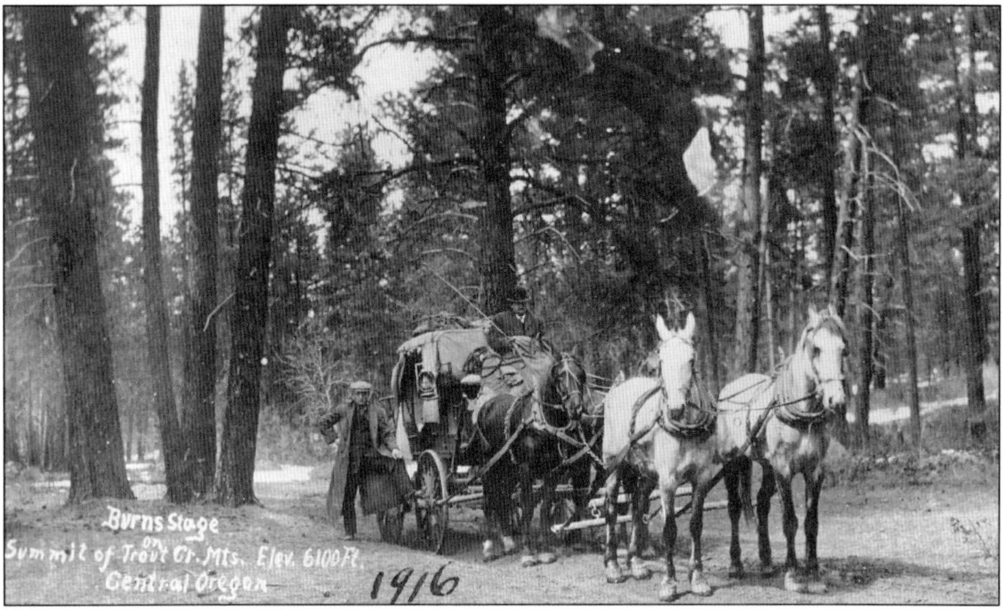

Stages were the primary method of travel until the advent of the automobile, and were still used even for a time after that. This is the Burns Stage that traveled from Burns to Canyon City. The photograph was taken about 1916 at the summit of Trout Creek. The passenger and the driver are unidentified.

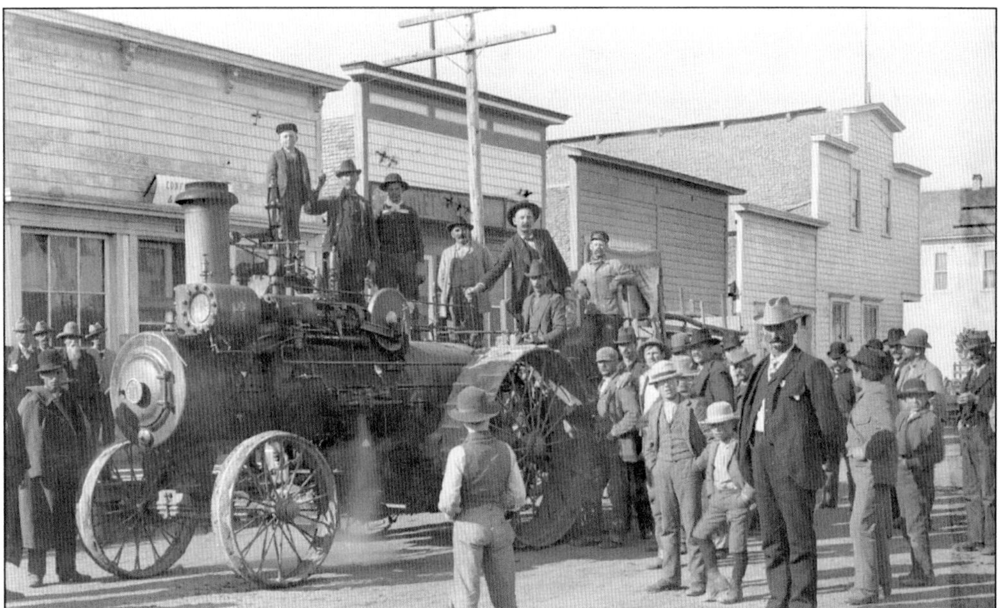

Hank Levens drove this 1900 steam tractor made by the Caterpillar Company to Burns from Vale in 1903. Standing on the tractor from left to right are S. R. Bead Howser, Chester Mace, Homer Mace, Hank Levens, Lowen Richards, and Charles Byrd. Others in the crowd standing to the right of the tractor include Charles Roper, George Sizemore, Frank Reider, Byron Terrill, and Pete Clemens.

The railroad entered Harney County by way of an extension from Ontario, Oregon. The Oregon Short Line extended to Vale about 1910, then on to Juntura in 1911. By 1914, the rail line had reached Riverside on the eastern edge of Harney County. Construction to Crane was completed in 1916. The last leg of the extension was completed in Burns in 1924. (Photograph by Lemons Studio.)

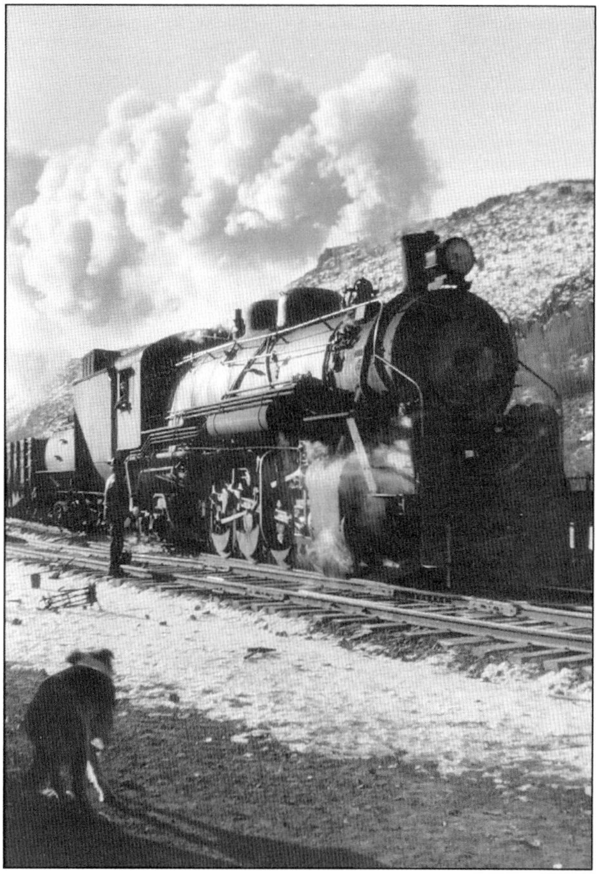

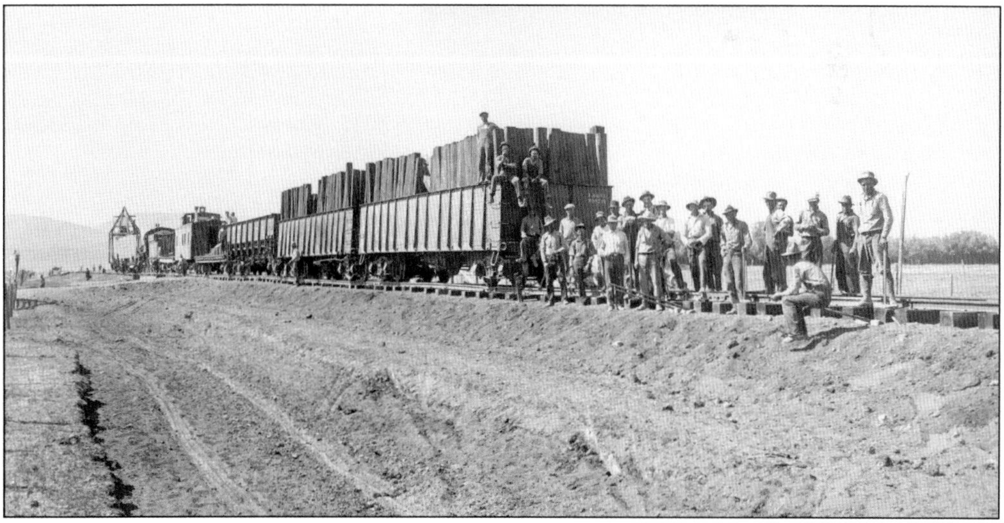

R. W. Heck photographed this group of rail workers before 1924, while the Oregon Short Line extension was being constructed between Crane and Burns. Locals were sometimes hired as contractors to prepare the right-of-way, and the mill supplied other crews. Construction and maintenance crews included Mexican and Japanese labor. The railroad company itself laid the track and the ties. (Photograph by R. W. Heck.)

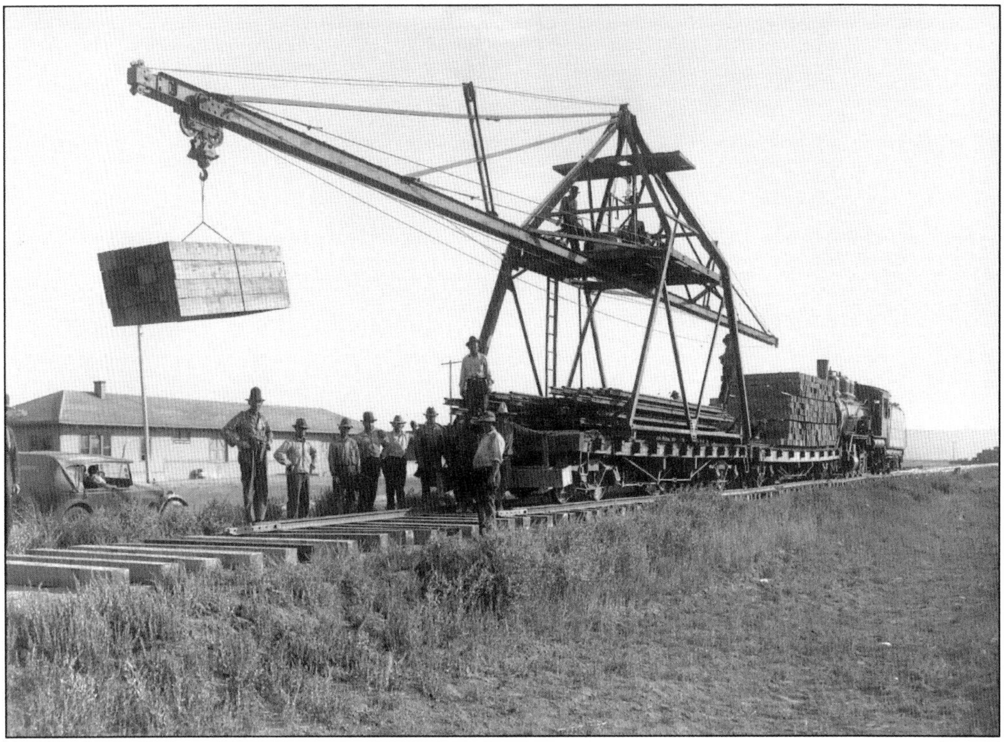

This machine was used to lay the railroad ties used in constructing the new track. It was mounted on a railcar that traversed the already completed track. This section of rail line is nearing the city of Burns. Note the Burns rail depot building in the background. (Photograph by R. W. Heck.)

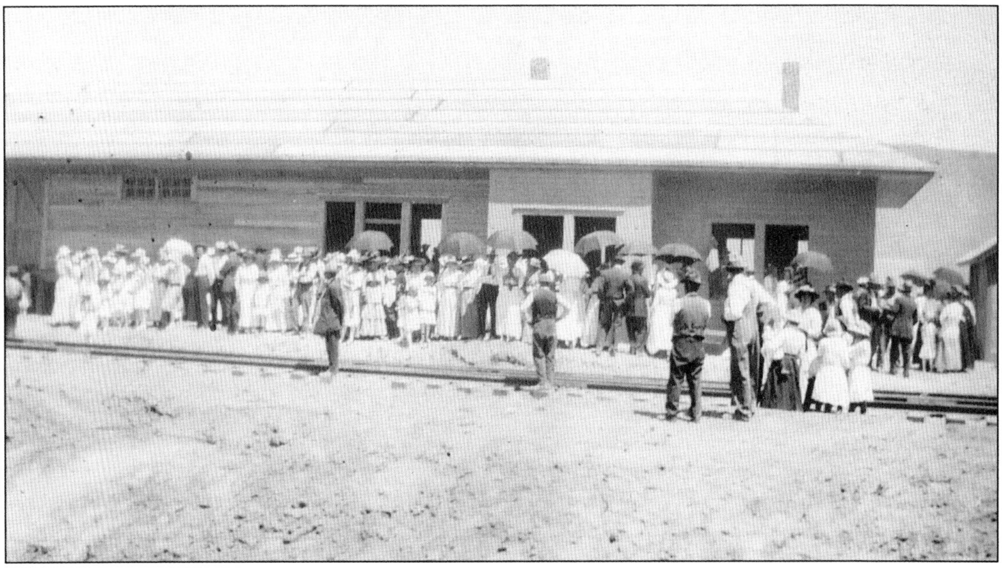

On July 11, 1916, the Union Pacific completed the extension of its rail line from Ontario to Crane. The rail line was operated by a subsidiary of the Union Pacific known as the Oregon Short Line. A gathering of over 2,000 people awaits the arrival of the first train at the Crane Depot. This was the Burns terminal for mail and freight until the line was further extended to Burns in 1924. (Courtesy Holy Family Catholic Church, Burns.)

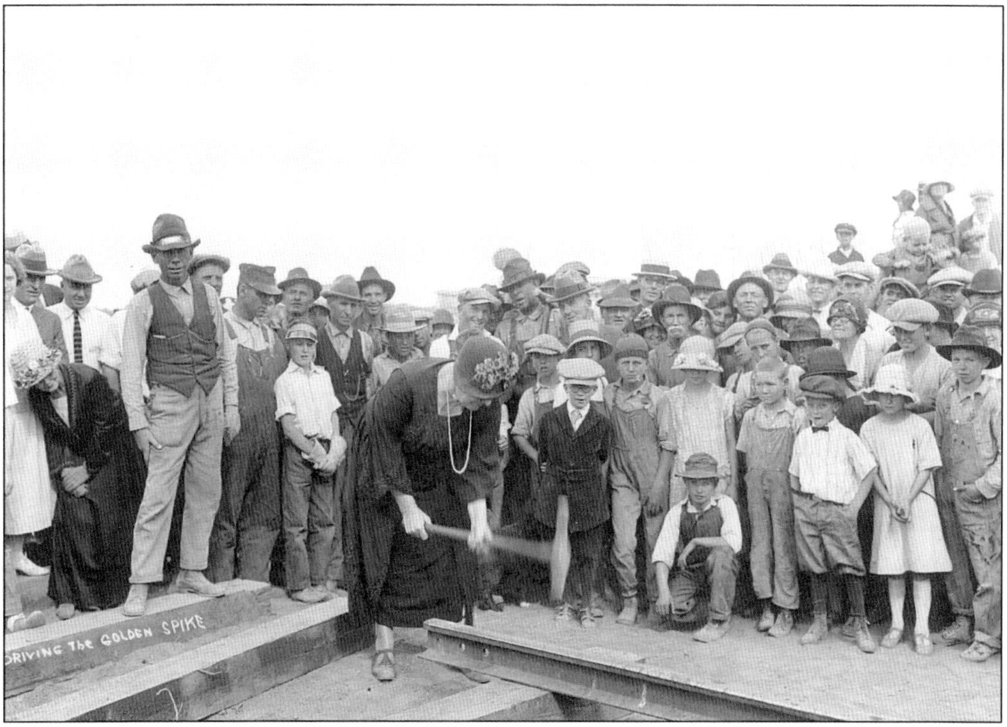

The Union Pacific Railroad completed an extension from Crane to Burns with the driving of the final spike by Jennie Cronin on August 16, 1924. The railroad played an important part in the development of Burns. Freighters no longer had to make the longer journey to Crane or Ontario to ship freight, stock, and supplies. Additionally, raw logs were brought from the forest to Hines Mill, and then shipped out for distribution. (Photograph by R. W. Heck.)

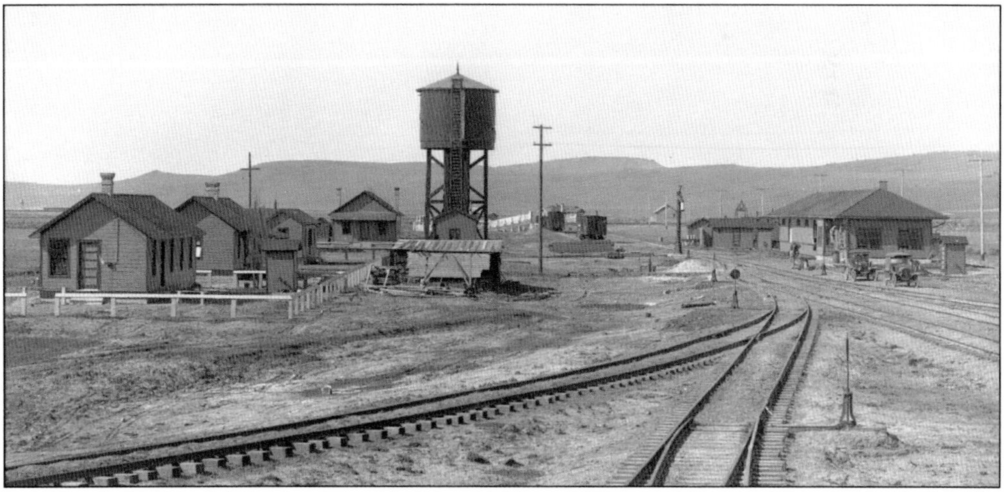

The Burns railroad depot was constructed on the southeast side of Burns, one block west of Main Street, on land previously owned by the Charles Voegtly family. There was some discussion about constructing the depot from stone but a frame structure was eventually completed. Shown here about 1929, the depot closed up in 1982 and was donated by Union Pacific to the Harney County Chamber of Commerce provided the building was removed from the railroad site. (Photograph by R. W. Heck.)

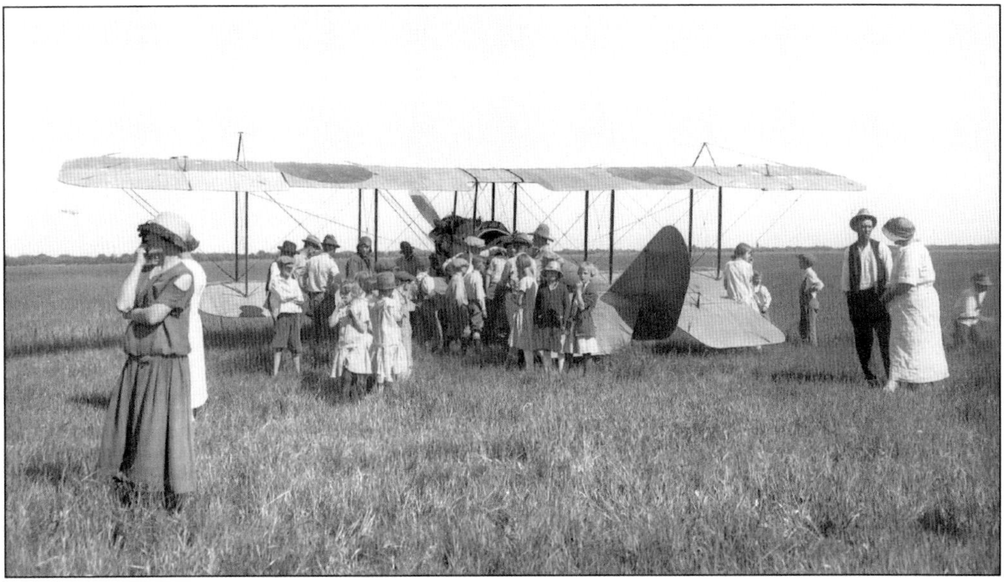

One of the earliest aircraft to land in Harney County was this Curtis JN4-D "Jenny" piloted by barnstormers R. R. Trask and Lt. W. D. Cannon. The plane landed in Sweeks hay field on August 13, 1920, after landing near the Double O Ranch the previous day due to a fuel shortage. Townspeople gathered around for rides in the plane.

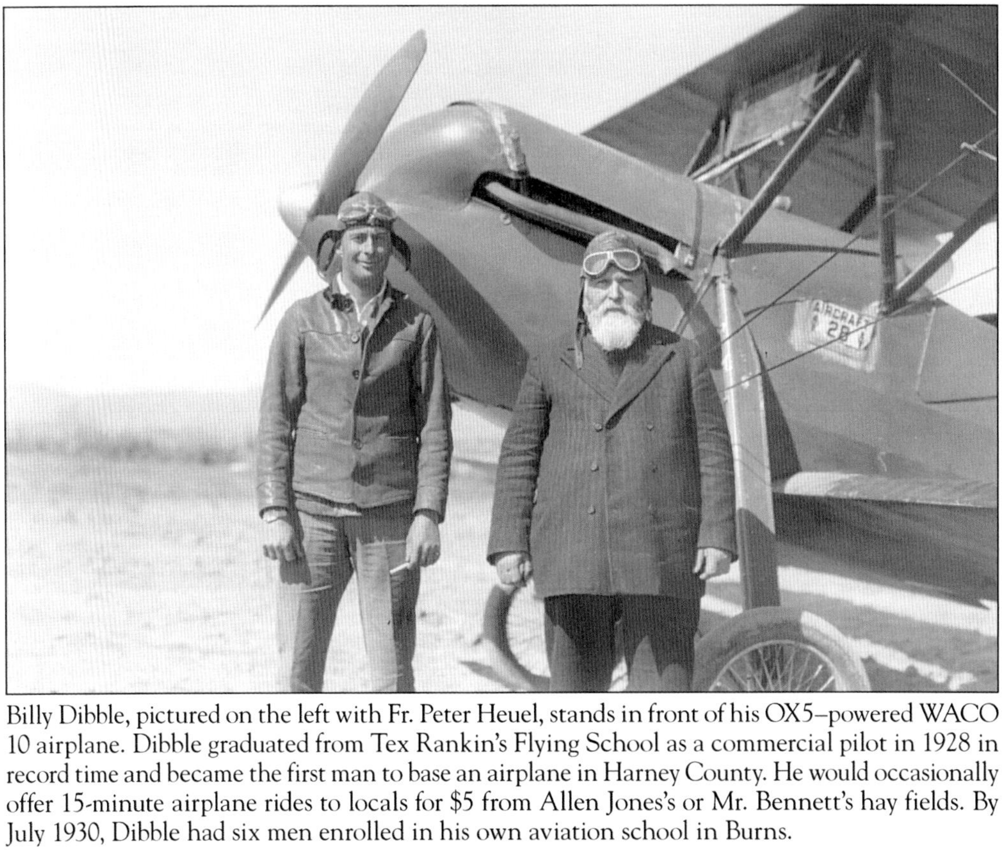

Billy Dibble, pictured on the left with Fr. Peter Heuel, stands in front of his OX5–powered WACO 10 airplane. Dibble graduated from Tex Rankin's Flying School as a commercial pilot in 1928 in record time and became the first man to base an airplane in Harney County. He would occasionally offer 15-minute airplane rides to locals for $5 from Allen Jones's or Mr. Bennett's hay fields. By July 1930, Dibble had six men enrolled in his own aviation school in Burns.

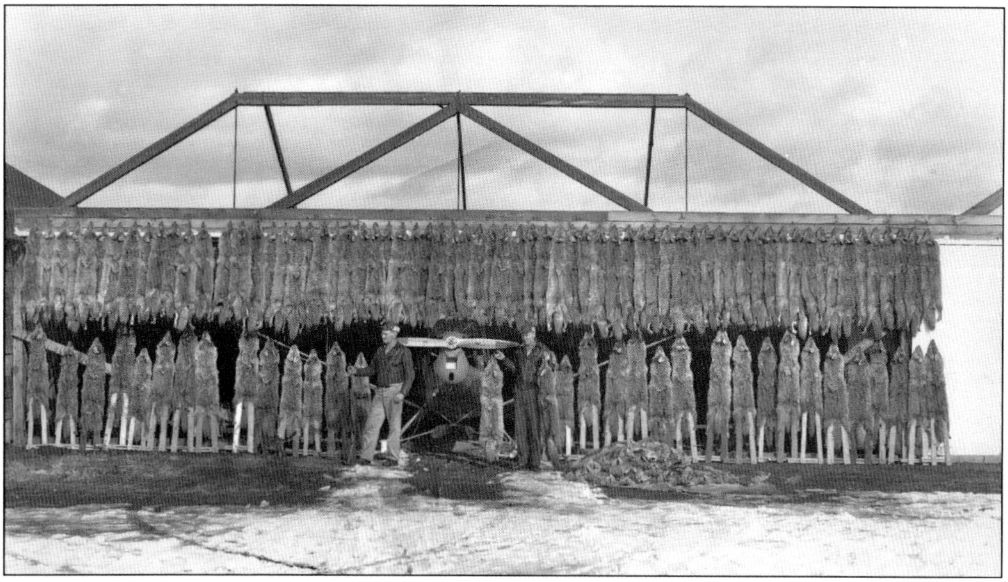

Bill Stevenson and Roe Davis pose in front of coyote pelts taken by the pair from an airplane in the winter of 1944–1945. The Oregon State Game Commission contracted aerial hunters for $12.50 per hour. In one season, Davis and Stevenson killed 247 coyotes, which brought in an additional $15 per hide. Another year, Davis took 400 coyotes from the air. Roe and his brother Oscar were two of the most active pilots in early Harney County aviation.

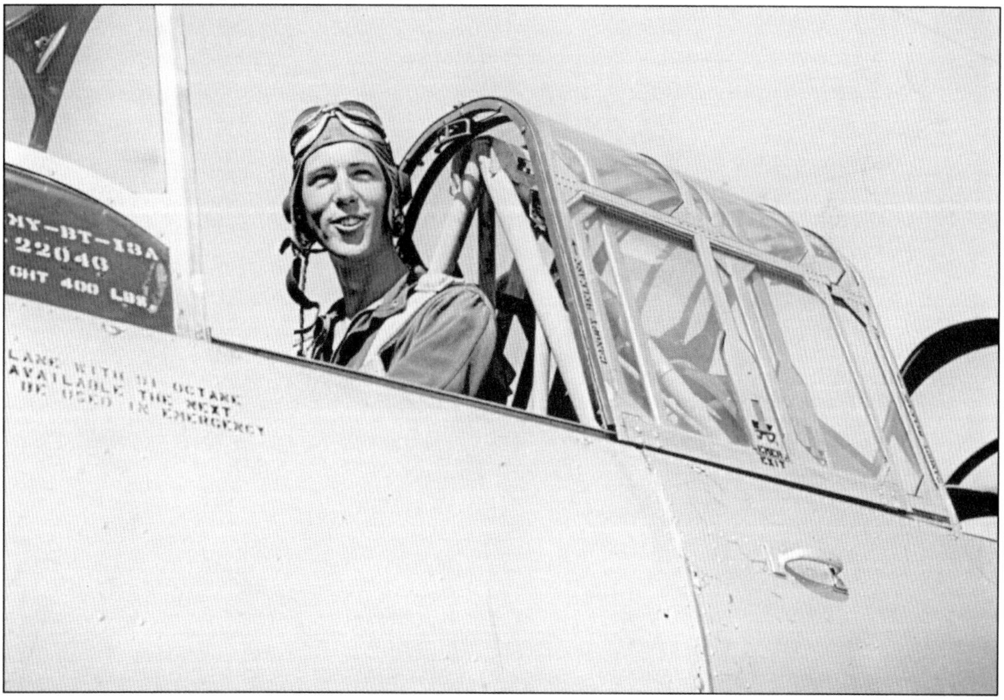

Dale and Daryl Eggleston were another pair of brothers who were early promoters of aviation in Harney County. Dale, pictured, served as a U.S. Army flight instructor in Texas during World War II. Brother Daryl at age 18 in 1935 became the first man to take his first solo in Harney County and the second person to fly solo from the new airfield. (Courtesy Dale Eggleston.)

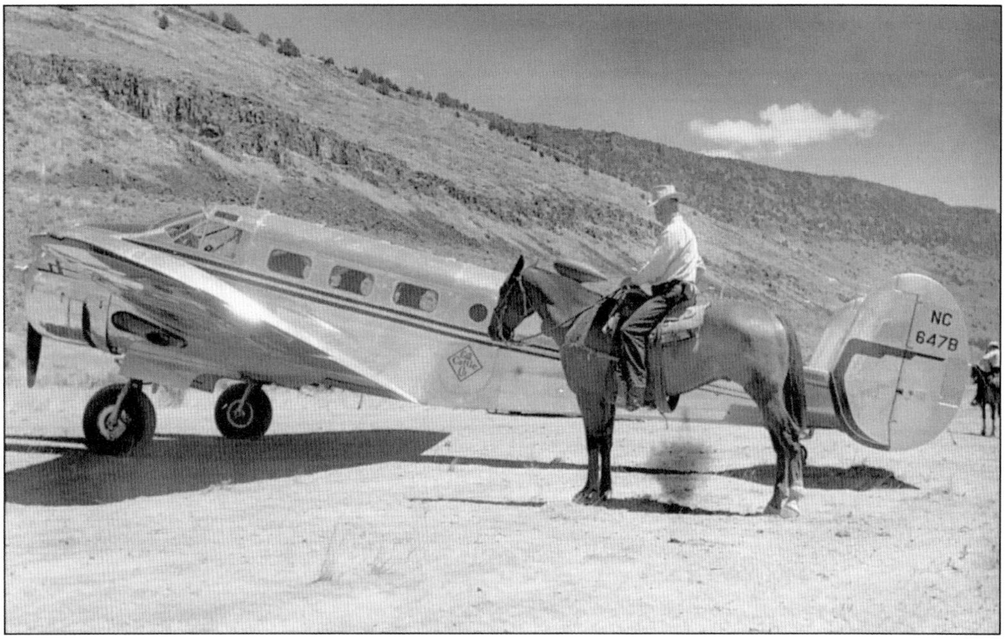

Aircrafts were used by the Gill Cattle Company of the Roaring Springs Ranch located on the western side of Steens Mountain. Flying in the dry, high-altitude climate and near the rugged peaks and canyons of Steens Mountain sometimes posed challenges for even the best of pilots. (Photograph by Lemons Studio.)

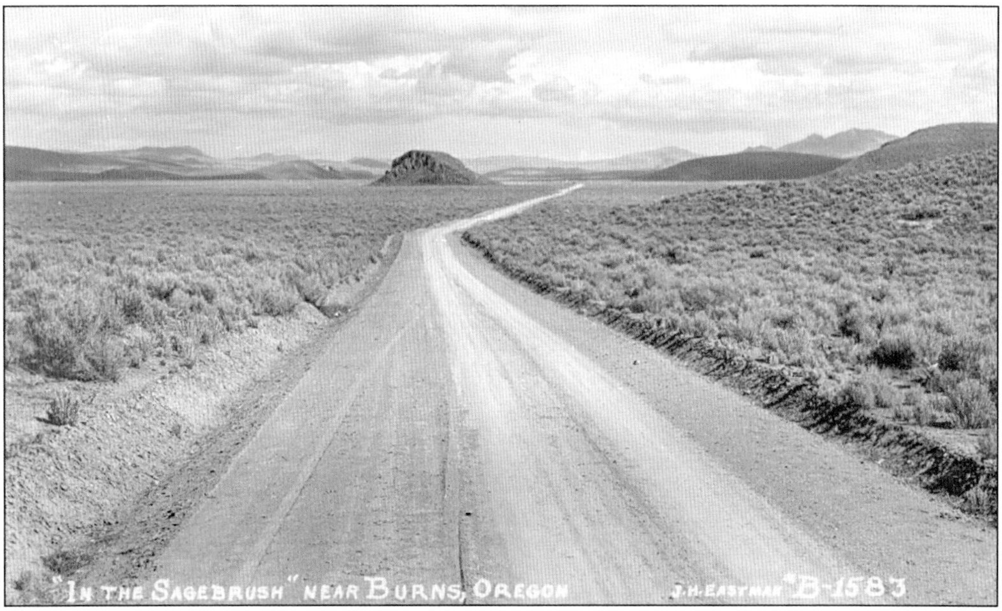

This view of the valley, probably taken during the 1930s, shows the vast open spaces and endless vistas encountered by early-day travelers. There are approximately 1,238 miles of county and state roads in a county exceeding 10,000 square miles. The majority of roads in the county remain unpaved. The most common season for travel was summer, as spring rains and snowmelt made for slick muddy roads and winter snows were difficult to navigate in early automobiles. (Photograph by J. H. Eastman.)

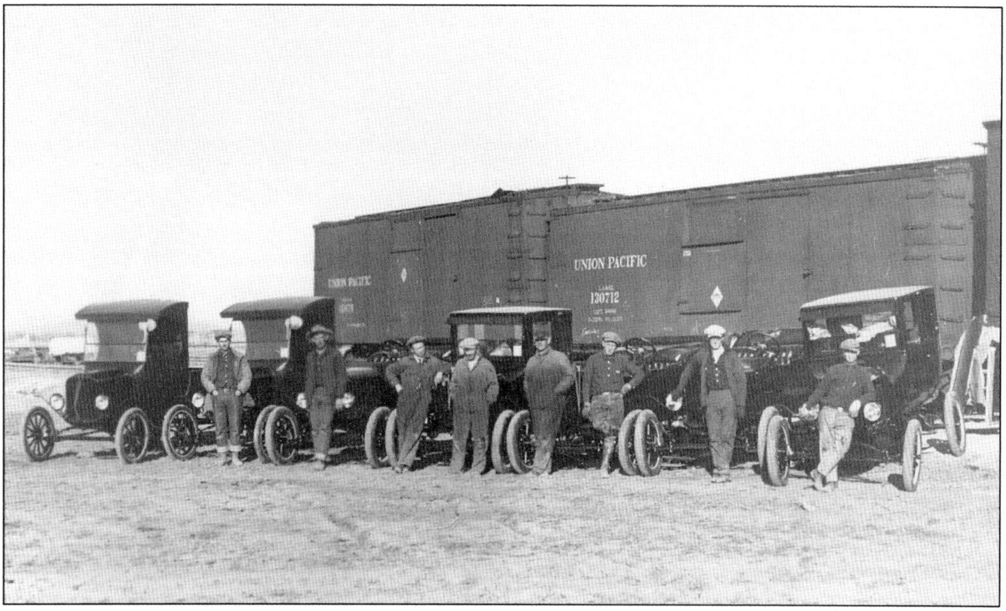

This railcar load of seven new automobiles was delivered to the Burns Ford Garage about 1915. Burns Ford is the second oldest Ford dealership on the West Coast and is the oldest continually operating business with the same name in Burns. J. L. McCulloch, pictured seventh from the left with the white hat, operated the Chrysler Garage in the corner of Main and Monroe Streets.

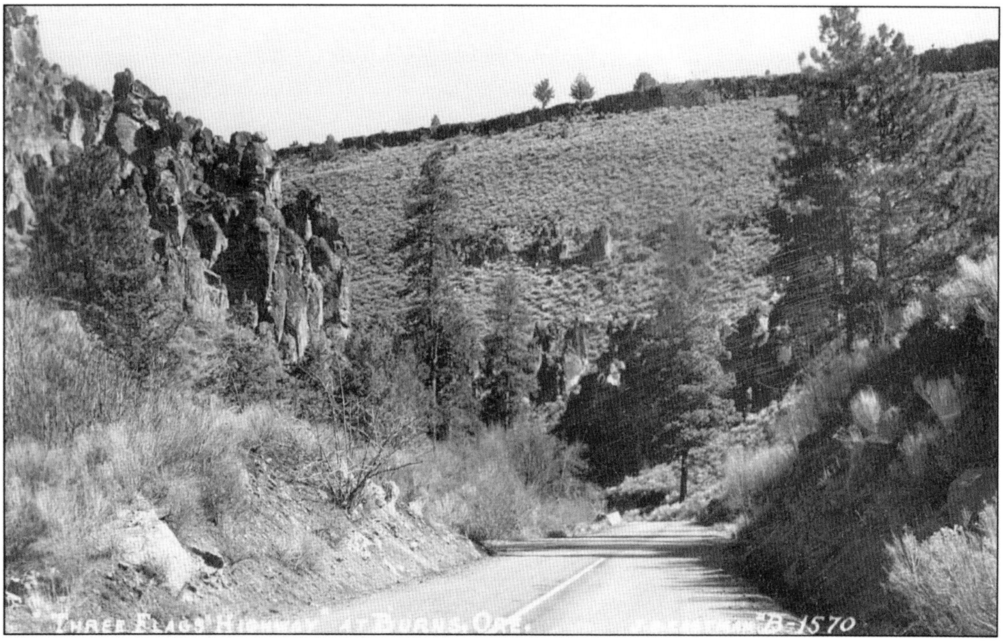

The Three Flags Highway officially opened in August 1953. It was an all-oiled north and south route from border to border in Eastern Oregon. Over 150 people gathered from at least four states to attend the ribbon-cutting ceremony at the Harney-Grant County line in Silvies Valley. A. A. Bardwell served as master of ceremonies. It was believed that this new highway would bring about better transportation to the region and encourage new industry. (Photograph by J. H. Eastman; courtesy Grant Gunderson.)

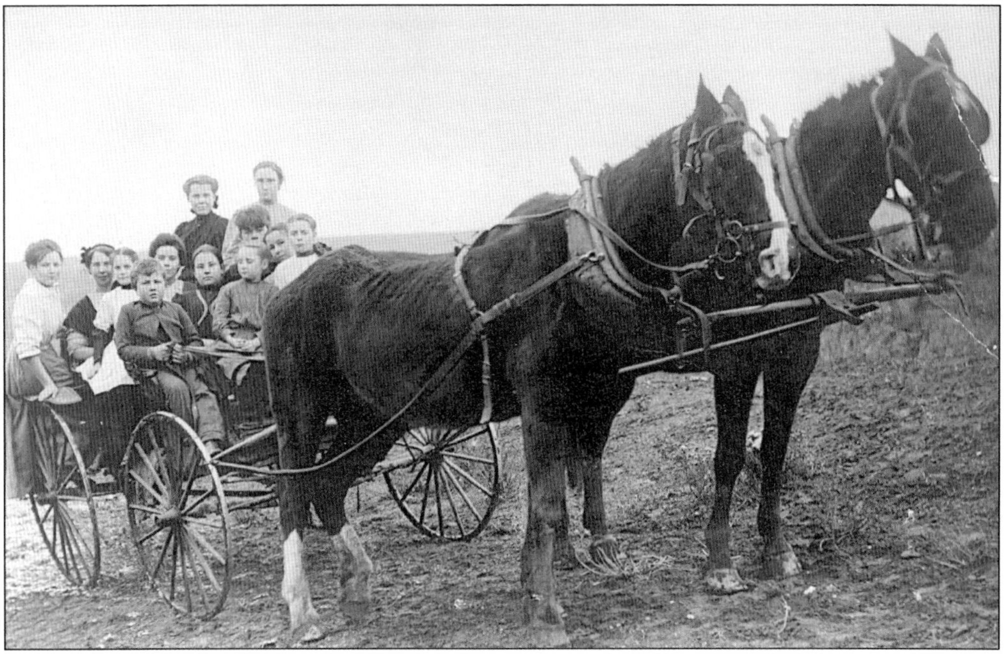

Pictured is a pioneer version of the modern school bus. Early-day schoolteachers performed a variety of duties. This teacher, known only by the initial C, relates that she brings half of her students to school every day in the "school auto." Two of the boys were absent the day of the photograph.

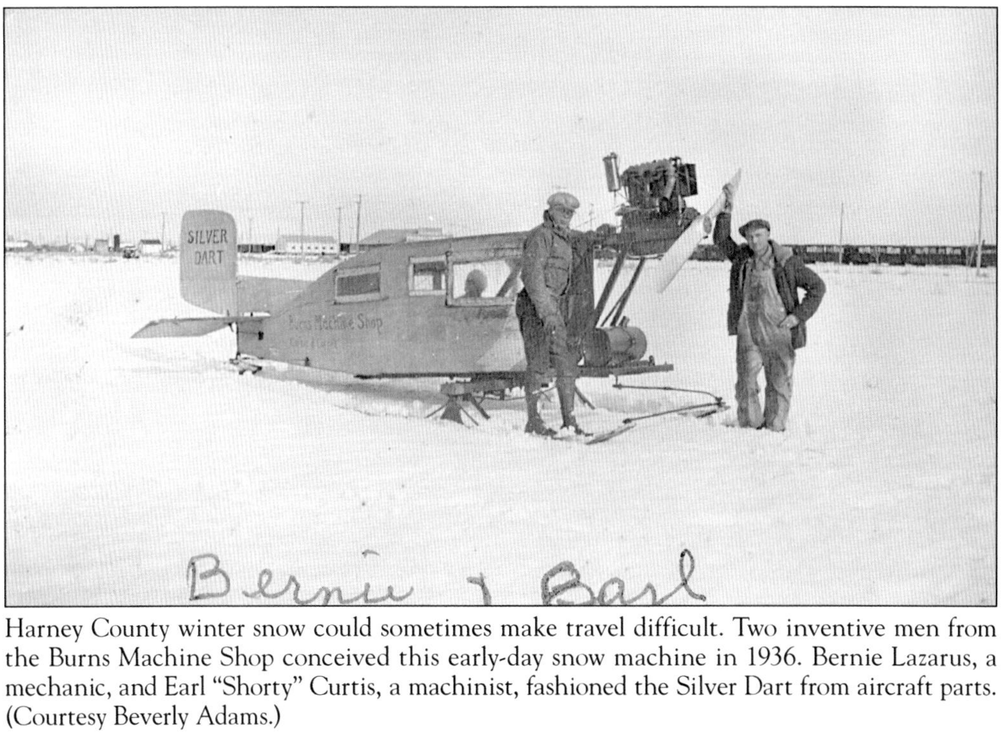

Harney County winter snow could sometimes make travel difficult. Two inventive men from the Burns Machine Shop conceived this early-day snow machine in 1936. Bernie Lazarus, a mechanic, and Earl "Shorty" Curtis, a machinist, fashioned the Silver Dart from aircraft parts. (Courtesy Beverly Adams.)

Five

Cultural Crossroads

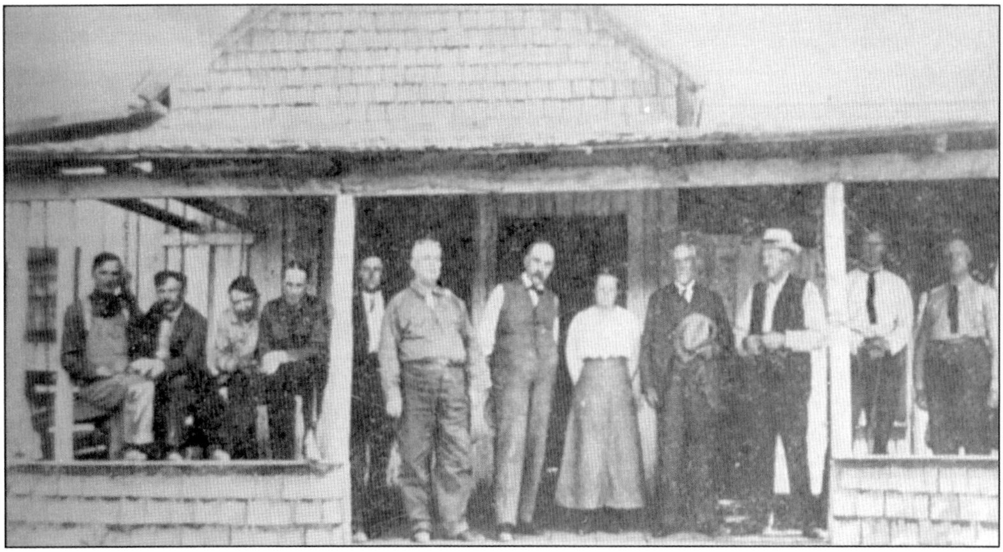

The Malheur Indian Agency was established by an executive order in 1875 and 1876. A large portion of Harney County was set aside for use by the Paiute and Snake Indians. Mismanagement by the commanders in charge led many of the Native Americans to drift away and caused general unrest among the various tribes subsisting in the county. Those who did not leave of their own accord were rounded up by the government and removed to other reservations. The reservation lands were then opened up to official settlement, although homesteaders and stockmen had been using the lands anyway. The agency building shown here also served as the Beulah Post Office.

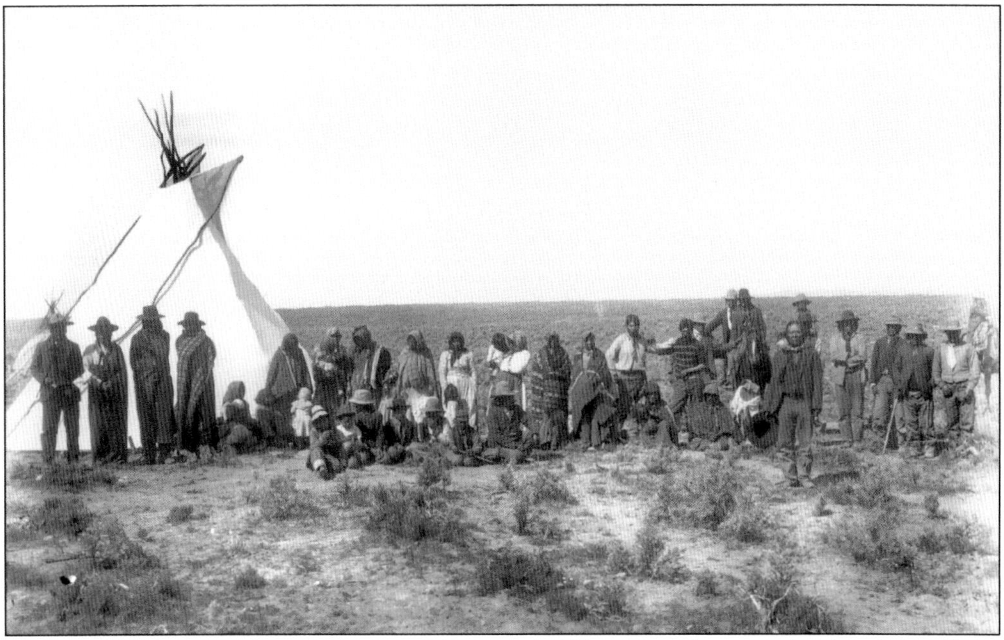

This group of Paiute Indians is shown at the site of "Old Camp" about 1915. After the Malheur Reservation was disbanded, the Paiute tribe was left with no land to call its own. Homesteaders and stockmen had already taken up the best land. Some of those who remained took up residence west of Burns. This collection of teepees and tents became known as Old Camp. (Photograph by R. W. Heck.)

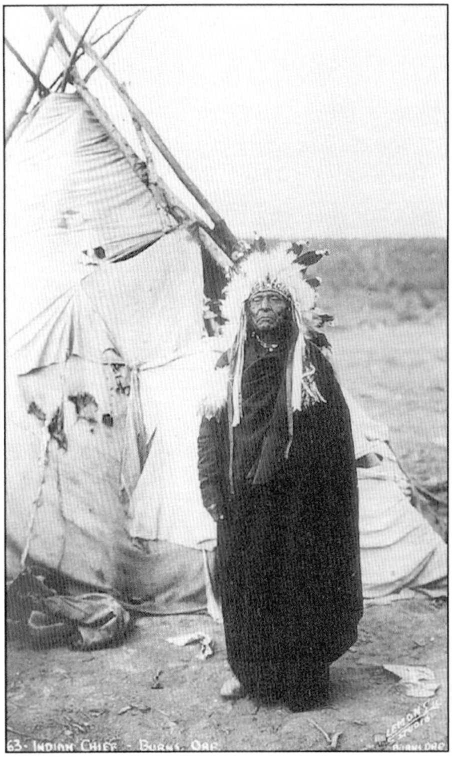

Chief Louie, dressed here in full regalia, was the well-known leader of the local Paiute tribe in the Harney Valley area. During the Modoc Indian uprisings in the 1870s, Louie acted as a scout for the U.S. Military, earning the nickname "Captain," though he was never officially appointed. The chief died in 1935 at approximately 90 years of age. (Photograph by Lemons Studio.)

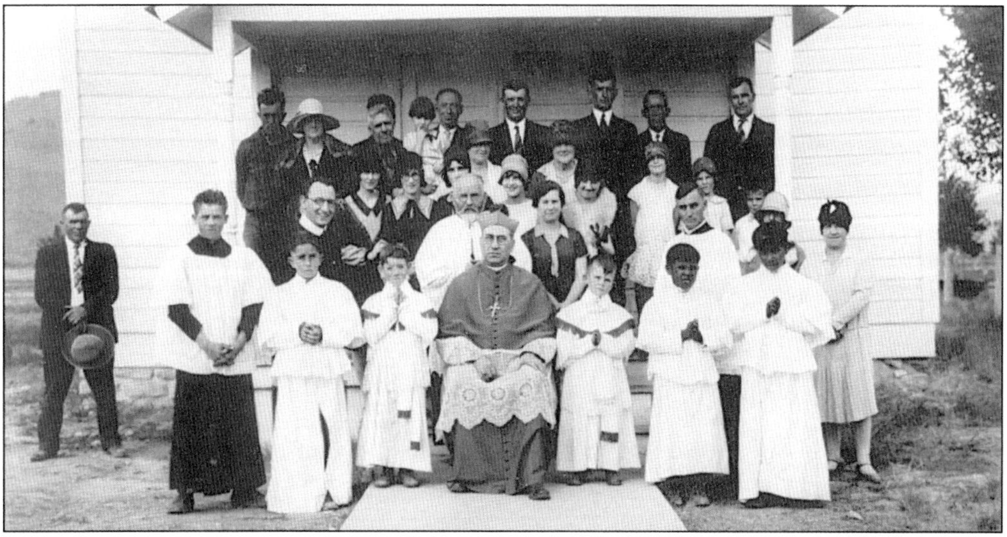

On October 1932, Bishop McGrath dedicated this chapel, which was built at Old Camp for the Paiute people. It was later moved to the reservation. Fr. Peter Heuel, who served the parish during the 1920s, was especially fond of his Paiute congregation. He encouraged the tribe to seek payment from the government for loss of lands of the Malheur Reservation. The result of the 35-year court battle was payment of $741 each to 850 members of the Burns Paiute tribe; however, the reparations were made based on 1890 land values of 28¢ to 45¢ per acre. (Courtesy Holy Family Catholic Church, Burns.)

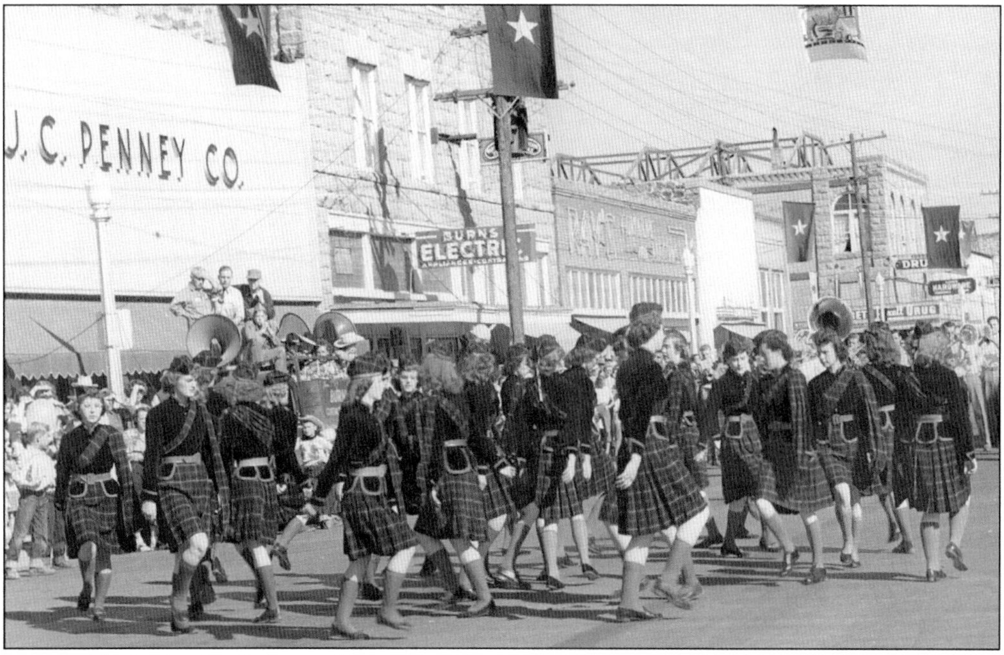

In 1952, the high school changed its mascot from the Bulldogs to Hilanders, and the school paper and annual became the *Bagpipe* and the *Bard*. The girls' pep club became the Bonnie Lassies, and the jaunty Scotsman that winks from the wall of the gymnasium became the mascot of the school and the town. The Bonnie Lasses are pictured performing during the fair parade on Broadway Street in 1952.

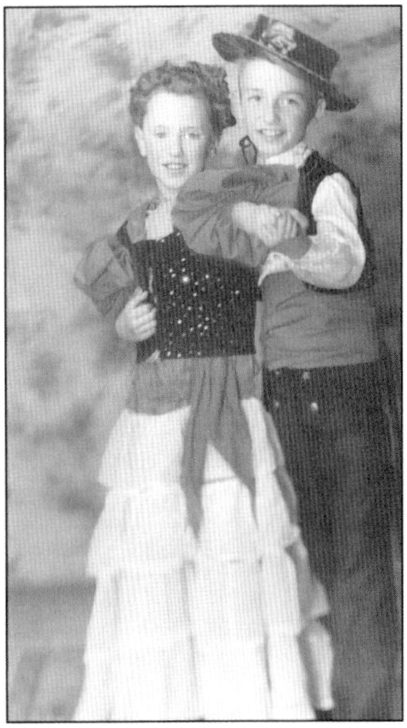

Frances Urizar and Frankie Osa are pictured in traditional Basque dress in the early 1940s. Frankie's parents were Marcelino and Margarita Osa. The family ran a boardinghouse where Margarita taught her children to dance to old Basque and Spanish phonograph records. Patty Yriarte remembers of her grandmother Margarita, " I always think of red velvet on our dancing dresses and gold rickrack whirling. And that smell, and crocheted slippers with sequins on them."

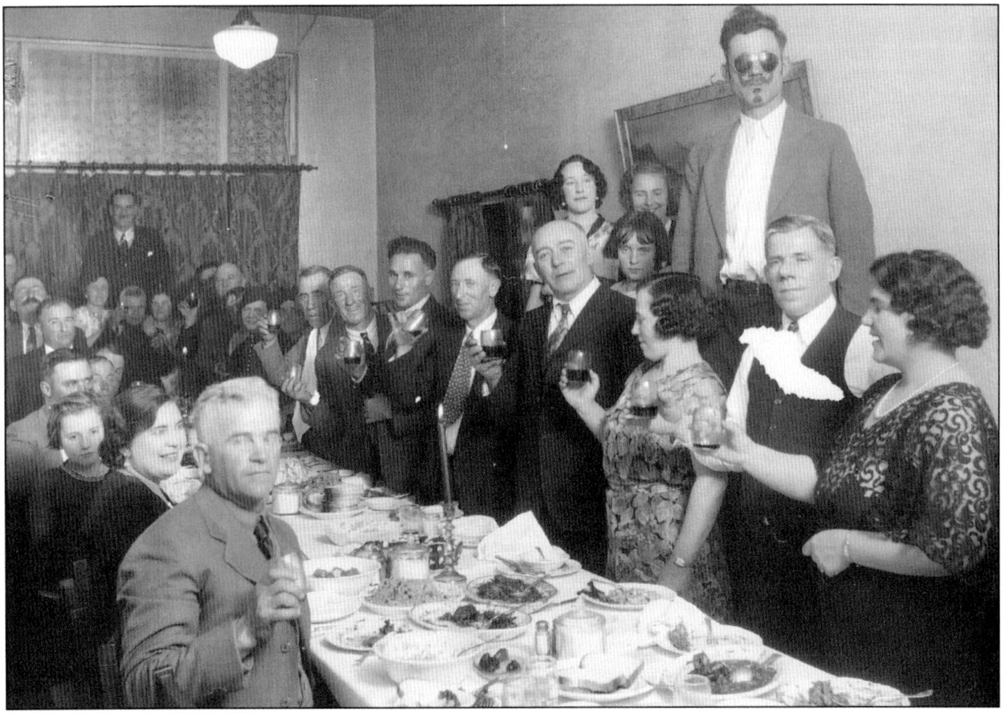

Burns was a hub for the Basque community in Harney Country. The Plaza Hotel and the Star Hotel among others were popular gathering places where Basques could socialize and practice traditional Basque customs. One such gathering is pictured here. The occasion and the date are unidentified. Pictured in the photograph are Dolly Obiague, P. Obiague, M. Ramirez, S. Arguinchona, Lisa Remaris, unidentified, Pete Ebar, Harold Cawlfield, Margarita Osa, unidentified, Martina Larraneta, Marcelina Osa, G. Frazier, unidentified, Mrs. D. Meyers, Mrs. B. Walker, unidentified, John Obiague, unidentified, Felix Urizar, B. Schroeder, C. Urizar, unidentified, Hattie Schroeder, M. Mendieta, I. Schroeder, M. Obiague, and J. Abasola.

Six

Community Patriotism

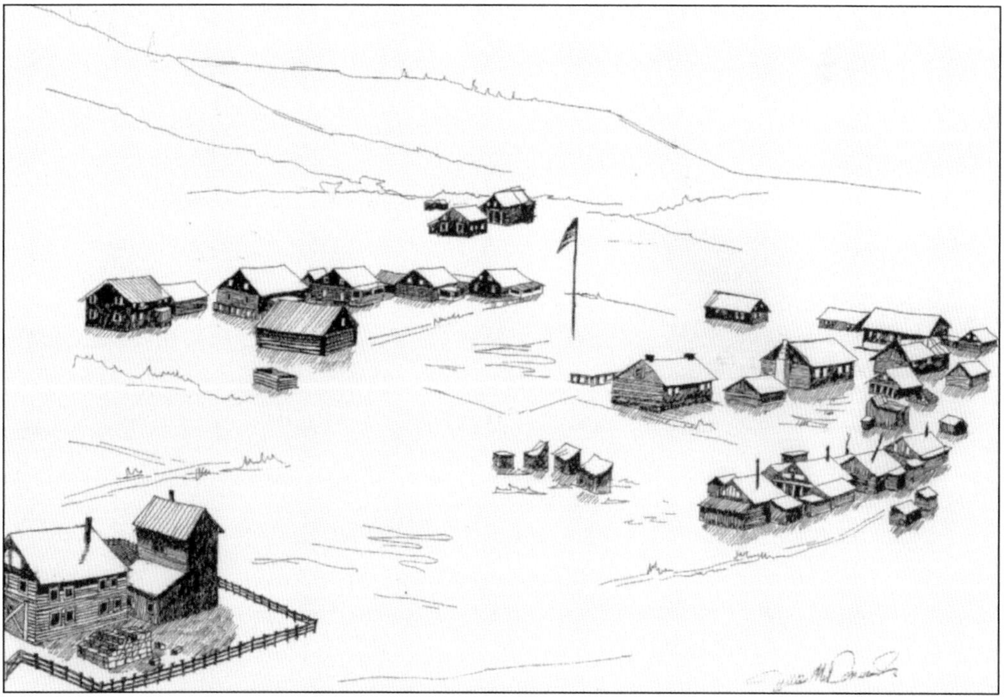

Camp Harney, seen here in a line drawing about 1872, was referred to by many names throughout its existence. Camp Wallen, Camp Rattlesnake, Camp Steele, Camp Crook, and finally Camp Harney in honor of Brig. Gen. William S. Harney. This was the first permanent settlement of white men in Harney Valley. The army's four-year campaign against the Eastern Oregon Native Americans ended with General Crooks's 1868 treaty meeting at Camp Harney. In 1873, Native Americans were quartered at the fort while the Malheur Reservation was being prepared. The first post office was established at the camp on August 10, 1874. Fort Harney was abandoned in June 1880. The buildings of the fort were dismantled over time and many were used in the growing settlement of Harney City, located about two miles to the south of the fort. Today nothing remains of the old camp. (Drawing by James M Donovan Jr.)

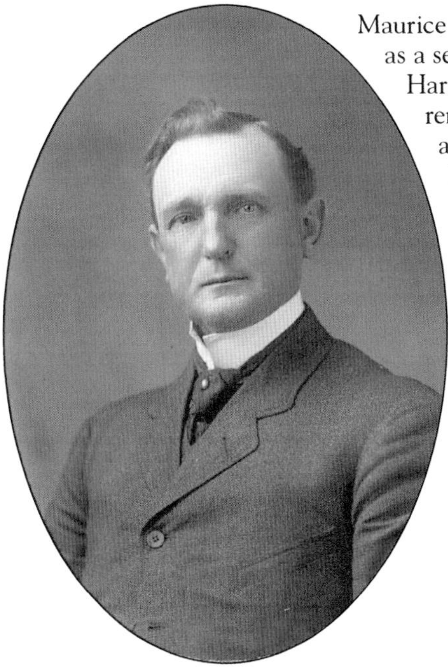

Maurice Fitzgerald arrived in Harney County on July 16, 1873, as a sergeant major with the U.S. Army stationed at Camp Harney. Upon disbandment of the camp in 1880, Fitzgerald remained in the county and was variously employed as a land surveyor, a contract mail carrier from 1880 to 1881, and a lawyer. In 1940, Fitzgerald penned "Harney County and Its Early Settlement and Development," one of the earliest published accounts of Harney County history.

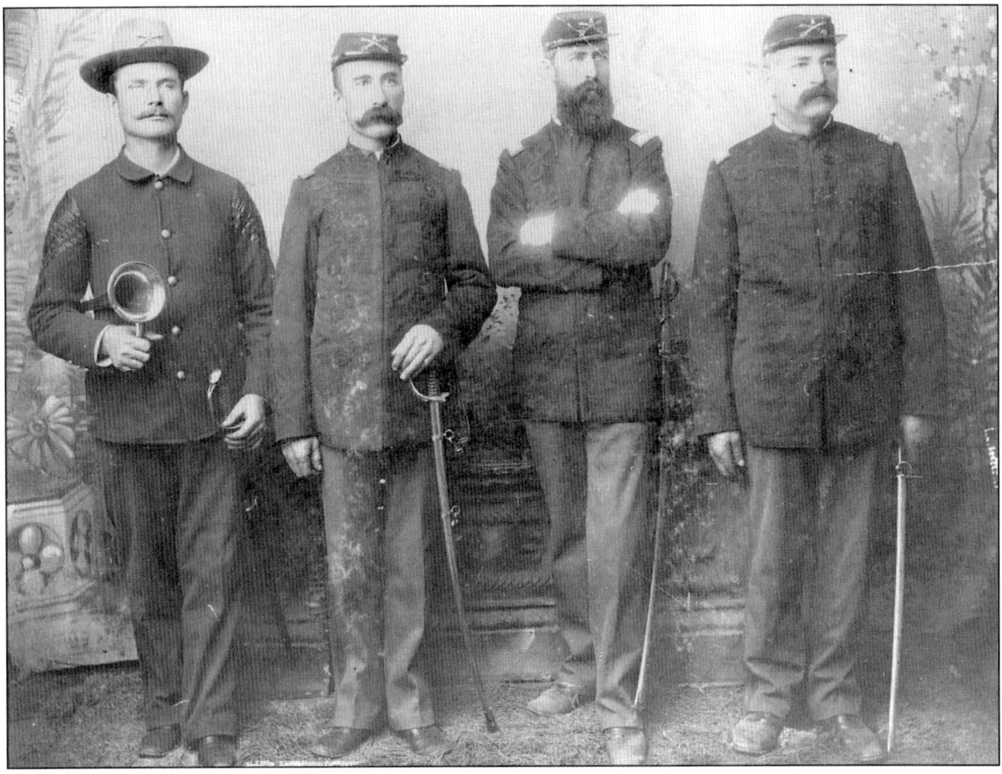

Colonel Mitchell organized Troop A of the Oregon National Guard in Harney County in September 1893. A. W. Gowan, third from the left, was appointed captain. Also pictured from left to right are Charles McPheeters; Harry E. Thompson, second lieutenant; and Samuel E. Joy, first lieutenant. The original roster lists 51 additional names. Troop A was disbanded in August 1896.

In 1882, Albert W. Gowan captained a wagon train to Union County, Oregon. Admitted to the Oregon State Bar in 1888, he was appointed clerk at the land office in Burns in 1890. In a special election in 1892, he was chosen to be representative to the state legislature from Grant and Harney Counties. Election as state senator for the district consisting of Morrow, Grant, and Harney Counties followed in 1894. Additionally, Gowan served as judge advocate for Oregon in 1895.

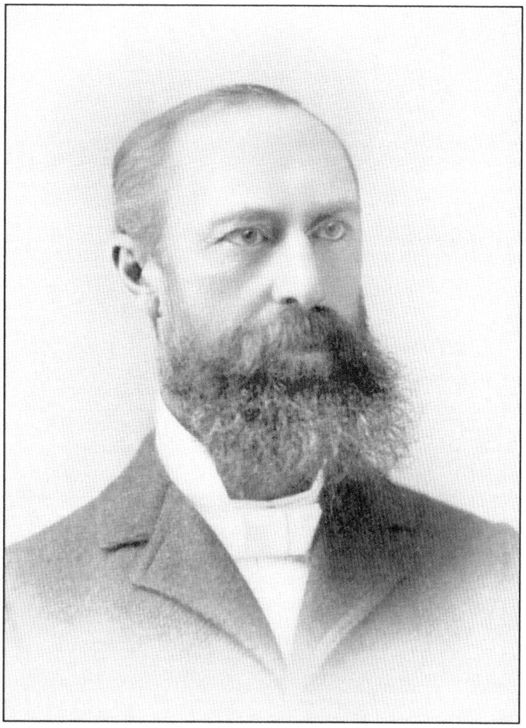

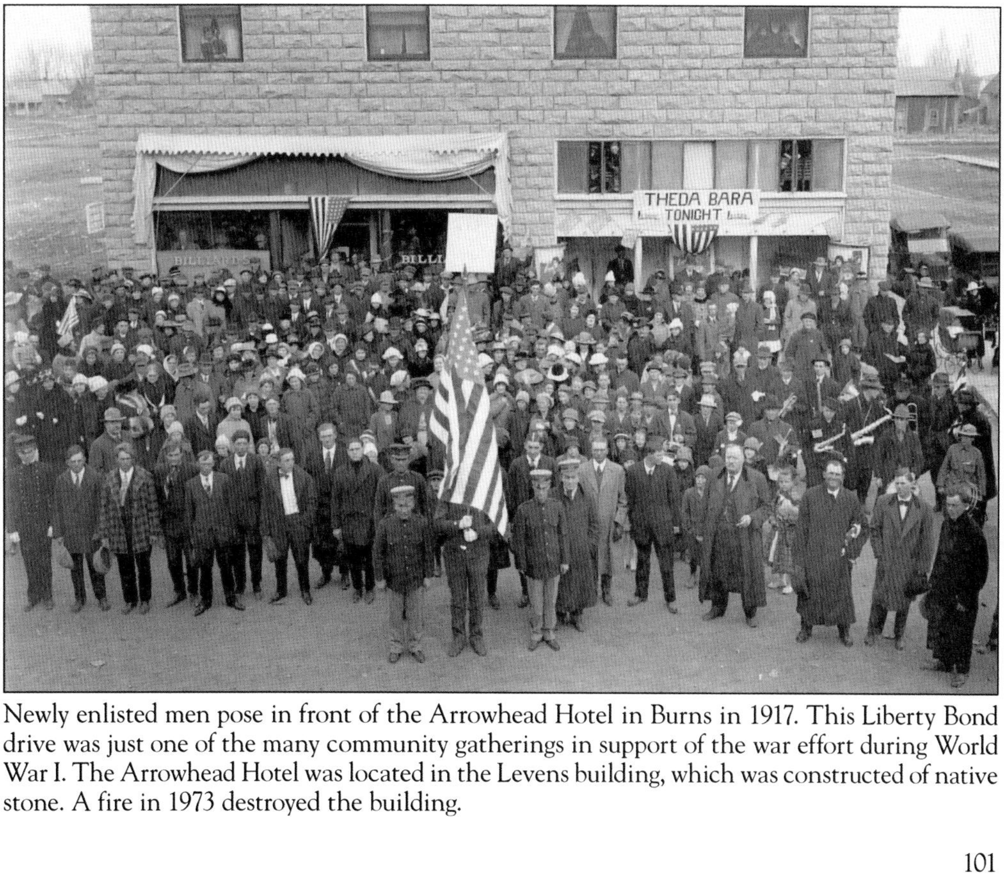

Newly enlisted men pose in front of the Arrowhead Hotel in Burns in 1917. This Liberty Bond drive was just one of the many community gatherings in support of the war effort during World War I. The Arrowhead Hotel was located in the Levens building, which was constructed of native stone. A fire in 1973 destroyed the building.

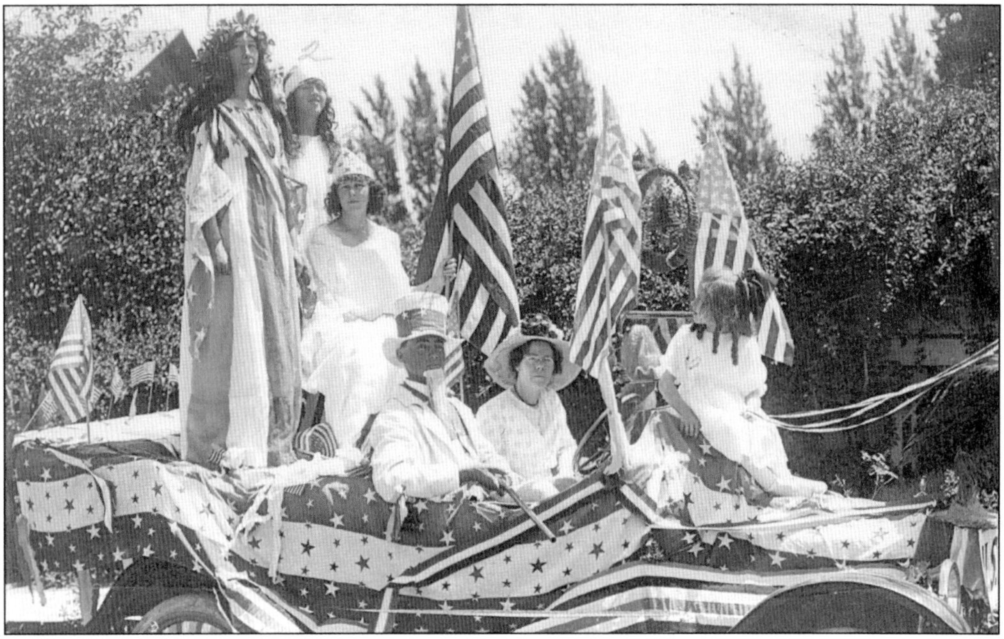

In Harney County, the Fourth of July was celebrated with festive parades. This parade float is decked with stars and stripes. The riders aboard are, from left to right, May Riggs, Celia Byrd Howser, Esther Sweek, Floyd Baker (Uncle Sam), Mary Caldwell Heck (driver), and Helen Garrett. (Photograph by R. W. Heck.)

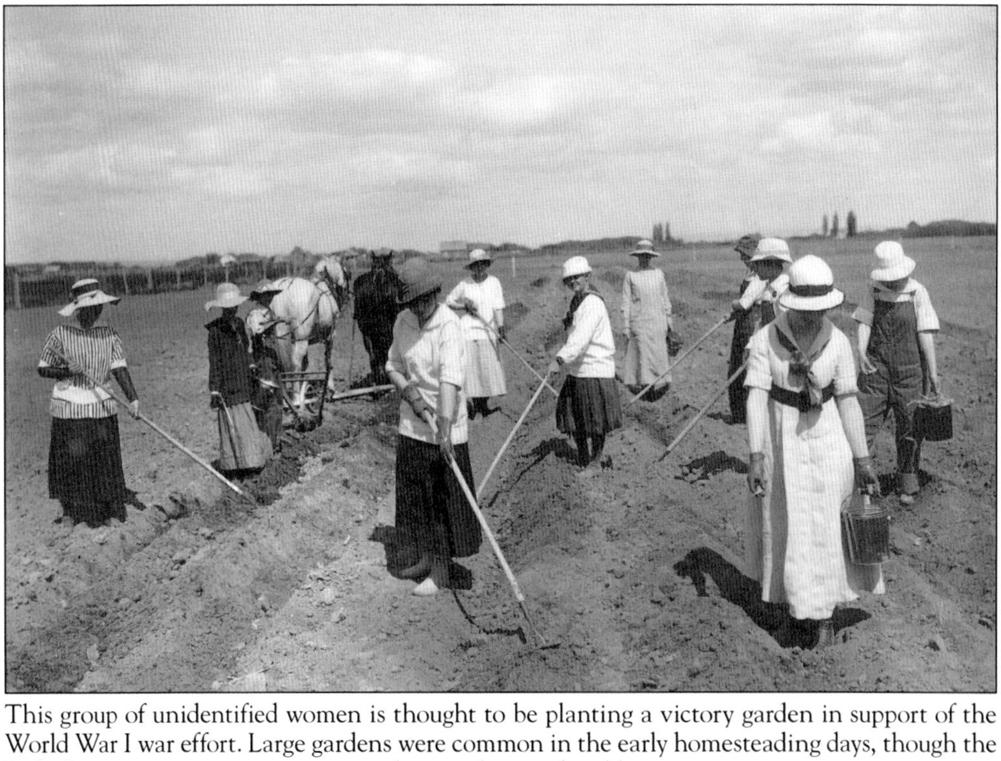

This group of unidentified women is thought to be planting a victory garden in support of the World War I war effort. Large gardens were common in the early homesteading days, though the high-desert growing season was very short and unpredictable.

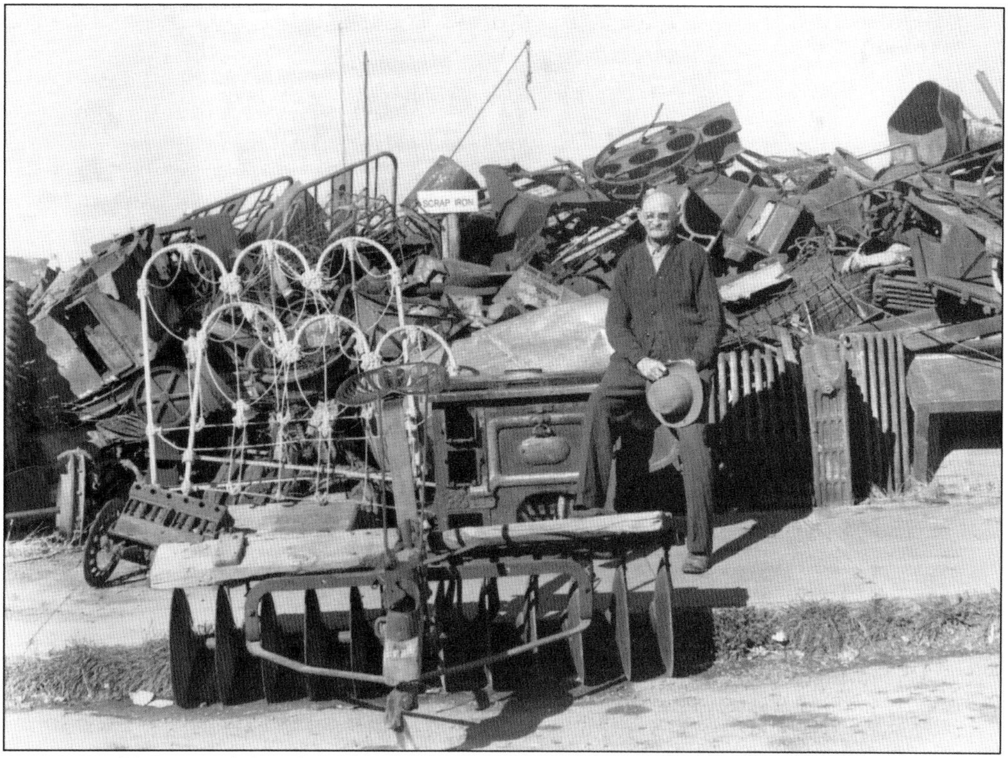

Newt Hotchkiss stands beside a giant pile of scrap iron gathered throughout Harney County. In October 1942, scrap-metal drives supporting the war effort contributed 904 tons from the county, with an additional 540 tons awaiting shipment and an estimated 300 tons left to be gathered for a total of 1,750 tons. A per capita estimate of 700 pounds of scrap metal far exceeded the national average of 200 pounds per person.

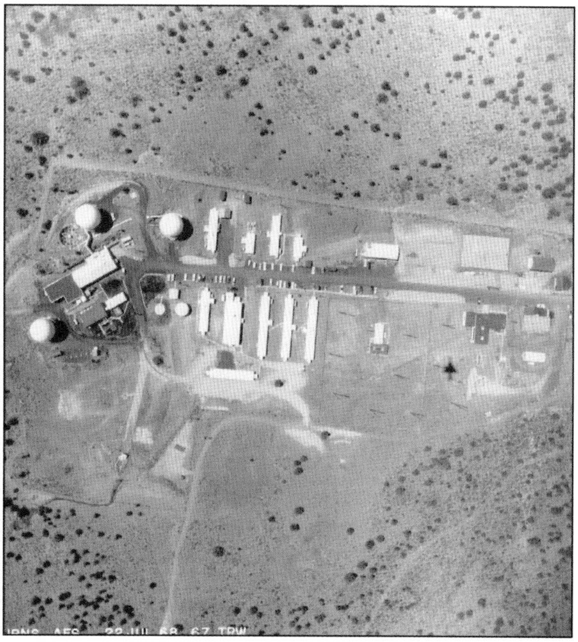

The Burns Air Force Radar Station, seen from above in July 1968, was operated by the U.S. Air Force Aerospace Defense Command from 1954 to 1970. Located at the top of Burns Butte overlooking the towns of Burns and Hines, the 18-acre site supported 38 buildings. The station served as an early-warning ground-radar site and communication receiver. The site was deactivated in 1970 and now stands abandoned. (Courtesy Pauline Brayman.)

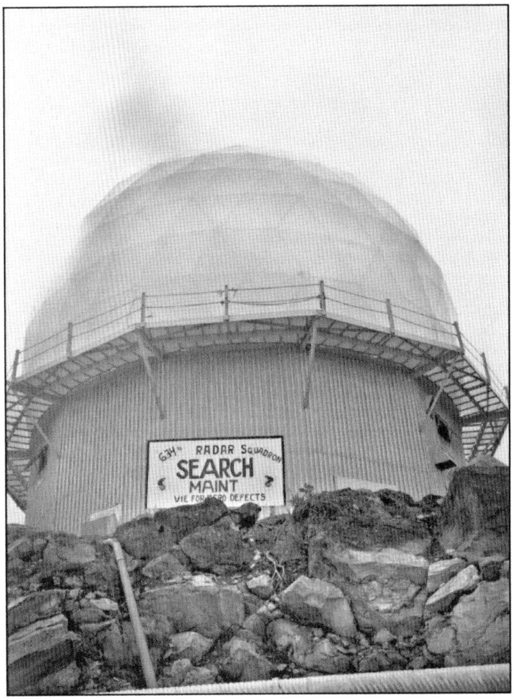

Under the command of Capt. Thomas B. Barnes, the 634th Radar Squadron of the U.S. Air Defense Command under the U.S. Air Force began operations of the radar base located on Burns Butte, about five miles southwest of Burns. The base began with 70 officers from Spokane, Washington. One radar was initially constructed and two more were later added.

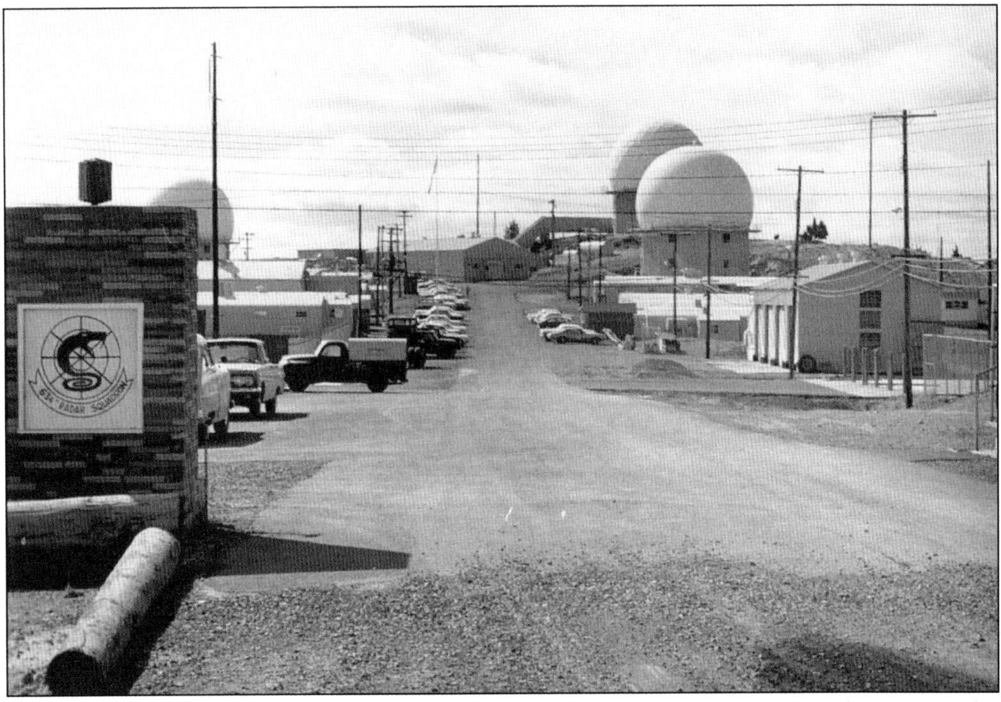

Domed observatories, seen in the background, were designed to scan the skies as far as 200 miles for signs of unfriendly aircraft. The station is one of many that constituted a radar net covering the Pacific Northwest. Three radar domes at this site were in operation as part of the "Pine Tree Line." The 634th Aircraft Control and Warning Squadron employed as many as 106 U.S. Air Force personnel and 20 civilians at the time of its closing in 1970. (Courtesy Pauline Brayman.)

Seven

JUST FOR FUN

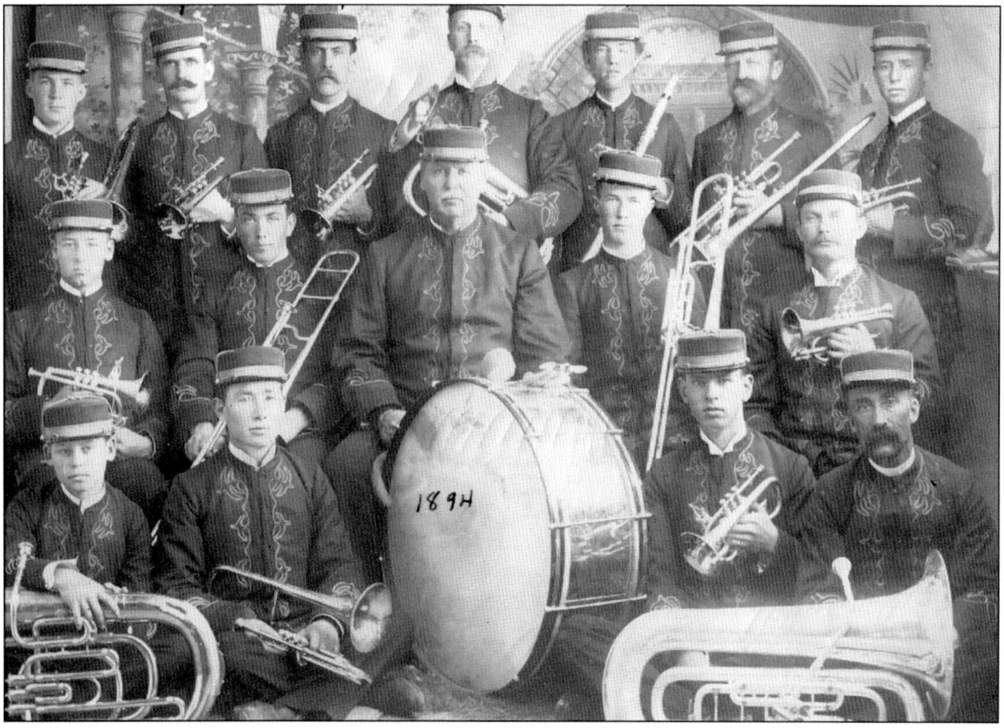

The Burns town band assembled for a group portrait in 1884. Members are, from left to right, the following: (first row) Frank Welcome, Julian Byrd, Adler Racine, and Harry Thompson; (second row) Al Welcome, Jack Regan, J. C. Welcome Sr., Chester Smith, and Charles McPheeters; (third row) John Sweek, Charles Kenyon, Joe Tupker, I. Geer, Delos Gould, William King, and J. C. Welcome Jr. (Courtesy Louanne Fugal.)

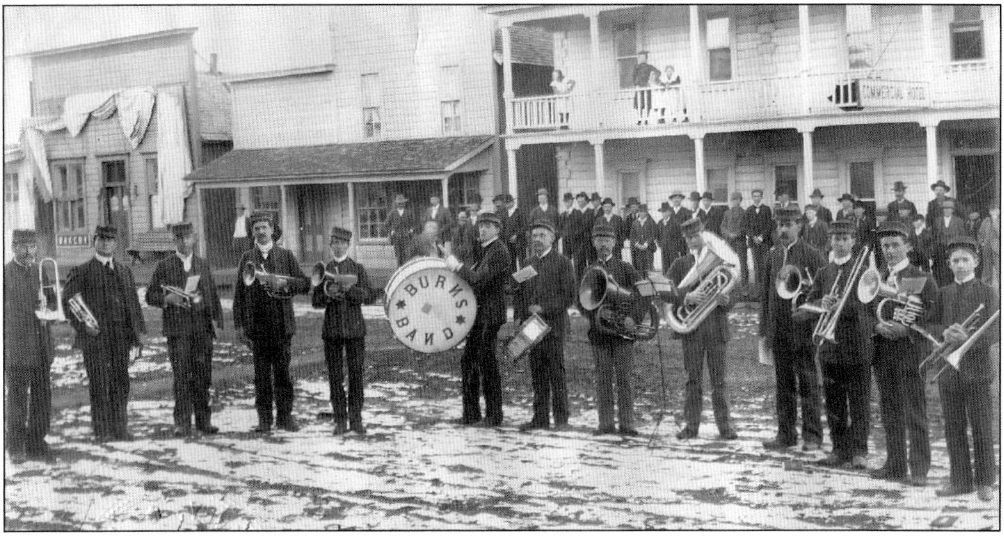

The Burns town band was made up of many well-known members of the community. Photographed in 1900, the group, shown from left to right, includes Roy Smith, Charles McPheeters, Al Welcome, Charles Kenyon, Nollie Reed, Delos Gould, Harry Thompson, Charles Byrd, Frank Welcome, Joe Tupker, Homer Reed, Conn Wyatt, and Graver Jameson. (Courtesy Louann Fugal.)

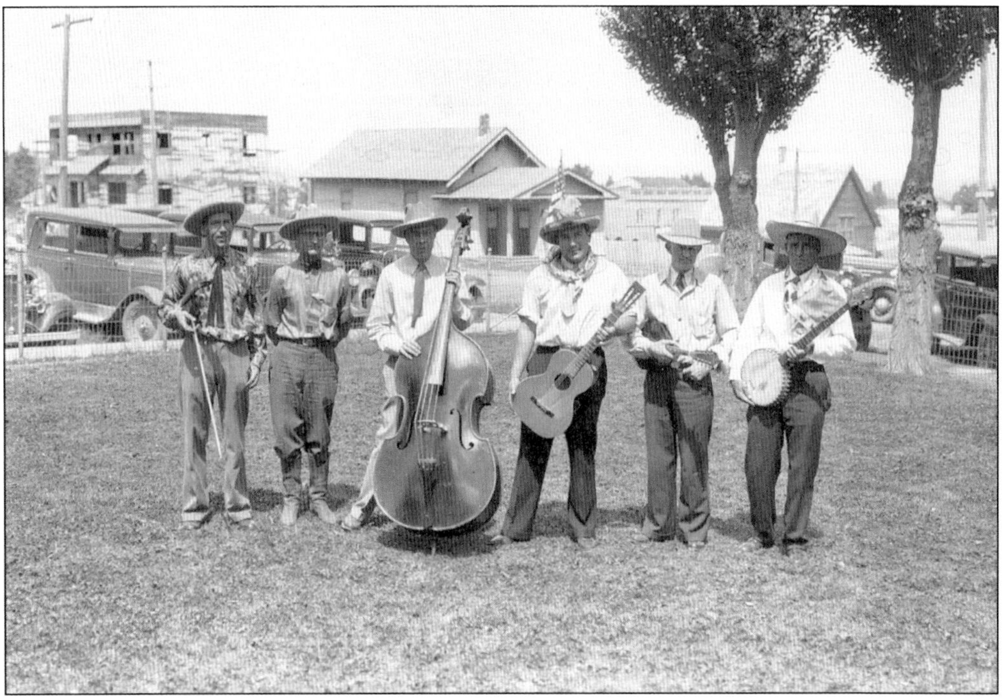

In the 1930s, a dance band composed of local professional men performed at functions around the county. Known as the Rattlesnake Rattlers, the band was composed of Alex Eggleston (fiddle), James Richardson (piano), George Mowery (bass), Charlie Schroeder (guitar), Hugh Miller (guitar), and unidentified.

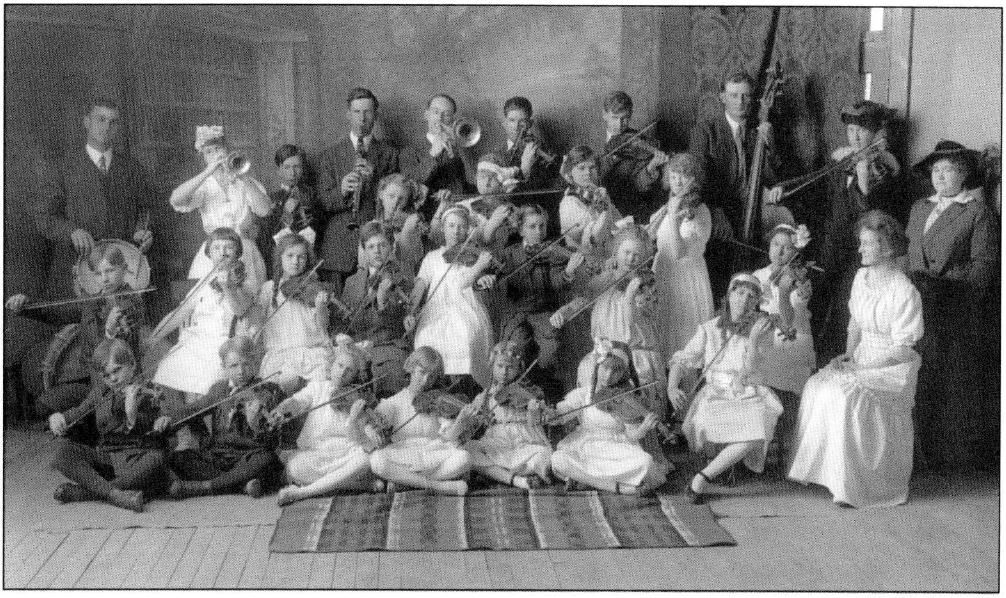

Mary V. Dodge, pictured seated, lower right, was a music teacher who moved with her civil engineer husband, Mott Dodge, to Burns in 1910. She established the Harney County Sagebrush Orchestra that would perform from 1912 until 1917. Beginning with a concert at Tonawama Hall in 1912, the group of up to 35 local young musicians played throughout the state of Oregon.

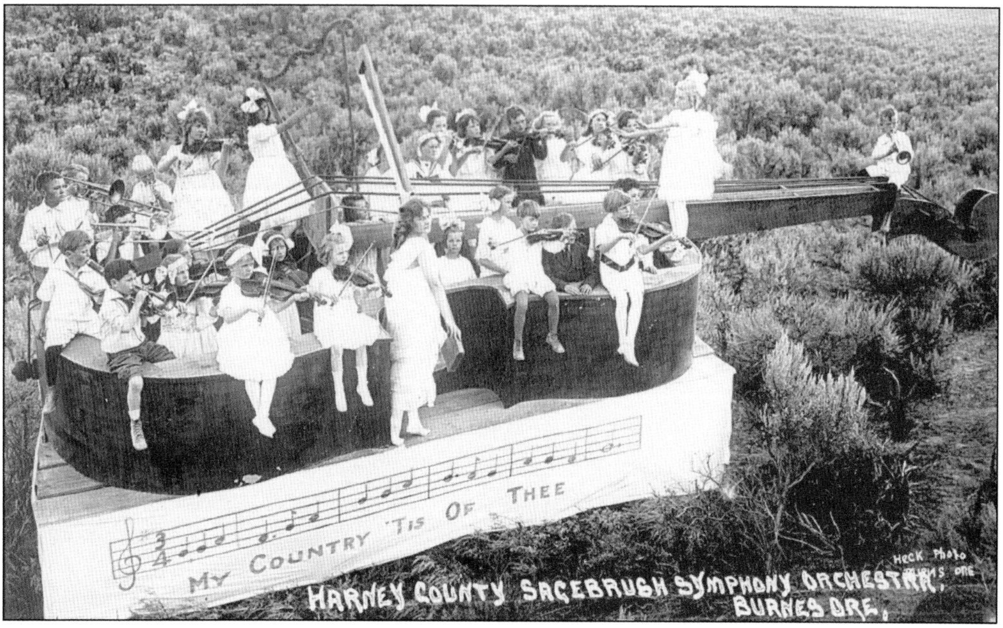

The Harney County Sagebrush Orchestra sits atop a float made in the shape of a violin for an appearance in the Fourth of July parade about 1915 in Burns. The float was constructed by local carpenter Dan Jordan, built to orchestra director Mary Dodge's specifications. The orchestra was composed of local youngsters who went on to tour the state of Oregon in a series of concerts. The boy in dark knickers playing the trumpet is Glenn Dodge, the director's five-year-old son. (Photograph by R. W. Heck.)

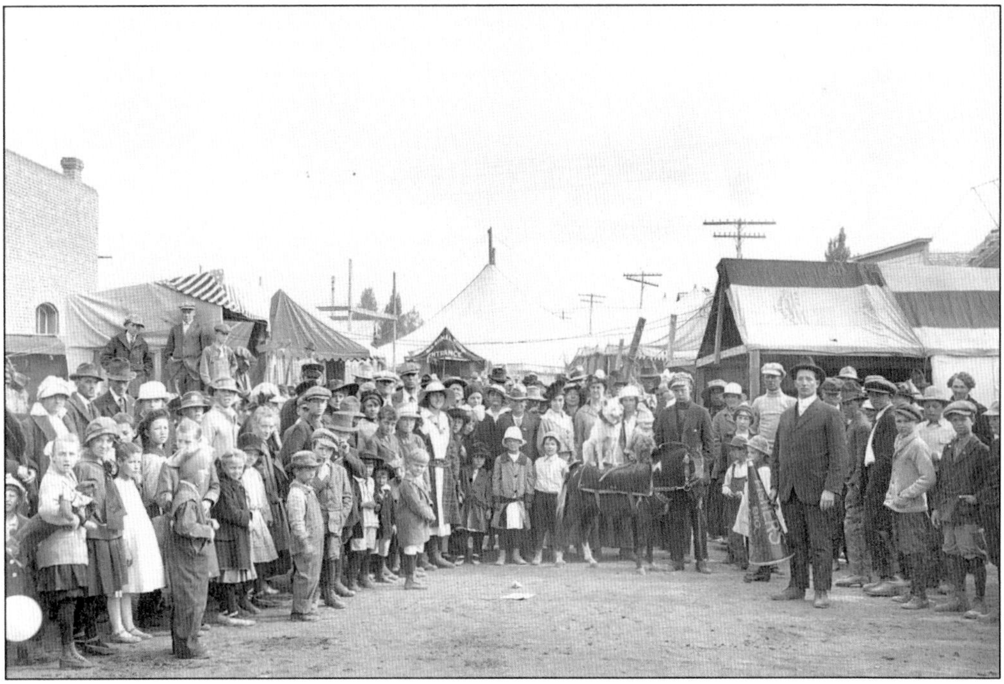

Dave Cawlfield and Rollin Gowan are among those pictured at this c. 1914 dog-and-pony show that set up operation on the corner of Washington Street, between Broadway Street and Alder Avenue in Burns. The man standing near the front of the crowd carries a megaphone proclaiming in bold letters "Fishers Big Shows." Traveling carnivals such as this were well-attended events.

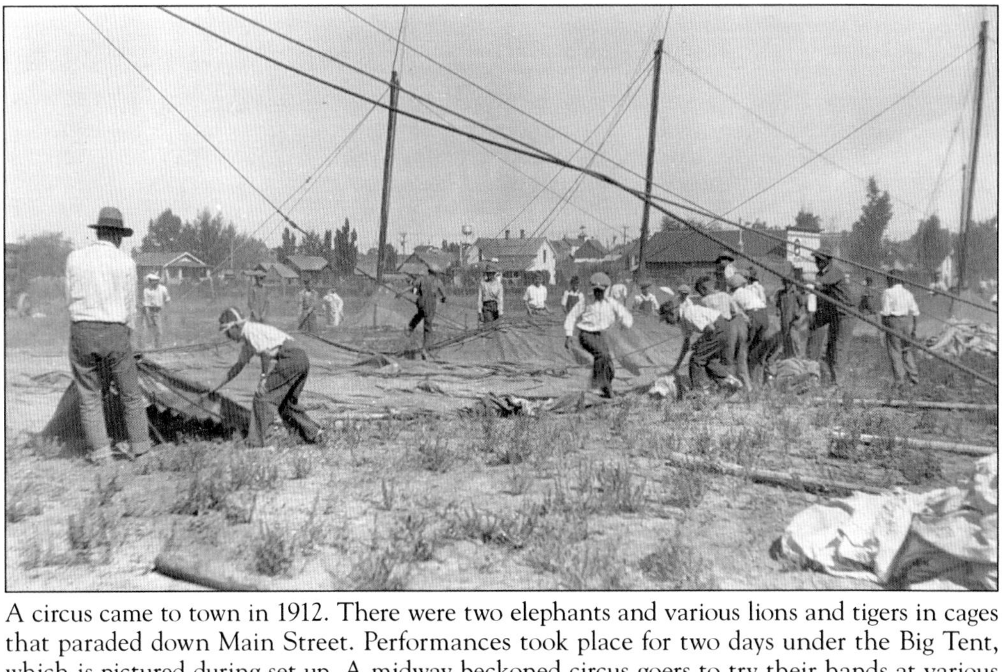

A circus came to town in 1912. There were two elephants and various lions and tigers in cages that paraded down Main Street. Performances took place for two days under the Big Tent, which is pictured during set up. A midway beckoned circus goers to try their hands at various games. Children were offered free tickets to keep the animals' water troughs filled. (Courtesy Dale Eggleston.)

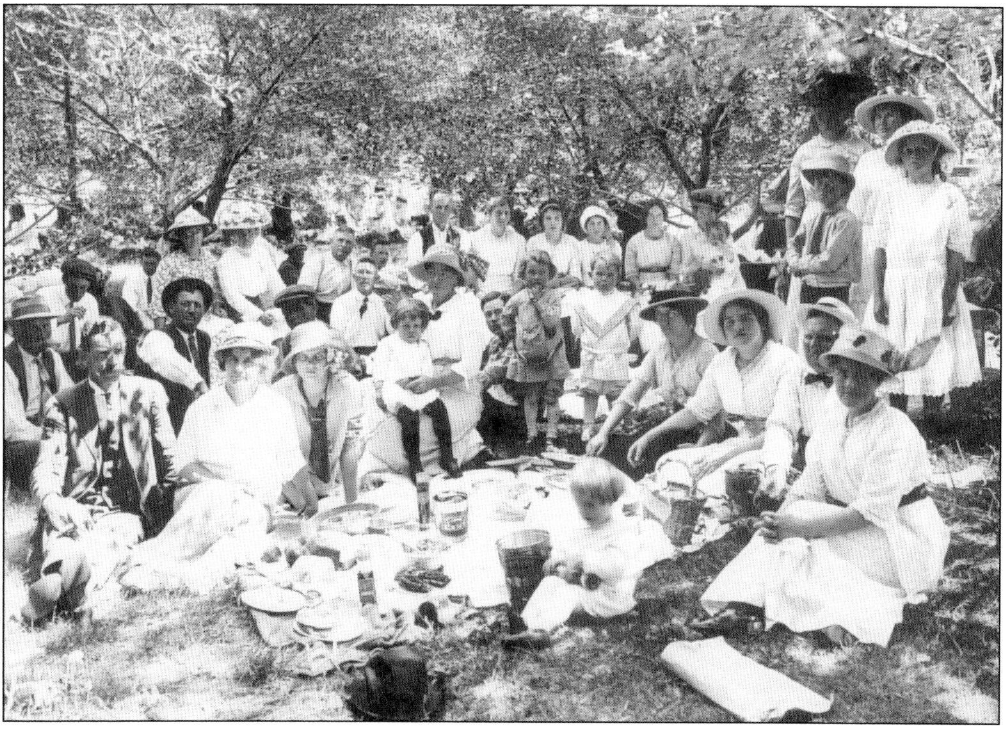

Picnics were a common way for early-day settlers to celebrate special occasions. Idlewild Park, located in the forest in the northern end of the county, and Crow Camp near Crane were popular destinations for escaping the heat of the high desert. This group posed at Crow Camp around 1915 and includes Ina Terrill Taylor, Edith Hayes, and Grant Thompson.

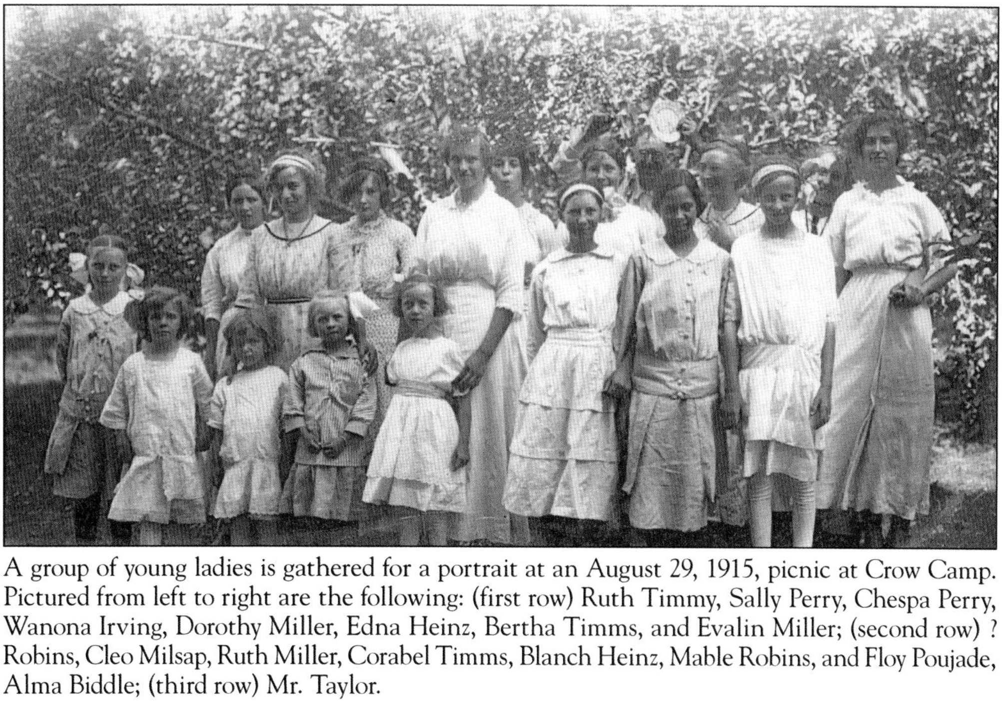

A group of young ladies is gathered for a portrait at an August 29, 1915, picnic at Crow Camp. Pictured from left to right are the following: (first row) Ruth Timmy, Sally Perry, Chespa Perry, Wanona Irving, Dorothy Miller, Edna Heinz, Bertha Timms, and Evalin Miller; (second row) ? Robins, Cleo Milsap, Ruth Miller, Corabel Timms, Blanch Heinz, Mable Robins, and Floy Poujade, Alma Biddle; (third row) Mr. Taylor.

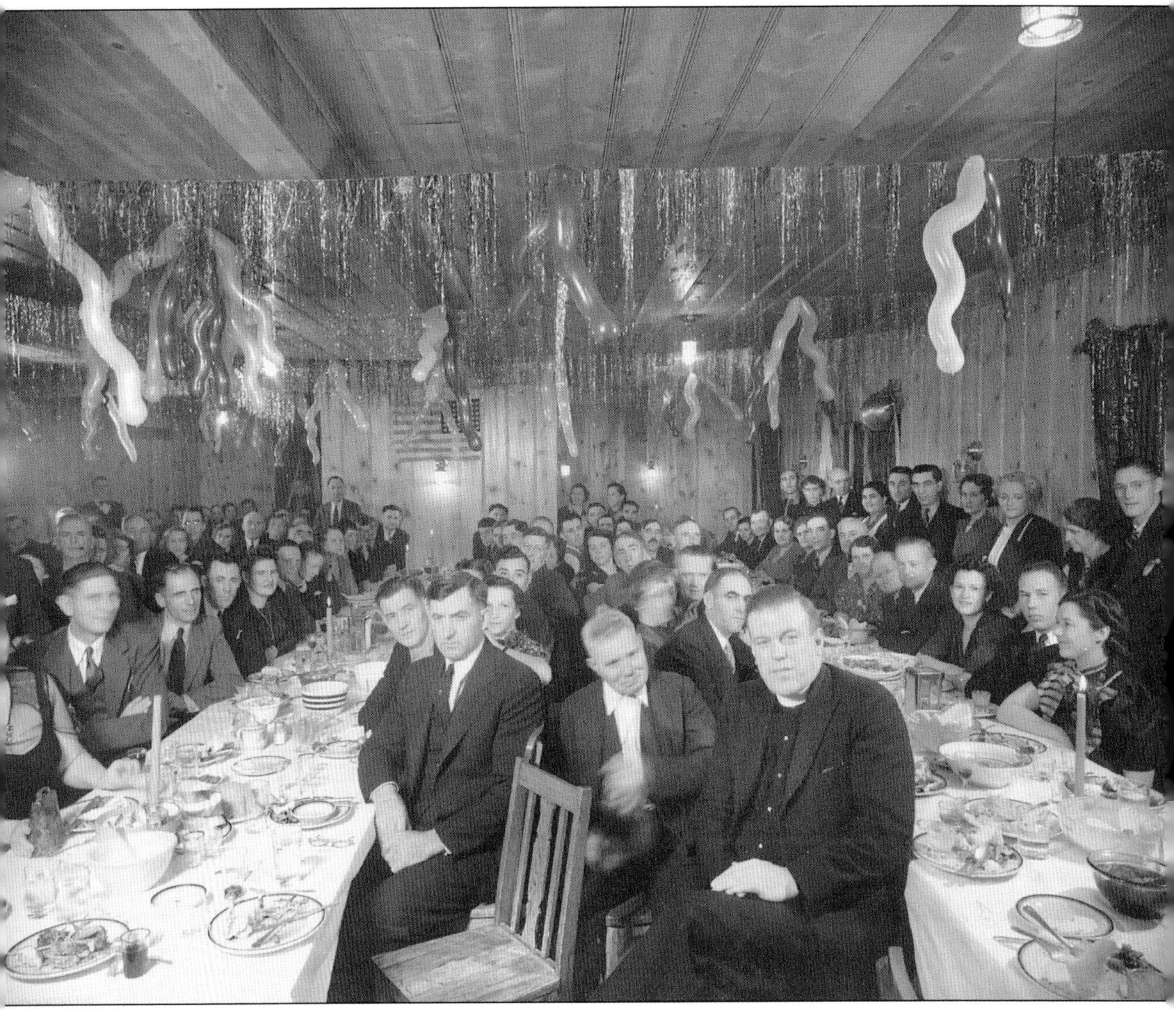

New Year's Eve was a time of celebration. Fr. Vincent Egan, pictured front right, rings in the New Year of 1938–1939 at a Basque dinner held at the west side Pine Room in Burns. A local news account gives the details of the events of the night. The fourth annual party was attended by 142 Harney County Basque residents and invited guests. Honored guest was "Tio" Antolin of Crane. He was thought to be one of the last pioneer Basque immigrants to Harney County. The banquet consisted of traditional Spanish-style dishes served by girls in Basque costume. Minutes before midnight, the group paraded to the business district where singing and dancing around a Christmas tree ushered in the New Year. The highlight of the evening was the introduction of the wine-filled bota. (Courtesy Holy Family Catholic Church, Burns.)

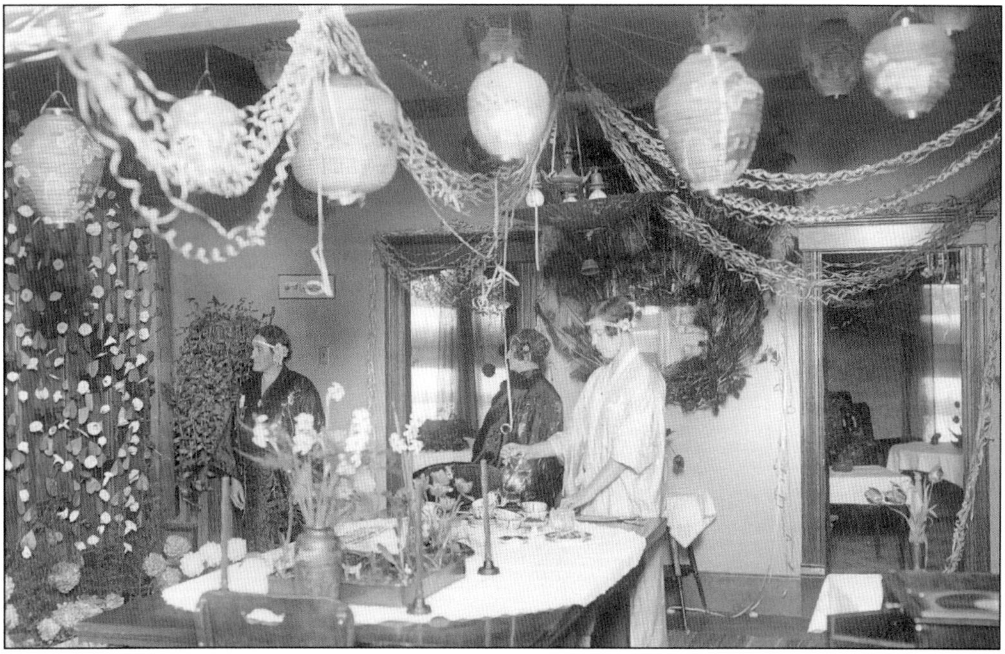

The first library in Harney County was formed in 1903 in the home of Phoebe Geary. Twelve ladies organized the Ladies Library Club, bought books, and paid dues of 25¢ per year. In 1923, the library moved to the old city hall building. Fund-raisers were held to raise money for the library club. This Chinese Tea–themed benefit was held at the Voegtly house around 1923. Pictured are Mrs. Charles Voegtly, Mrs. Gimberling, and Eunice Voegtly.

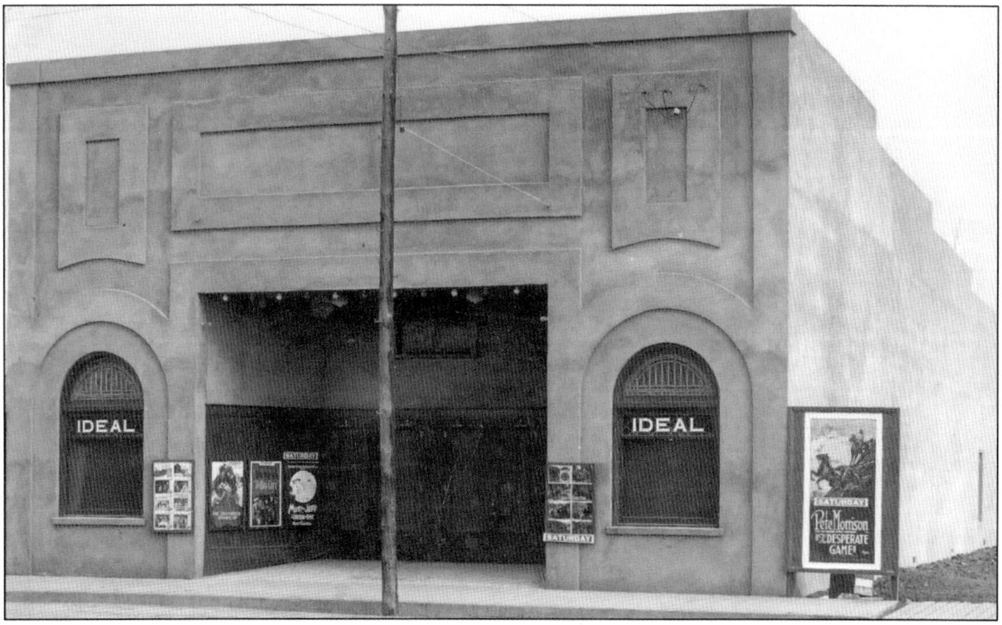

The Ideal theater building was constructed in 1926. A pipe organ and a stage were installed during the silent films era. By 1929, the theater had upgraded to showing "talkies." A fire in 1932 destroyed the stage. The theater operated until sometime in the 1950s. The building now houses a restaurant. (Photograph by R. W. Heck.)

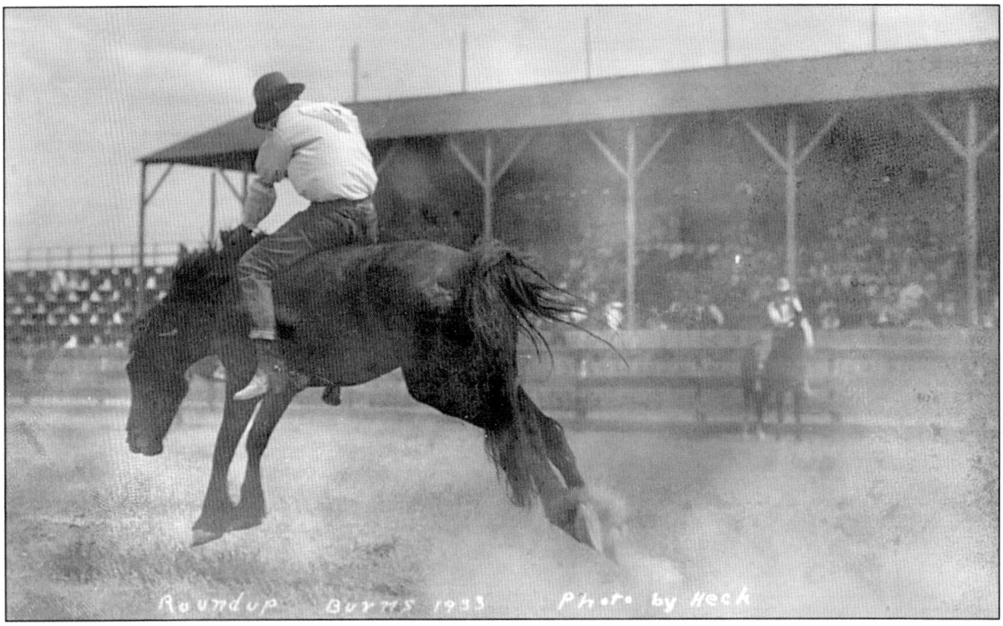

True to the official slogan, "Ride 'em High," Harney County cowboy Alan "Jiggs" Catterson is shown here riding bareback during the 1933 Harney County Roundup. The *Harney County News* of 1922 offered this jingle to accompany the roundup, "Ride 'em high and scratch 'em low, Says Uncle Si, let 'em gro, Peekolee, peekolee, cabreeno." (Photograph by R. W. Heck; courtesy Frank Catterson.)

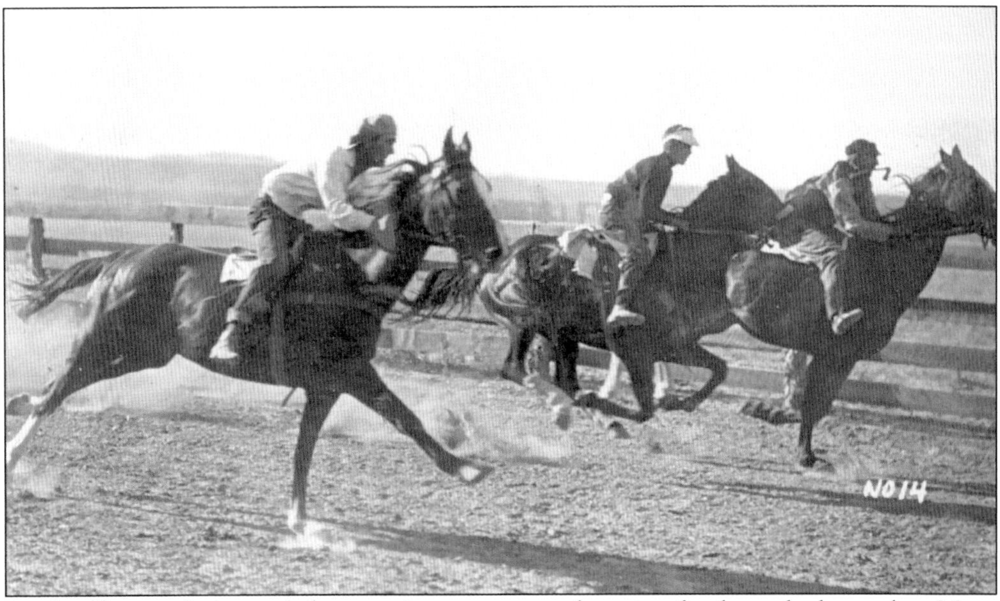

In a land known for its stock, horse racing was a natural pastime for the early-day settlers. Many townspeople owned racehorses, trotters, and pacers. The Burns Jockey Club was formed as early as 1897. The first official mile-long track was built in 1888 in Burns. Races were primarily held during Fourth of July celebrations but beginning in 1900, horse races were held in conjunction with the fair. The Harney County Fair, Rodeo, and Race Meet continues as the oldest race meet in the state of Oregon. (Courtesy Bonnie Smith.)

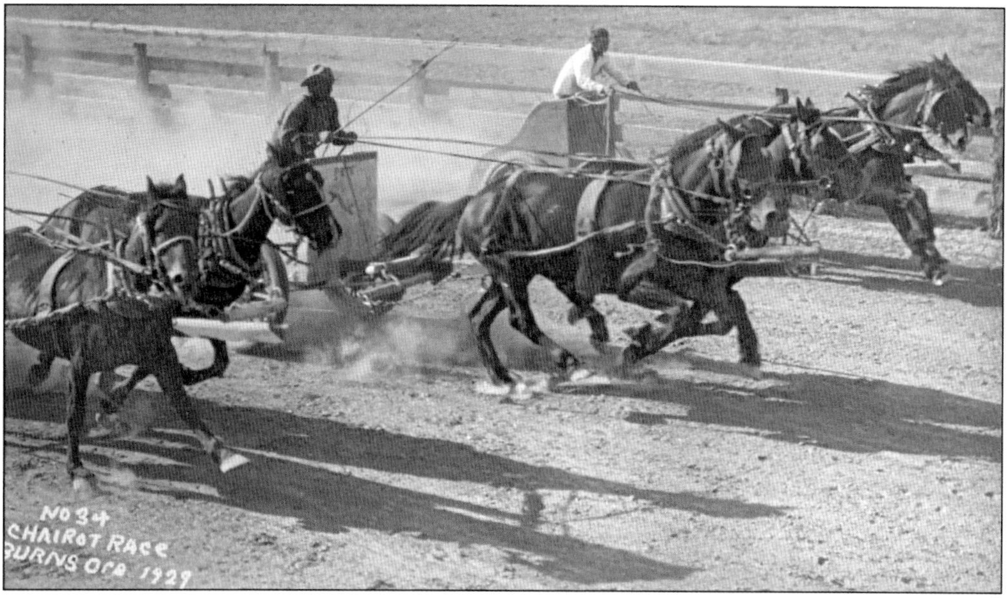

One of the more unusual events of the Harney County Fair, Rodeo, and Race Meet was the chariot races. The races were also known as the Roman races. Pete Elmose, left, is shown here competing during the 1929 event. (Photograph by R. W. Heck; courtesy Bonnie Smith.)

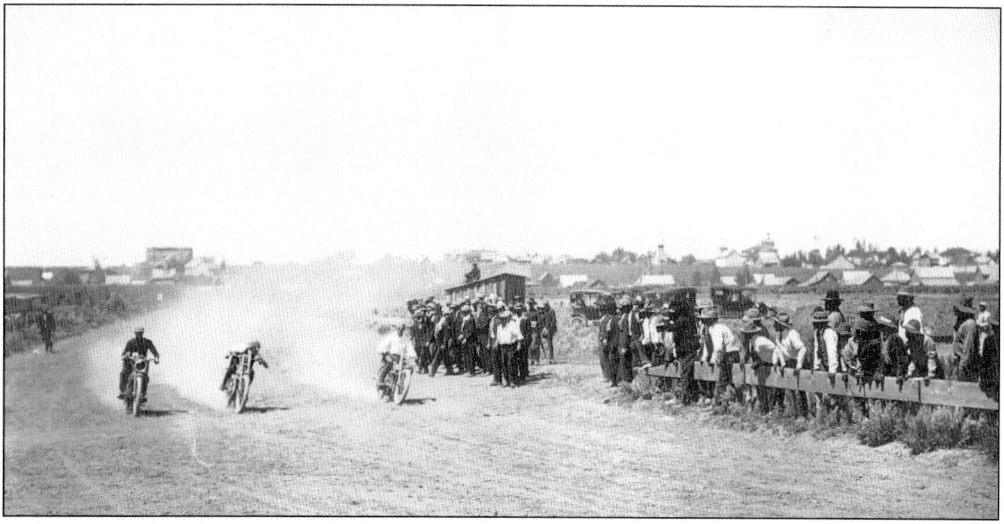

A large crowd gathers to watch daredevils on two wheels make their way around the track. Motorcycle racing was a popular event during the Burns Fourth of July celebration in 1916. This round of riders included Frank Triska, Ludwig Johnson, and ? Peterson.

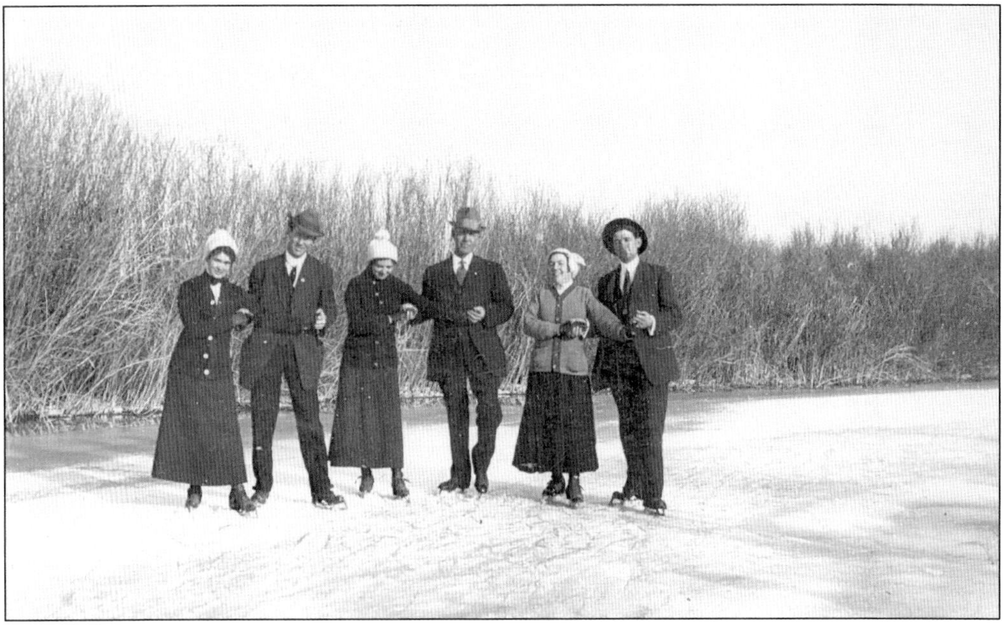

Ice skating was a popular pastime during the long, cold winter months in Harney County. Sometimes schoolchildren could ice skate to school. Others recall skating parties held on the shores of Malheur Lake. This group of skaters shown in 1912 includes Billy A. Coleman, Chester and Eliza Hamilton, and Chet Smith and his first wife.

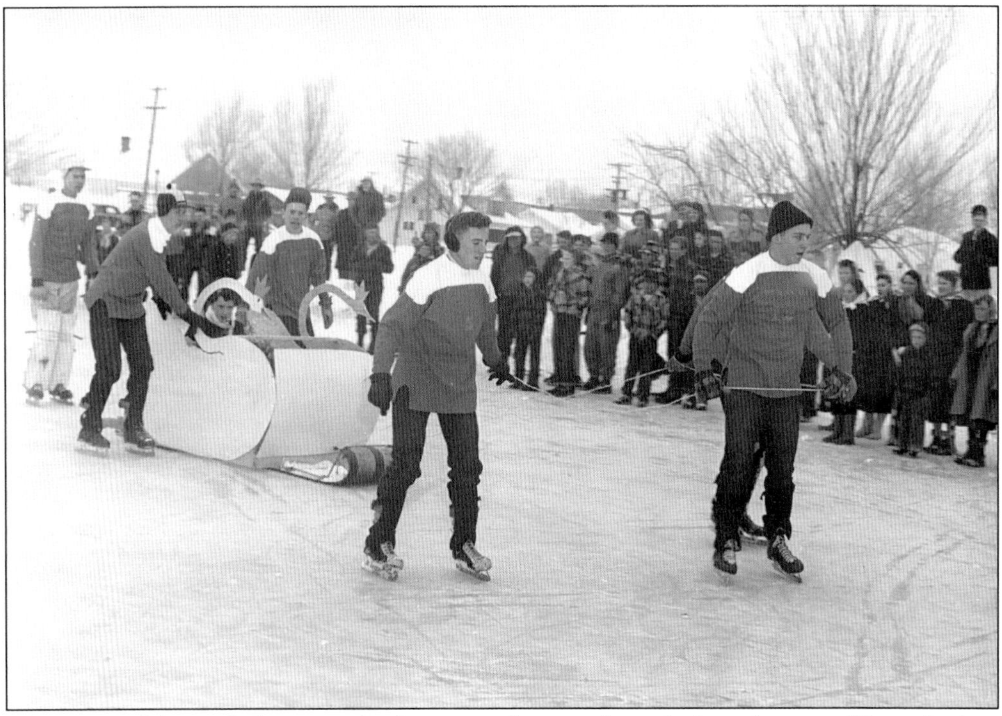

This group of skaters belongs to a hockey team that was formed when the city of Burns had an ice skating rink. The rink was located on East Washington Street at the current location of Washington Park.

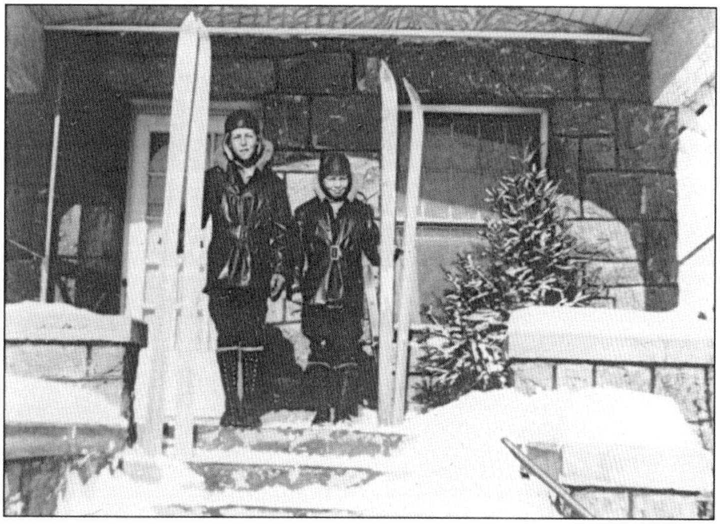

Wintertime in Harney County usually meant lots of snow. Daryl and Dale Eggleston are shown here on the front porch of their house with new skis. At one time, the Forest Service had a small ski area located near Idlewild campground north of Burns. There was no towrope or ski lift, so skiers had to climb up the hill using their own power. (Courtesy Dale Eggleston.)

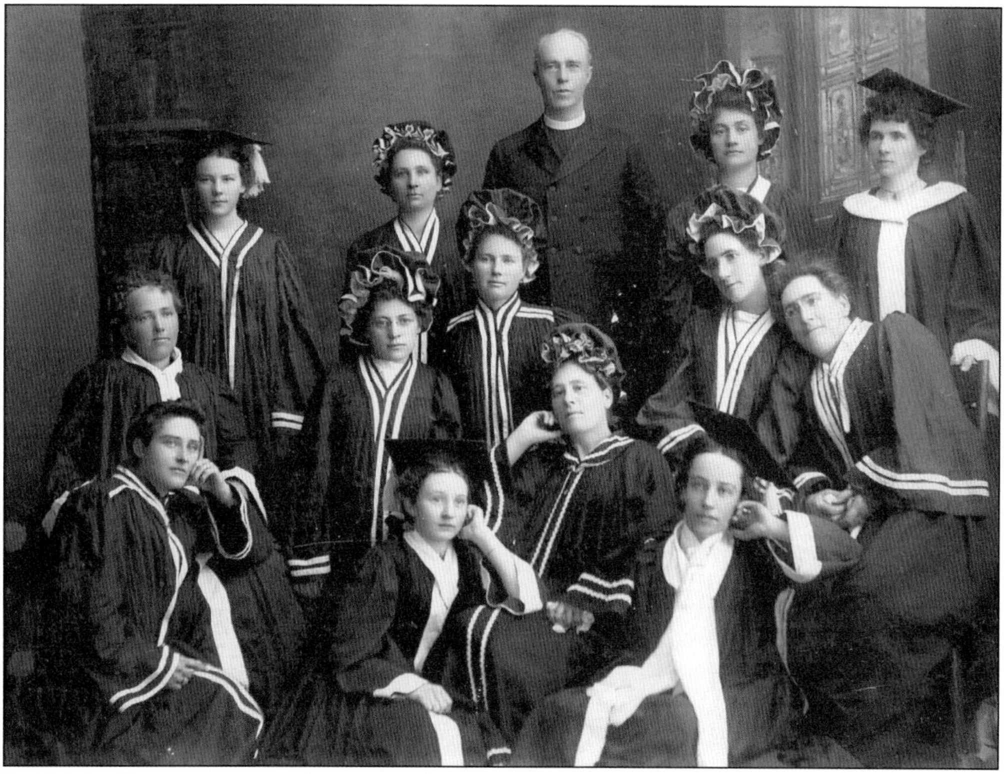

Fr. H. J. McDevitt appears with a group of young women thought to be a church choir or Catholic school class. Members identified are, from left to right, (first row) Charley Foley, Bessie Fitzgerald, Mrs. Cecil, and Mrs. Irish; (second row) Mrs. George Shelly, unidentified, Mrs. Thomas Allen, Mrs. Charley Kenyon, and Mrs. Louis Woldenberg; (third row) Jennie Racine Renolds, Mrs. Harry Smith, Father McDevitt, unidentified, and Mrs. Lee Caldwell. McDevitt became resident pastor of the church in 1899 and was transferred to Tillamook near the end of 1902.

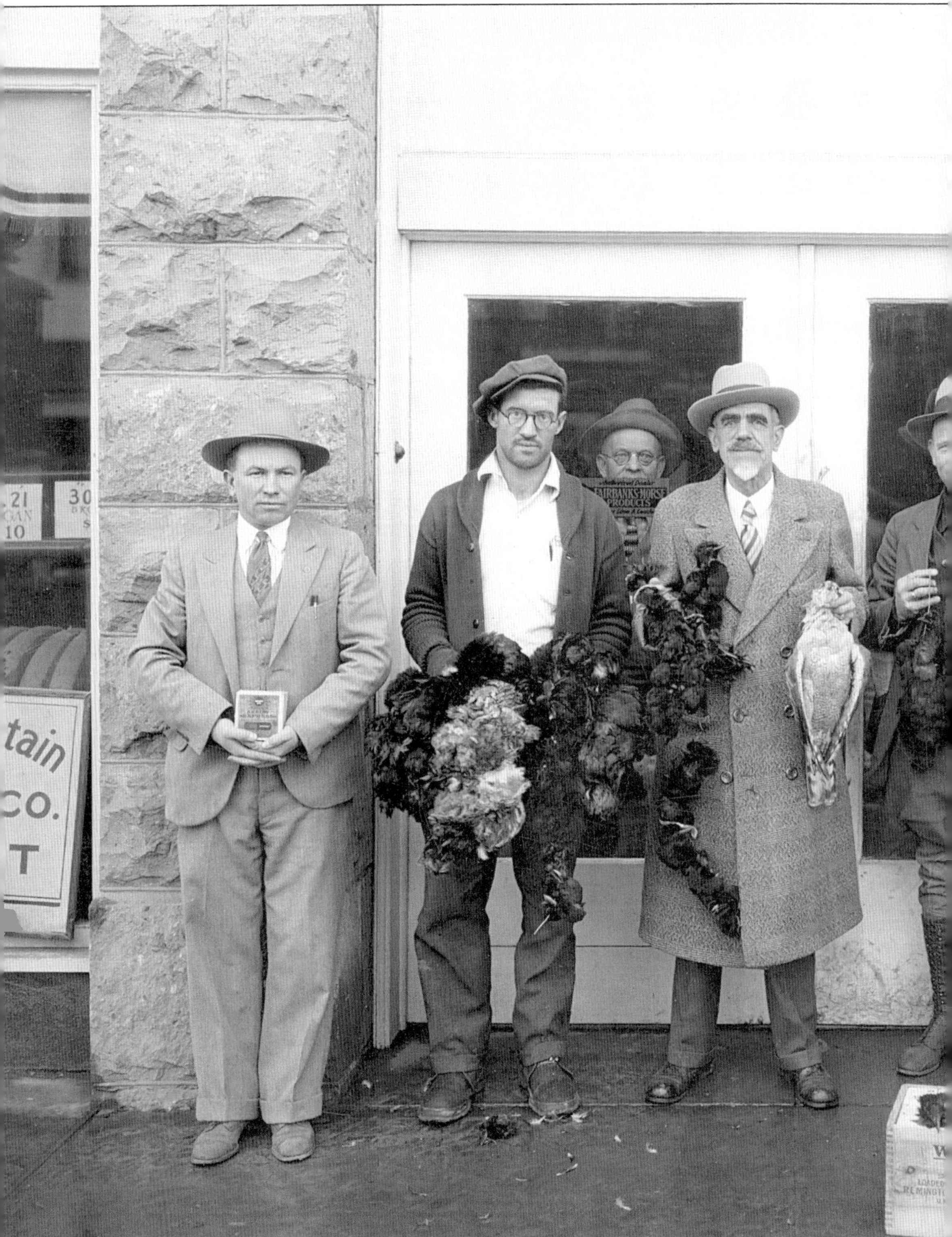
FAIRBANKS-MORSE
PRODUCTS
21
30
10
tain
CO.
T
REMINGTON

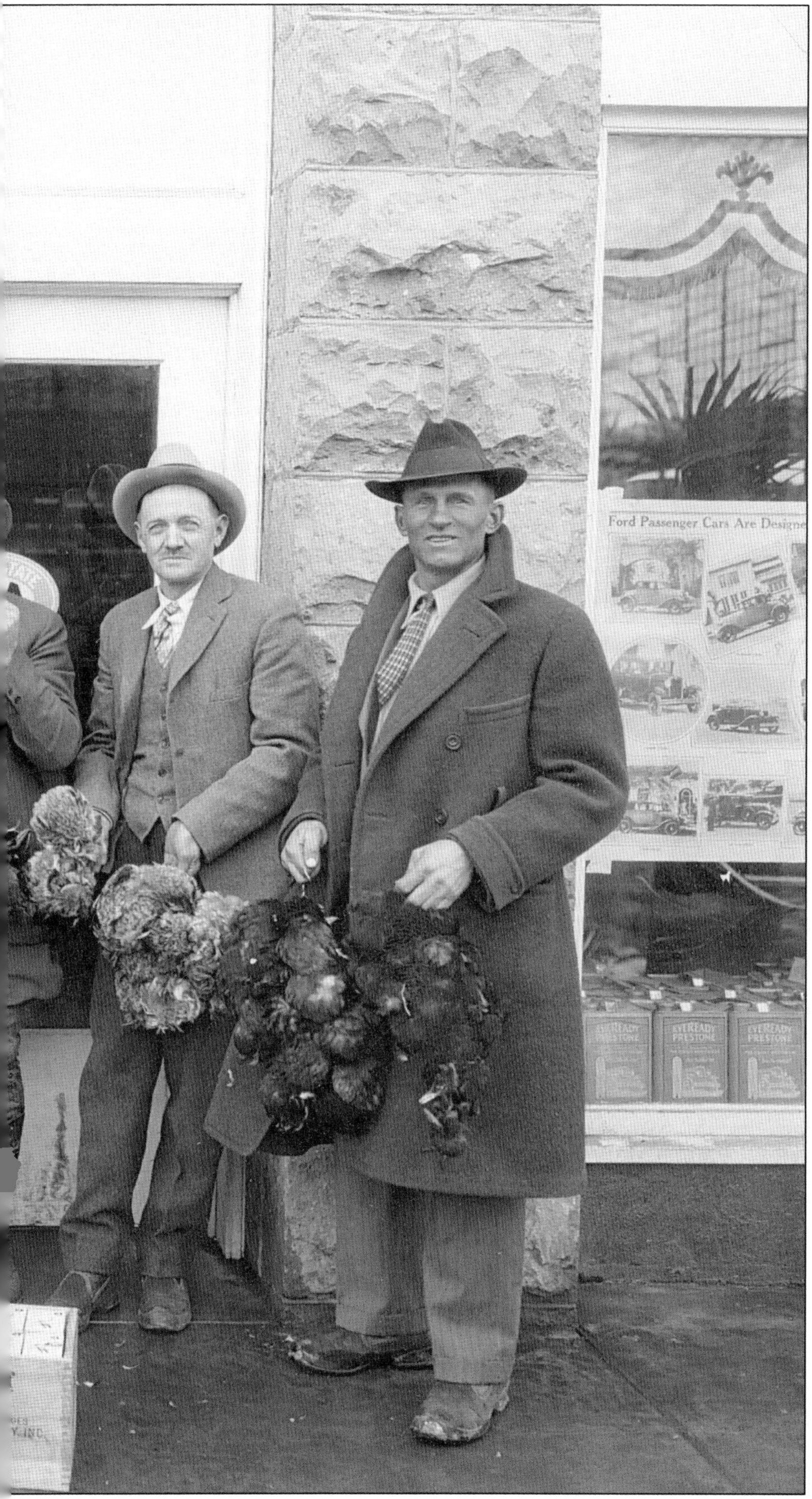

Selected members of the Harney County Game Protective Association competed in a raven and owl shoot in January 1932. At the close of the event, 325 birds were reported to be brought in. The team headed by Dr. L. E. Hibbard bagged 217 birds while James McCulloch's team tallied 108. Dinner at the Knickerbocker was provided by the losing team. Posed standing in front of the Burns Ford building with the quarry are, from left to right, Poleman Skeins, Jim McCulloch, Johnny Loggan (behind door), Dr. Hibbard, Irving Hazeltine, George Benson, and Frank Triska, district game warden in 1915.

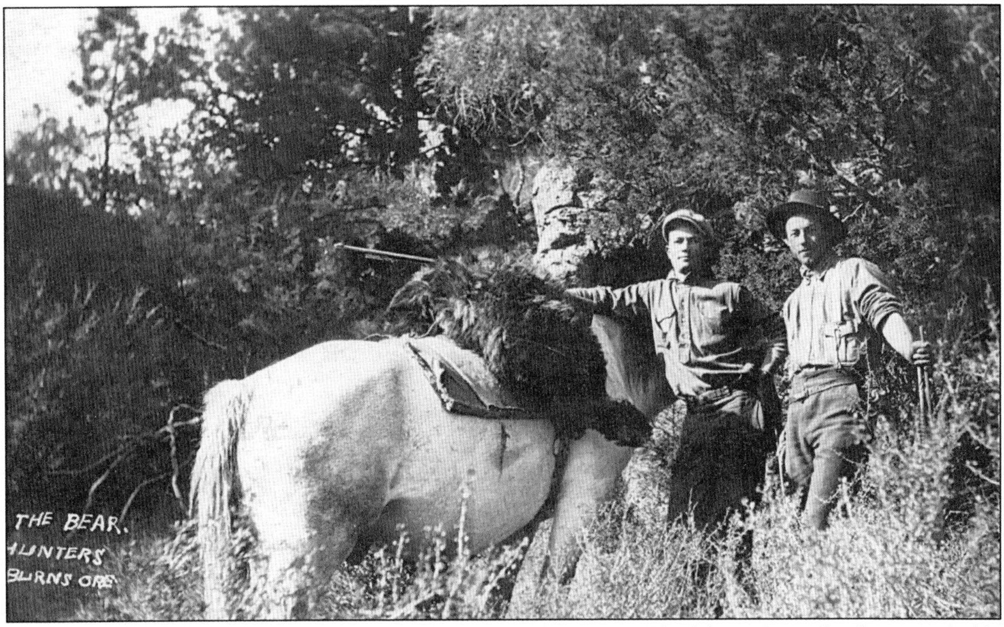

Two bear hunters from Harney County are posed packing out a black bear from the forest probably somewhere north of Burns. On May 10, 1919, one of these men wrote, "This is like the place we are going to cut wood. There are lots of bear about five miles from where we are going. They have got a little baby bear here in town for a pet. W. ?. M."

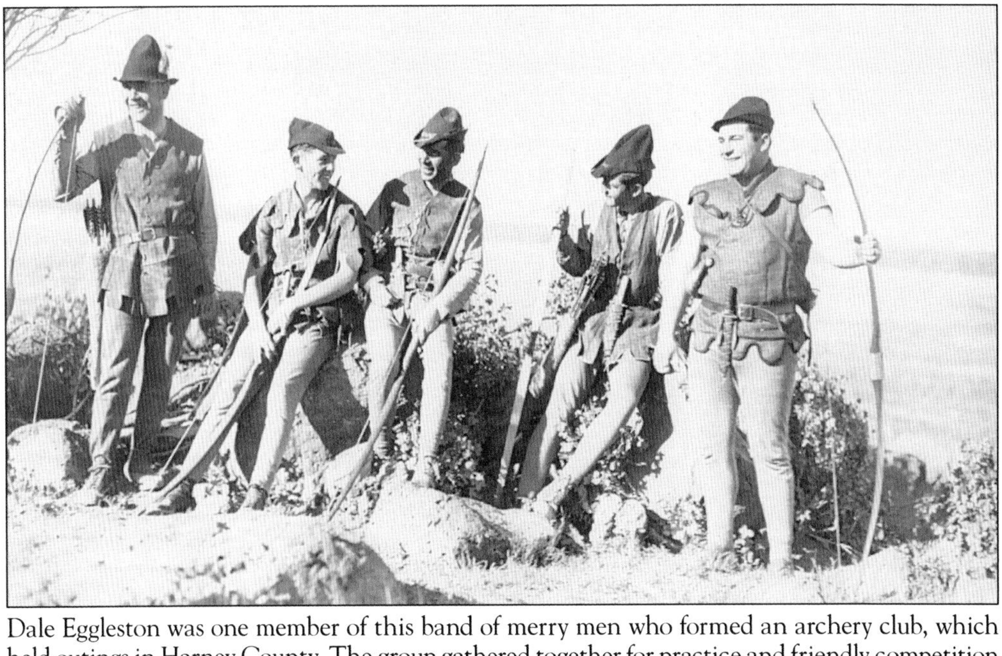

Dale Eggleston was one member of this band of merry men who formed an archery club, which held outings in Harney County. The group gathered together for practice and friendly competition with wooden longbows. (Courtesy Dale Eggleston.)

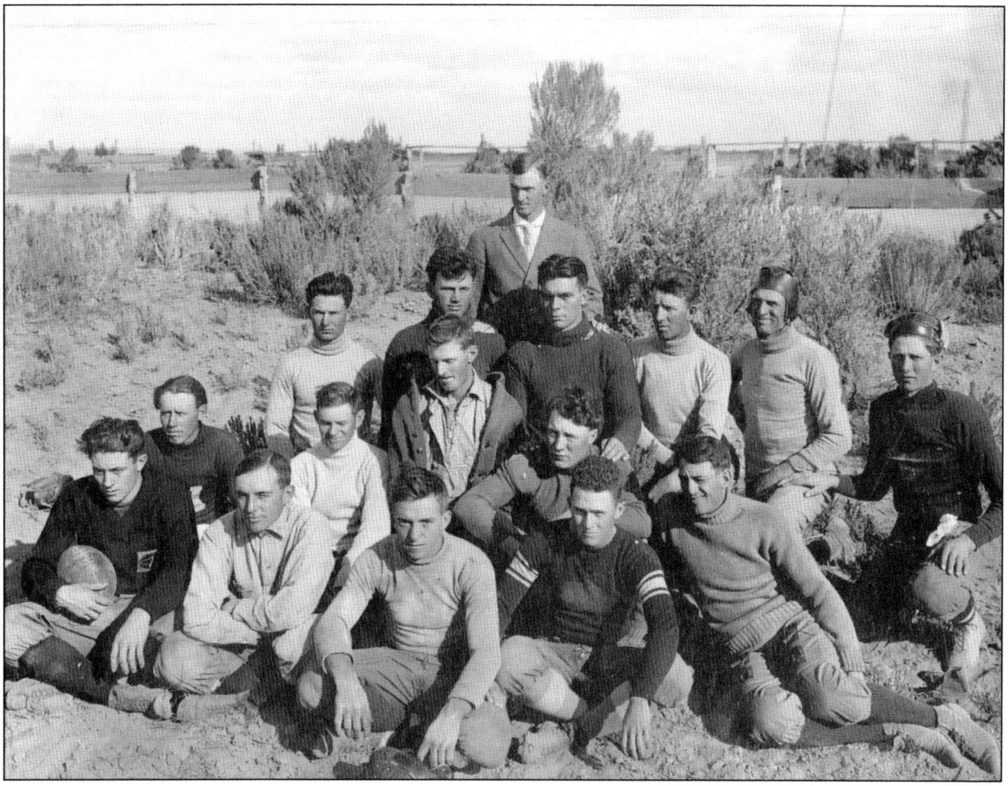

The Burns football team is pictured here in 1915. Some of the young men identified are Culver Page, Lee Miller, Clarence Young, Gus Bardwell, Earl Hagey, George Bevens, Bill Young, John Sayer, and George Coolie. The team outmatched the John Day Huskies on October 26, 1915, by a score of 27-0. Games were typically played in the field located at Miller's Cove.

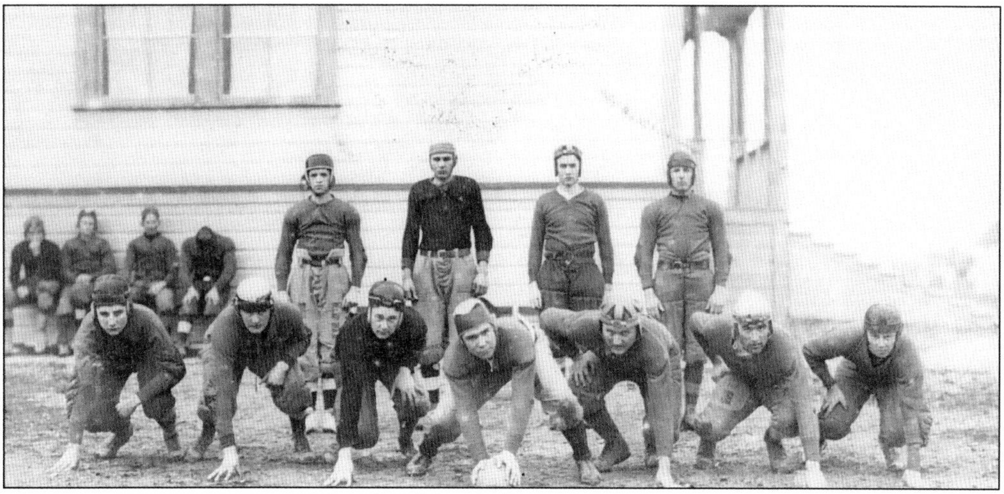

The 1920 Harney County High School football team poses, ready for action, on the gridiron. Members of the team pictured include Hal Hibbard (center), Ray Horton (right guard), Harley Hotchkiss (right tackle), Frank Reineman (right end), Willis Swett (left guard), Walt Cooley (left tackle), Rex Clark (left end), Rollin Gowan (quarterback), Ray Voegtly (fullback), Jim McCulloch (halfback), and Wes Welcome (halfback).

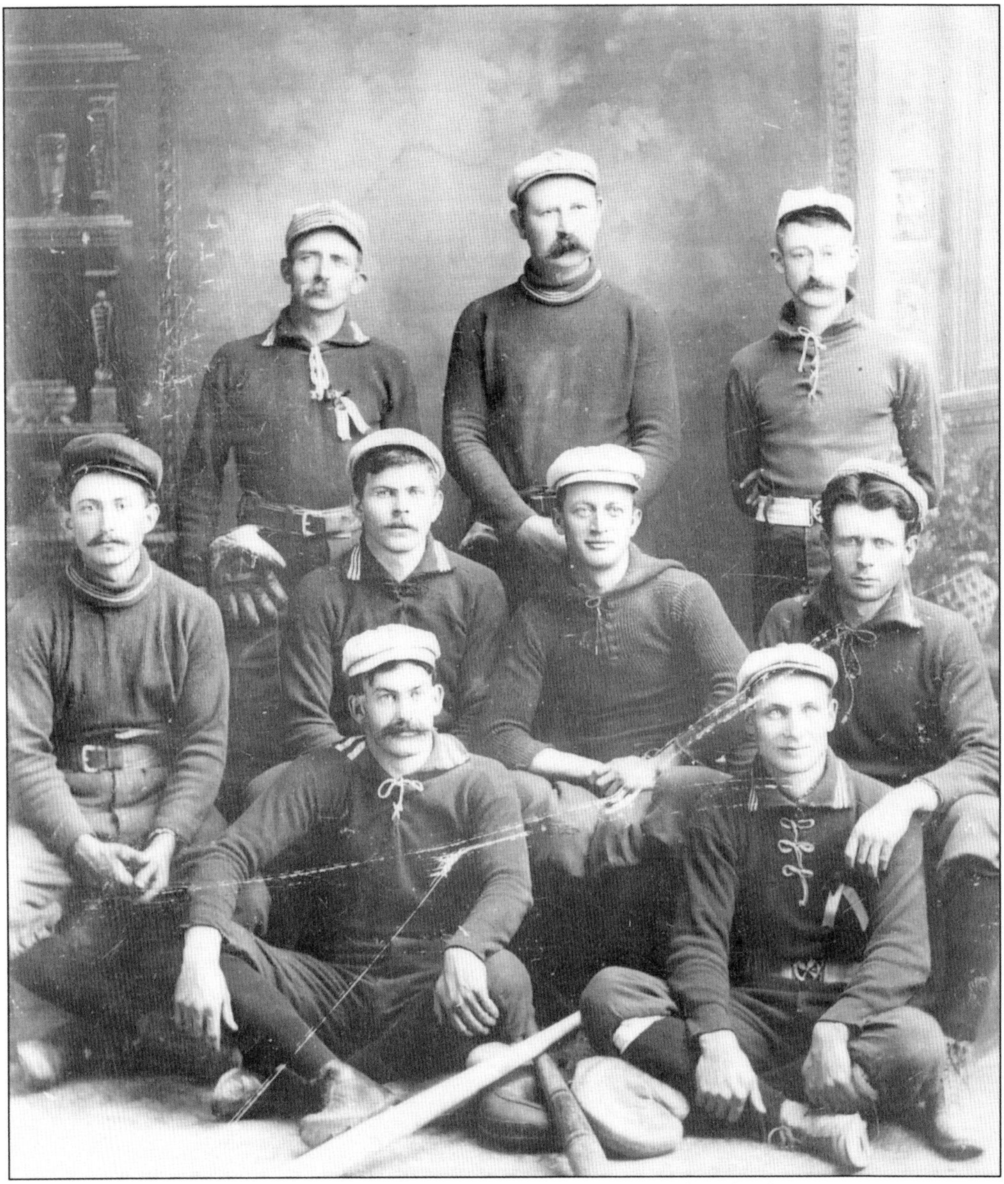

Some of the players on the Burns City baseball team pictured here played a three-game tournament against Canyon City in September 1899. The first game was played for a purse of $200, while the following games offered a prize of $150 each. The first game in the series was won by Canyon City 19-11. A news account relates that is was not good playing on the part of the winning team but rather bad playing on the part of the Burns team, accounting for the outcome. Canyon City again carried off the prize for the second game, outplaying Burns to a score of 18-10. The third game was beset by injuries to catchers Gowan and Wood, a sprained foot to Jack Stephens, a split finger to W. A. Gowan, and a bruised elbow to W. W. Wood. Burns emerged victorious at the close of the game. Pictured from left to right are the following: (first row) Charles Cochrane and Tom Sagers; (second row) John Thomas, George Waters, Winn Gowan, and Ed Esmond; (third row) Jack Dennis, Bob Angervine, and William Barrows.

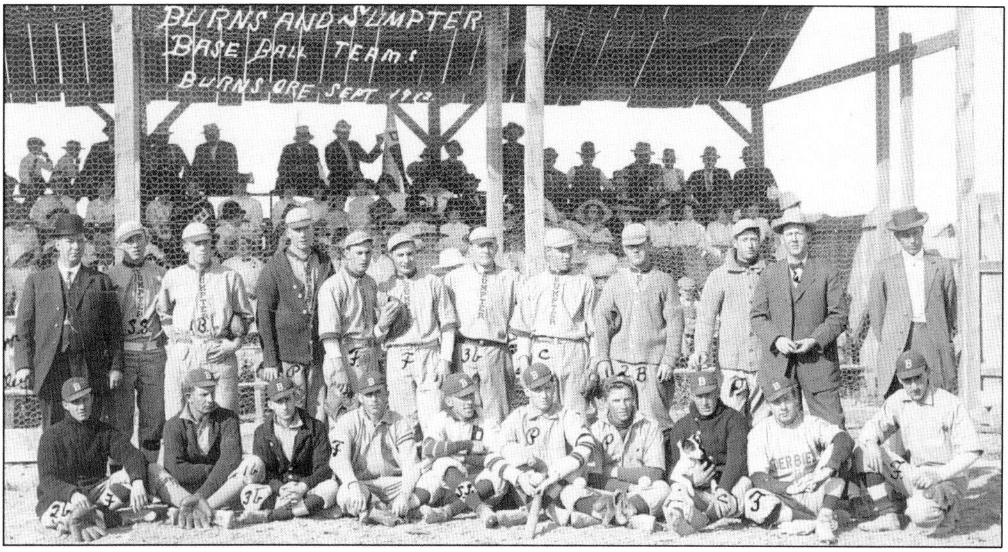

Baseball has long been a popular pastime among the early Harney County residents as far back as 1899. Communities around the county, including Burns, Harney, Crane, Drewsey, Catlow, and Sunset Valley, competed in lively tournaments. During one particular game in 1912 when the Burns team played in Sumpter, the catcher, Clarence Young, proffered his excuse for dropping the balls. His car had four flat tires, and he got blisters on his hands trying to pump them all up. The photograph shows the Burns and Sumpter teams that played for the Amateur Championship of Central Oregon in 1913.

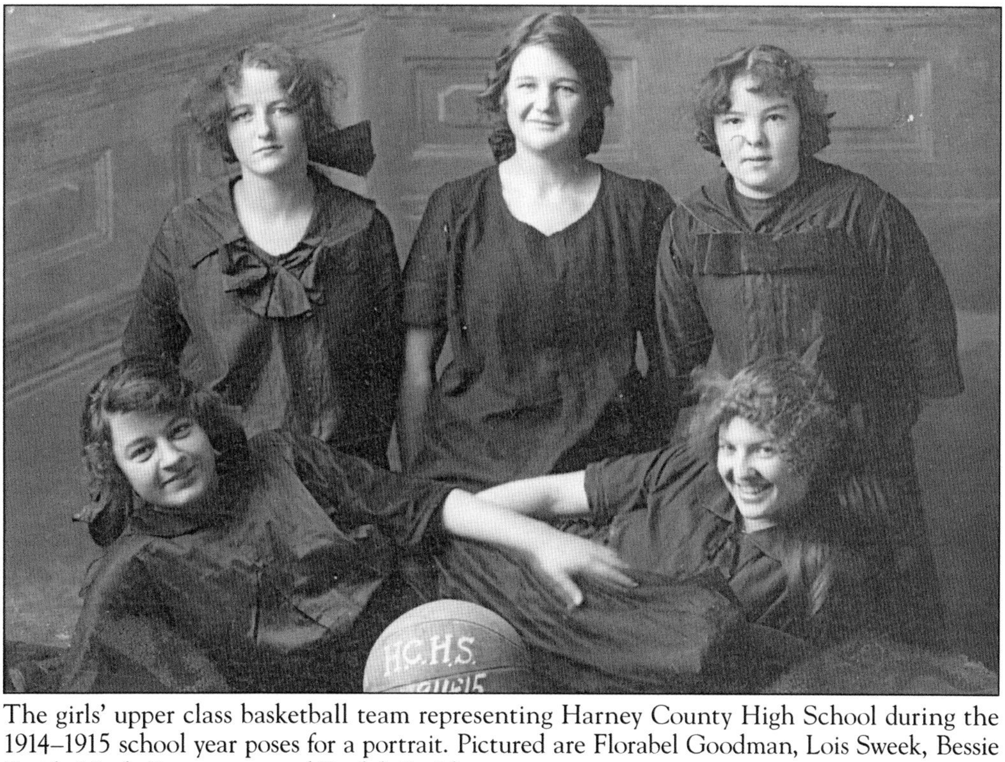

The girls' upper class basketball team representing Harney County High School during the 1914–1915 school year poses for a portrait. Pictured are Florabel Goodman, Lois Sweek, Bessie Smith, Verda Sturtevant, and Beulah Smith.

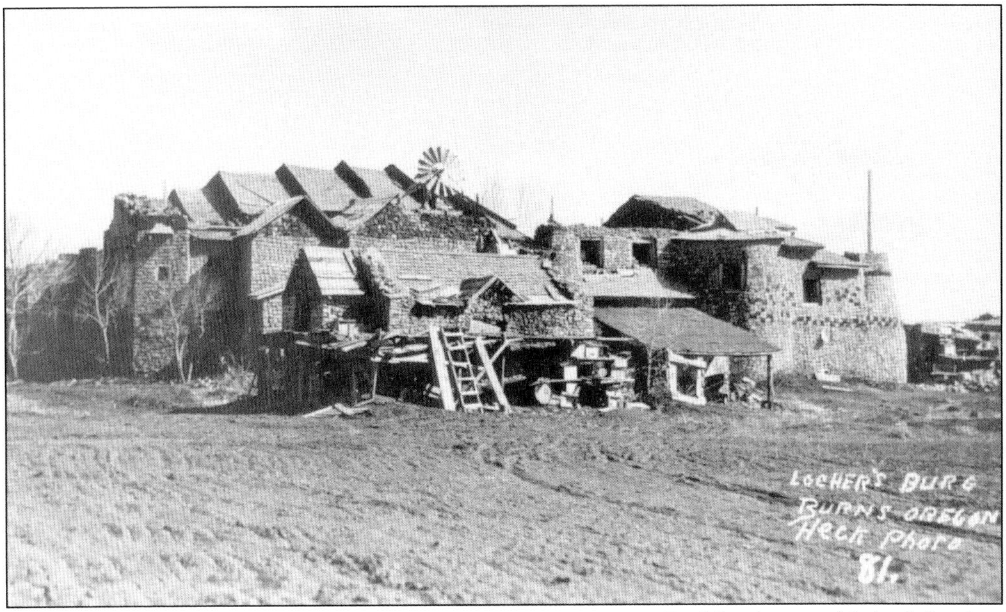

After arriving in Harney County in 1887, German immigrant Paul Locher established the first brewery and later built Locher's Hall in Burns where social events were held. Reminded of the castle in which he was born in his native country, Locher began construction on an enormous mud and stone building around 1916. Locher's Castle as it was known, was a maze of haphazard rooms that was never lived in or completed. After Locher's death, a later owner tore down the building. Nothing remains of the structure except a pile of rocks. (Photograph by R. W. Heck.)

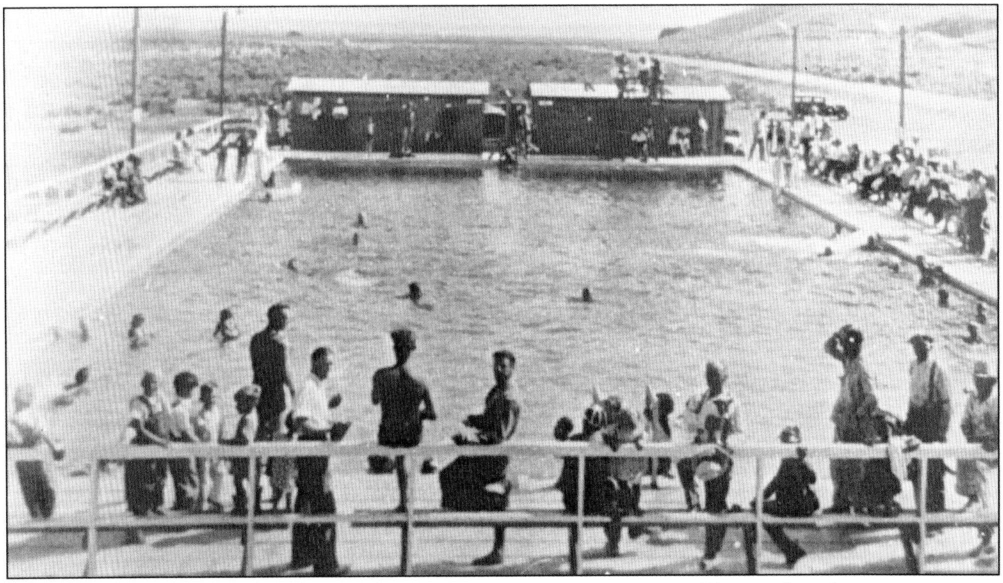

Construction of the 50-foot-by-100-foot community swimming pool located at the warm springs near the Hines Lumber Mill was begun in May 1935. The pool was built completely out of wood supplied by the Hines Lumber Mill and paid for by raffles The facility included dressing rooms, showers, and footbaths, and a promenade around the border. The water was supplied by an artesian spring with a constant temperature of 68 degrees. When full, the tank held 240,000 gallons of water and a pump recirculated the water 400,000 gallons per day.

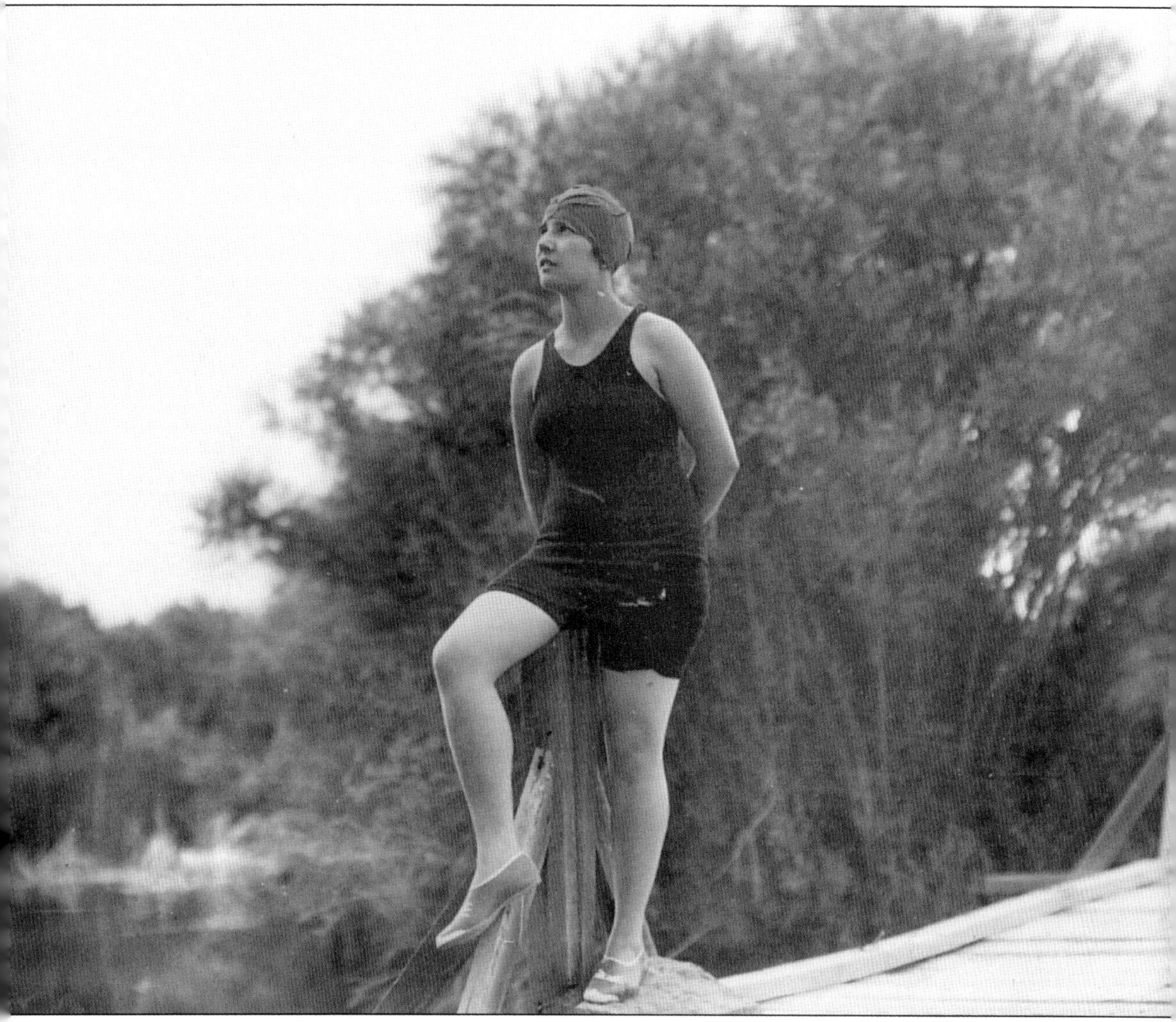

In July 1926, Evelyn Oliver Jordan won a local bathing beauty contest held in connection with the Oregon convention of the American Legion. She qualified to travel to Marshfield, accompanied by her parents, Mr. and Mrs. Glenn Oliver, to compete at the state level. Miss The Dalles came away with the first place judge's decision while Miss Oliver finished fourth. C. K. Bartley, one of the Harney County post's delegates, related that the crowd of 20,000 applauded Miss Oliver for five minutes at the final showing and an attempt was made to recall her again to the stage. Miss Oliver clearly won the prize for popular admiration according to Bartley. None of the other contestants created such a stir among the spectators. The Harney County Legion Post won a certificate of merit at the convention for posting a 100 percent increase in membership.

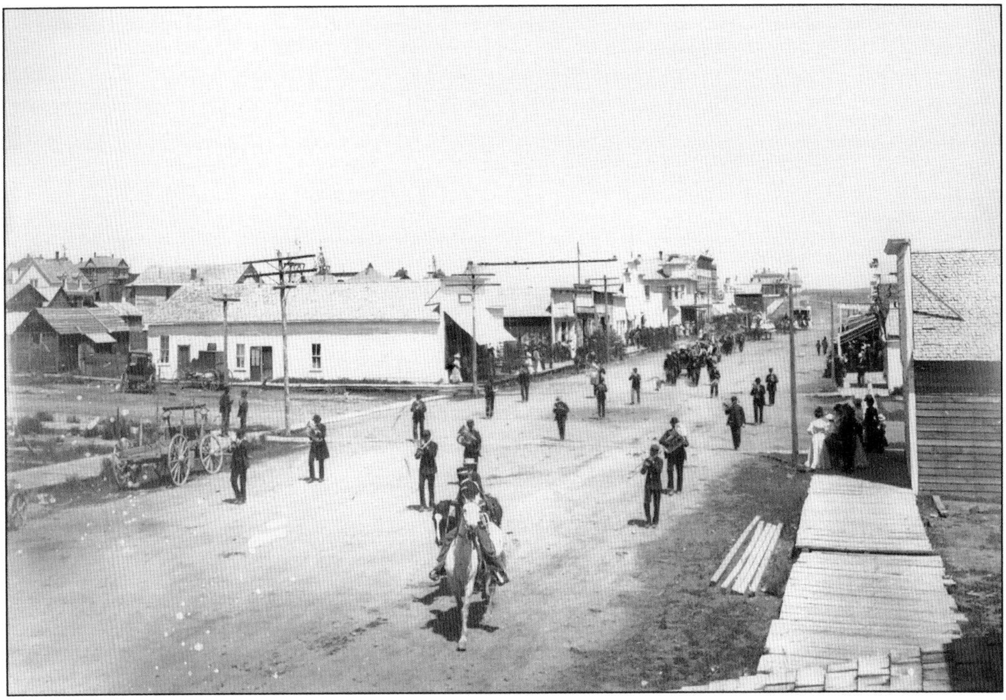

A brass band and horse-drawn floats parade down the Main Street of Burns in celebration of Independence Day in 1900. Note the wooden sidewalks lining the streets. Main Street was not paved until 1929.

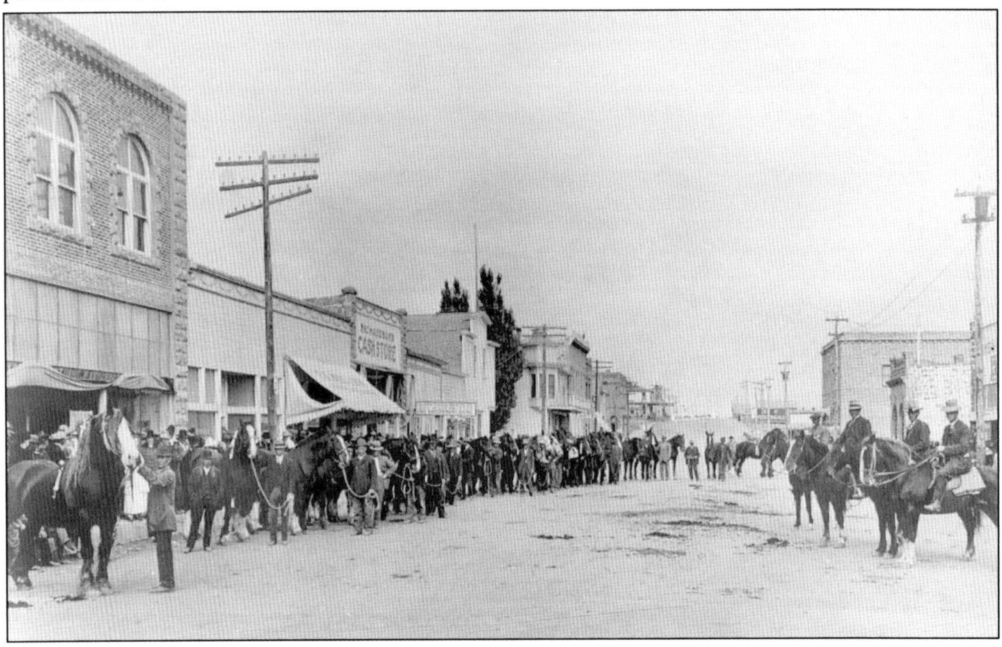

This assemblage of men and horses gathered on Main Street in Burns appears ready for a horse race or a parade. Note the Richardson Cash Store in the background near the center of the block on the left. This building was constructed in 1902. This photograph was taken about the mid-1910s.

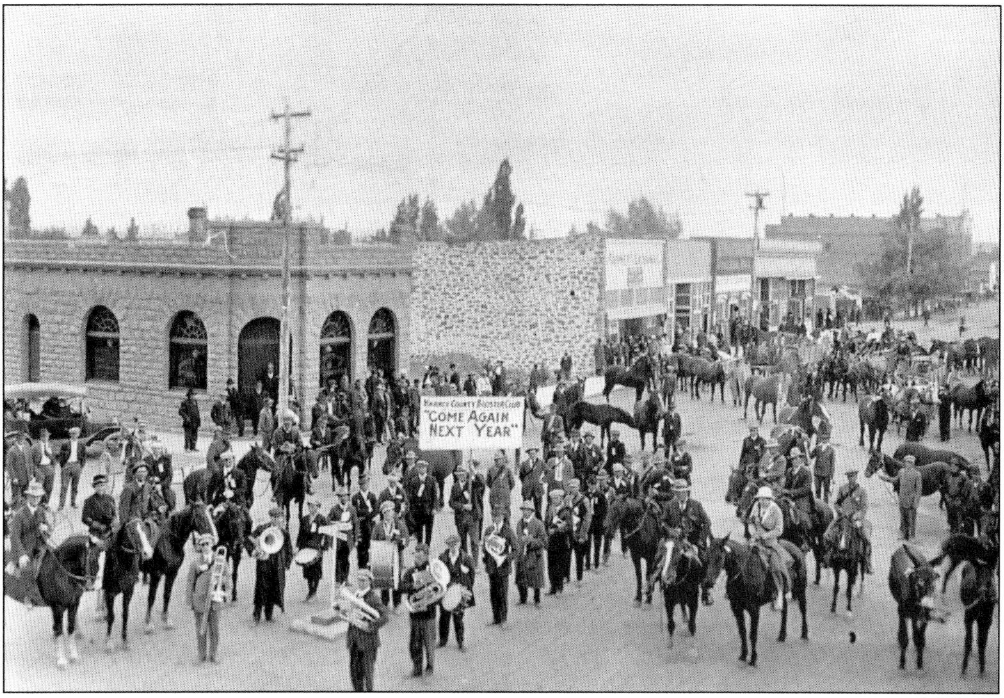

Sponsored by the Harney County Booster Club, a banner held high above the crowd proclaims, "Come Again Next Year." The parade was held between 1914 and 1929 on Main Street in Burns. The stonework building in the background is the Harney County National Bank, which was constructed in 1907. (Courtesy Lurie Whiting.)

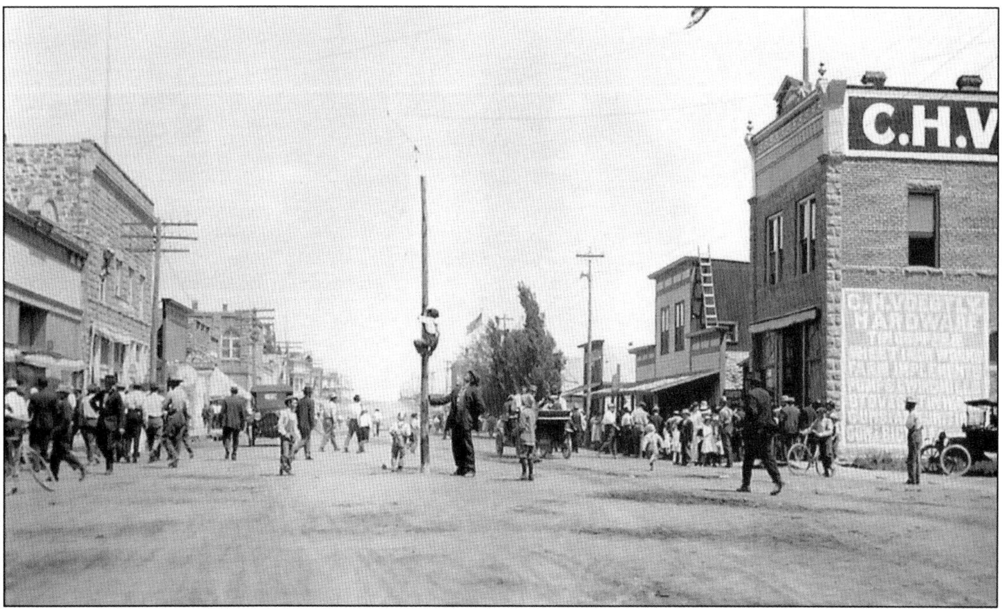

A watchful eye studies the youngster attempting to scale a greased pole set up on Main Street in Burns in 1915. The reason for the event is unknown. The distinctive C. H. Voegtly building is visible on the corner of the block to the right. (Courtesy Lurie Whiting.)

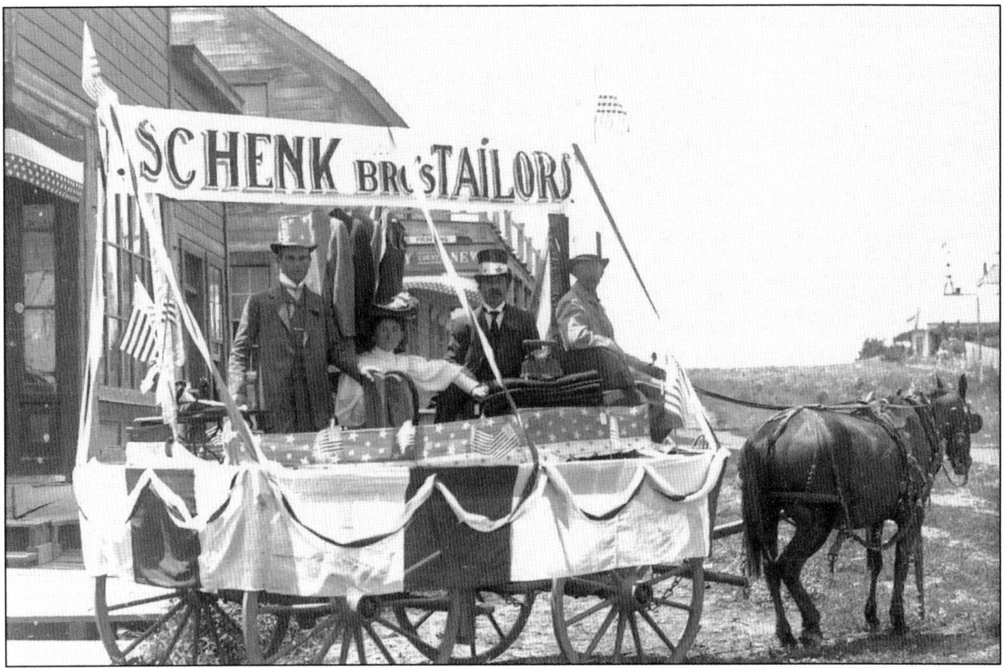

Around the beginning of the 20th century, the Schenk Brothers Tailors entered this festive float in a Fourth of July parade. The office of the *Harney County News* can be seen underneath the banner.

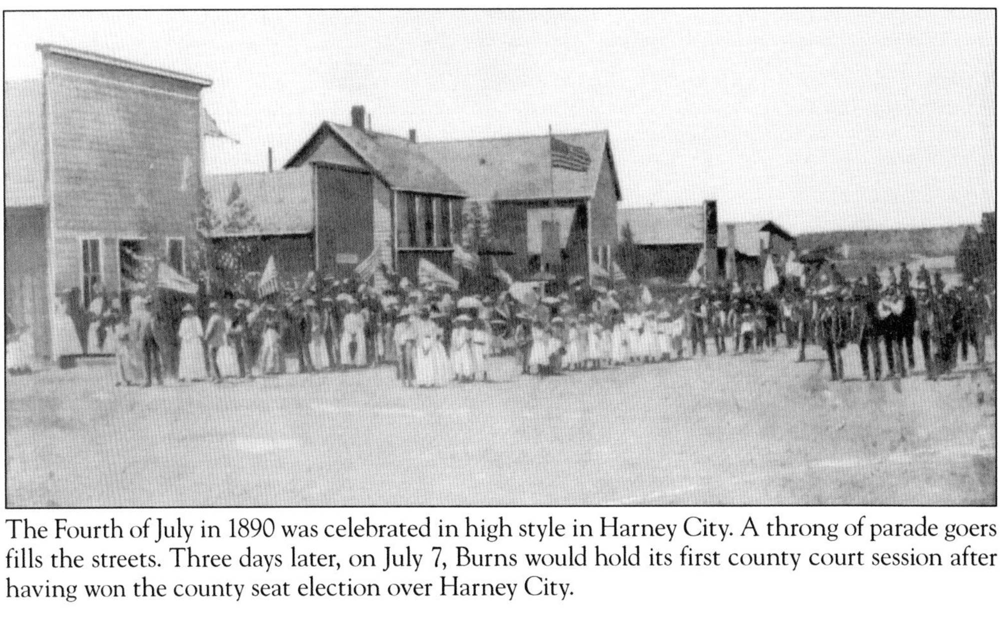

The Fourth of July in 1890 was celebrated in high style in Harney City. A throng of parade goers fills the streets. Three days later, on July 7, Burns would hold its first county court session after having won the county seat election over Harney City.

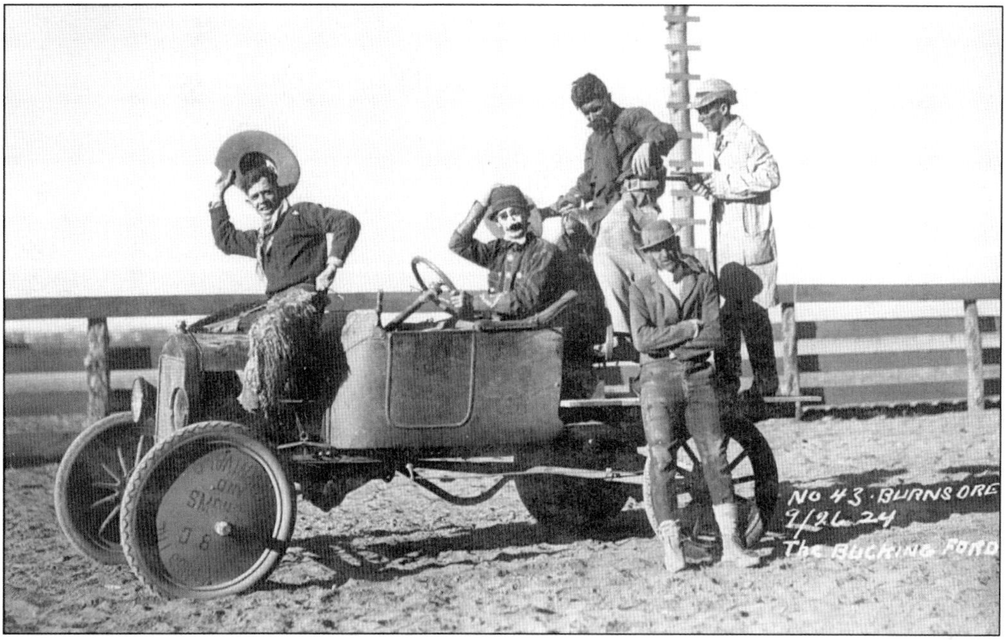

Rodeo clowns mug for the cameras aboard the "Bucking Ford" at the 1924 Harney County Roundup. Lettering on the front left wheel reads, "Don't miss the big shows and carnival!" (Photograph by R. W. Heck; courtesy Jack and Bonnie Smith.)

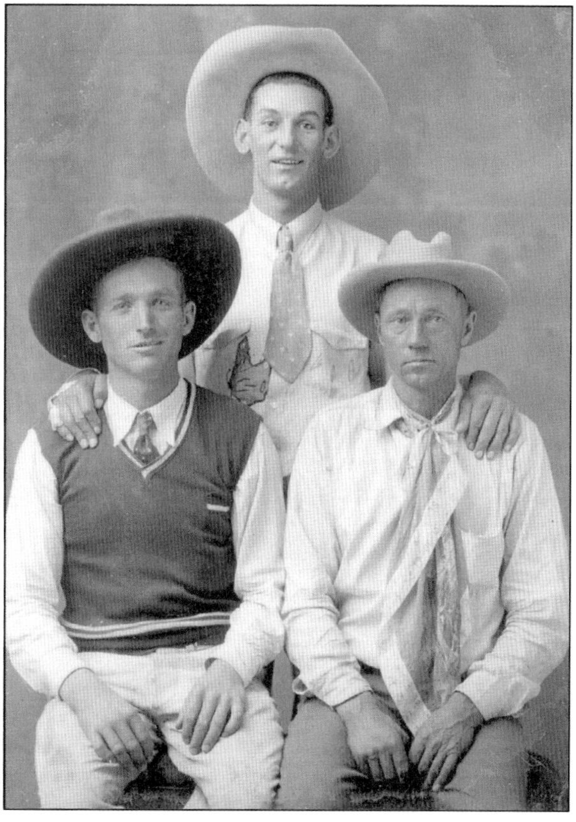

First place winner Charles McPheeters (sitting, left) poses with second and third place winners Ross Dollarhide Sr. (sitting, right) and Smoky Osborn (standing). The three competed at the 1933 Harney County Roundup.

Discover Thousands of Local History Books Featuring Millions of Vintage Images

Arcadia Publishing, the leading local history publisher in the United States, is committed to making history accessible and meaningful through publishing books that celebrate and preserve the heritage of America's people and places.

Find more books like this at
www.arcadiapublishing.com

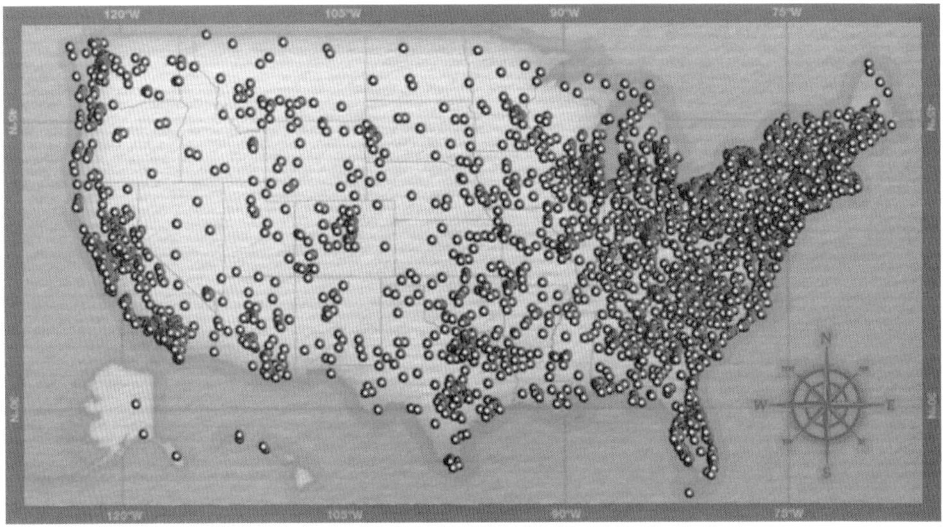

Search for your hometown history, your old stomping grounds, and even your favorite sports team.

Consistent with our mission to preserve history on a local level, this book was printed in South Carolina on American-made paper and manufactured entirely in the United States. Products carrying the accredited Forest Stewardship Council (FSC) label are printed on 100 percent FSC-certified paper.

MADE IN THE USA